The Blessings of Specific Times

Faḍâ'il al-Awqât

by

Imâm al-Bayhaqî

Translated from the Arabic with annotation

by

Abdul Aziz Ahmed

First Edition April 2018

ISBN 978-82-690767-0-7

Published and distributed by:

Bardiy

Oslo, Norway

info@bardiy.org

Book design and typesetting by

Bardiy, info@bardiy.org

Translation: Abdul Aziz Ahmed

Editor: Chad Alan Earl

Proofreading: Chad Alan Earl

Contents

Foreword by Shaykh Afeefuddin al-Jaylani

All praise is to Allah who created humankind, guided them and blessed them with time. May there be prayers and salutations upon our master, the Messenger of Allah, the liege lord of all existent things.

After the aforementioned, there is not the least doubt that time and taking advantage of time are among the greatest concerns of humankind. This is because time is connected to every aspect of our lives.

We, as believers, know with certainty the importance of time in our lives, for Allah, the Transcendent and Exalted, has made this clear in the Noble Book by His glorification of time and expounding upon its value. He swore oaths by portions of the day and night to show us the importance of those portions. As this is the case with portions of the day, then what of its entirety? He – Transcendent is He – swears by the dawn and on another occasion by the mid-morning and elsewhere by the last part of the night. All of these indicate the importance of specific times by which we may attain His Pleasure. Indeed, Allah has established worship, such as the five daily prayers, the fast, pilgrimage and all the other forms of worship within specific times, so that we will pay attention to the time as well as to the actual worship. The Messenger ﷺ said about the prayer, when asked which act is most beloved to Allah, 'prayer *in its time*'. And this is why we must plan our time and take full advantage of the days of our lives before they end.

As it is said, there are only three types of day: The first is the day that has passed and all that is left of it is recompense, if it was good then good, and if it was bad then bad. The second is the Last Day, which is the awaited day that is before us. This we have no control over. Once we have taken our steps upon it, we do not know where we will end up. We don't know whether we will be in a good state (and we ask Allah for his bounty), or whether we will be in wretchedness (and we ask Allah for His pardon). We don't know whether we will find ourselves full of joyfulness or endlessly empty. The third is the day we are presently in. It is an opportunity to attain both the good of this temporal world and that of the eternal world.

Praise be to Allah for His blessing in that He inspired our respected brother Abdul Aziz, the one who has high aspiration and determination. He motivated Shaykh Abdul Aziz Ahmed to do the majestic work of translating *Kitâb Faḍâ'il al-Awqât* of Imâm al-Bayhaqî in which the author strives to explain the importance of what Allah has provided for us in specific times, and their blessings. So good fortune to our brother Abdul Aziz for this accomplishment! May Allah shower him with goodness for the effort of translating and clarifying this work, and may He provide him with the highest level of steadfastness and firmness in all the aspect of his life that occupy him and in the difficulties he faces and the striving he does and that Allah blesses his time and makes this book that you have before you of universal benefit. May Allah reward you with goodness.

Afeefuddin al-Jaylani

Kuala Lumpur, Malaysia

10th Jumâdi al-Âkhir 1438H, 9th March 2017.

Foreword by Shaykh Muhammad bin Yaḥya bin Muhammad al-Ninowy

All praise is to Allah, the Most Gracious who taught the Quran, created humankind, made subservient to him the whole of creation, made the angels prostrate to him, and preferred him over the Jinn. He opened for him doors of proximity, love and faith. He made certain periods of time more special than others, and preferred some years over others, some months over others, some nights over others, and some days over others. He made the Night of Power better than a thousand months.

He swore an oath by the mid morn, by the dawn, and by 'the ten nights'. In all of this, He, the Transcendent One, is the One who facilitates closeness for His slave, and is the Opener of the doors of gnosis. He is the one who pours upon him His blessings and His satisfaction, the One who makes manifest the lights of His proximity, and is the One who throws to him the secrets of His mercy. He increases him in love and happiness with his Lord whenever he exposes himself to the breezes of His proximity, stands before Him, humbles himself before Him, adulates Him, reads His verses, and tastes the subtleties of intimate discourse with Him and receives His beautiful reply. Whoever tastes knows, and whoever knows increases and drinks more. Allah has blessed those moments because it is in them that He sends His mercy and His breezes so that we can direct ourselves towards Him. He ordered us to be sincere in these moments so that we can witness Him. He repeats and increases His bounty at these times so that we can realise through the lights of His attributes. There is no known limit to His generosity during those nights and days so that He may gather us at the well of His Essence. With this, He called us to the importance of time, its limits and its immense value, and warned us about its loss. And Allah has said in an oath: *'By Time, indeed humankind is in a state of loss,'* and then He explained that the exceptions to this loss are those who understand the value of time, and use it to express faith and do righteous actions. He, the Exalted, said, *'Except those who believe and do righteous actions, for they will receive a reward unfailing.'*

May there be most perfect and complete prayers and salutations upon the one from whom the secrets dawned, and from where lights were brought forth. In him, realities were elevated. He was the manifest light and the straight path of guidance for humankind. Allah, the Exalted, gave him knowledge of all things, and taught him that which he did not know. He made him the elect of the Arabs and the non-Arabs.

He had the greatest knowledge of Allah of all His creations. He was the most aware and most conscious of them. He illumined the path of those who desire to journey to Him. He clarified the milestones for those who travel the spiritual path. Through him, Allah guided neglectful hearts, opened deaf ears and blind eyes. He guided us to the value of time, and of each and every breath. For the Messenger ﷺ said, "I was sent; and I and the final hour are like these two", and he joined his index and middle finger.[1] This was to warn the believer about the shortness of opportunity and tightness of the respite, so that one flees to one's Lord and benefits from these festivals and times, and divests oneself of the world, its preoccupations and its deceptions, and connects to Allah, the Exalted, in remembrance, gratitude, vigilance, and truly bearing witness in all his states, thoughts, words, actions, and times of stillness. By this, the lights of his Lord rise, and tranquillity and peace descend upon him, and he joins the people of felicity of both worlds.

After the aforementioned, I was asked to write a foreword to the book the *Blessings of Specific Times* by the Imam, the Ḥafiẓ al-Bayhaqî, may Allah the Exalted show him mercy, translated by the esteemed, the skilful, the sagacious, the beloved teacher Abdul Aziz Ahmed, may Allah the Exalted preserve him and look after him. I hastened to do this, even though I am not qualified to do such a thing, in the hope that I will be counted among the ranks of those who supported the Noble Sunnah and spread it to the East and West, be it only by this meagre effort. I ask Allah to count us among its people, and seal our lives upon it; and that He gathers us with the one who established it, upon him be peace and salutations in this world and the next, and between the two.

Imâm al-Bayhaqî was one of the leaders of the Muslims and among their greats. He was the Imâm, the scholar of the Principles, the ascetic, the jurist, the conscientious. He was unique in his time in his memory and was exceptional among his peers in his critical ability and meticulousness. He was one of the greatest students of the Imâm al-Ḥâkim, may Allah's mercies and pleasure be upon all of them. He used to record and memorise *ḥadîth* from when he was young and excelled in the Principles of the Religion. He then travelled seeking the *ḥadîth* of our master the Messenger of Allah, upon him be peace and salutations.

He was an ascetic, satisfied with very little, beautified by his asceticism and scrupulousness, being one who knew and acted upon his knowledge. He was one who gathered knowledge of *ḥadîth*, jurisprudence, the science of criticism of *ḥadîth* and the divergent opinions among the scholars of *ḥadîth* and jurisprudence and the principles of the religion.

---

[1] Related by al-Bukhârî (5301) and Muslim (2951).

The book *Blessings of Specific Times* is a book about blessings (*faḍâ'il*), and it is appropriate that it is noted and published as many consider it to be one of the Imâm's lost texts. In it, Imâm al-Bayhaqî specifies the Sacred Months and takes care to describe the extra blessings they contain compared to other months. It is compiled in the manner of the People of *Ḥadîth,* and it contains more than three hundred *ḥadîth* related by fifty-one of his different Shaykhs. May Allah shower His mercies upon all of them.

The book informs us of the value of time and the importance of making an effort to expose oneself to Allah's breezes. This is a sign of enabling grace and intelligence. May Allah shower mercy upon al-Wazîr bin Hubayra for what he said in a beautiful poem, which was exemplified by our Shaykh, the scholar who gathered all the Islamic Sciences, Shaykh Abdul Fattâḥ Abu Ghudda, may Allah, the Exalted, shower him with His mercy:

Time is more precious when you enrich yourself by preserving it,
And I see it is the easiest of all things for you to waste

The felicitous is the one who is enriched by the time Allah blesses him with, exerts himself in his days and hours, and realises the need for the actions that lead to safety in this world and the next, and in doing so rises above all the things that may bring him down and hastens to proximity to the Lord of the worlds and skies. Perhaps he will expose himself to a cool breeze of closeness or a lightning spark of light or a breath of love, for surely Allah has spiritual breezes by which He sends His mercy to those of His servants who expose themselves to them. They will never be miserable.

(وَمَا يُلَقَّاهَآ إِلَّا الَّذِينَ صَبَرُوا وَمَا يُلَقَّاهَآ إِلَّا ذُو حَظٍّ عَظِيمٍ)

And no one will be granted such goodness except those who exercise patience and self-restraint, none but persons of the greatest good fortune.

(Fussilat 41:35)

I ask Allah, the Exalted, to bring benefit through this book and grant our brother, Shaykh Abdul Aziz that which he loves and pleases him, and that He makes us stick to the Quran and its elect, and to the *ḥadîth* and its people; and that He seals our lives upon that and gathers us with the source of the Way, upon him be the prayers and salutations of Allah the Exalted in this world and the next. I say this in a state of praise, prayer and salutations.

Muhammad bin Yaḥya bin Muhammad al-Ninowy al-Shâfi'î, may Allah, the Exalted, grant him pardon, in the blessed month of Rajab 1438 years after the Hijra of the Greatest Prophet, upon him be prayers and salutations.

In the Name of Allah, Most Gracious, Most Merciful

Translator's introduction

Allah, the Mighty and Majestic, swears an oath by time. He says:

(وَالْعَصْرِ)

(إِنَّ الْإِنسَانَ لَفِي خُسْرٍ)

(إِلَّا الَّذِينَ آمَنُوا وَعَمِلُوا الصَّالِحَاتِ وَتَوَاصَوْا بِالْحَقِّ وَتَوَاصَوْا بِالصَّبْرِ)

By (the token of) Time

Verily Man is in loss

Except such as have faith, and do righteous deeds, and (join together) in the mutual teaching of truth, and of patience and constancy.

(al-'Asr, 103:1-3)

One only swears an oath by something that one holds in high esteem. For Allah to swear an oath by 'time' shows its value and importance. The reason why *He* holds it in such high regard can be seen in the verses that follow the oath. They indicate that failure to appreciate time results in total loss. The only way to avoid that loss is by using our time to *'do good deeds'* and *'join together in the mutual teachings of truth, patience and constancy.'*

Time is divine. The Messenger of Allah ﷺ said: "*Do not curse time! For Allah is time!*"[2] Although the statement is metaphorical and the Messenger ﷺ does not imply that time is actually our God, once again, it is a clear indication of the importance of time. The Messenger ﷺ is telling us that recognising Allah through

[2] Related by Muslim (*ḥadîth* number 2246).

the changing events of time helps us to understand those events and allows us to see His constant Majesty and Beauty through the ever changing world. It helps us to live our lives in tune with time, and opens up the possibility of living in accordance with the Lord of Time. The first step towards living in accordance with the Lord of Time is to stop cursing time and to stop taking a negative view of its occurrences, but rather, to recognise that there is a greater power and wisdom behind these events. That is why the first step towards avoidance of the total loss described in the verses above is to have faith. The second step is to utilise time, and to do as many good deeds as possible in the limited time that the Lord of Time has granted us.

The importance of this book should be seen in this context. It is about something that Allah and His Messenger hold in high esteem. It helps us to appreciate Allah's patterns and wisdom, and offers direct guidance as to how to get the best from each moment of our lives.

Almost all of it is from the Messenger of Allah ﷺ. It is a collection of *ḥadîth. Ḥadîth* are the words and reported actions of the Messenger of Allah ﷺ. They are supplemented in this book by explanations from the early generations of scholars and clarification by its compiler, Imâm Abû Bakr al-Bayhaqî.

In an effort to determine the most correct translation, I have referred to classical commentaries which include those of Imâm al-Nawawi, Ibn Rajab and 'Abdul Raûf al-Munâwi[3]. I also had the opportunity to refer some of the *ḥadîth* to the scholar of *ḥadîth,* Shaykh Muhammad bin Yaḥya al-Ninowy. I am extremely grateful to Shaykh Afeefuddin who clarified one of the most difficult *ḥadîth* and to our editor, Chad Earl, who was meticulous in his work and corrected many of my errors. I pray Allah rewards them abundantly. Wherever I have had to add words to render the meaning comprehensible in English, I have enclosed my additions in brackets.

---

[3] Imâm al-Nawawî (d. 676H/ 1277CE) was one of the great scholars of *ḥadîth.* His commentary on the *Collection of Imâm Muslim* is one of the most important sources for understanding the meaning of the Prophetic tradition. Imâm 'Abdul Ra'ûf al-Munâwi (d.952H/ 1545CE) was a later scholar based in Cairo during the Ottoman period. His commentary on *al-Jâmi al-Saghîr* of al-Suyûṭî is a comprehensive explanation of thousands of *ḥadîth* drawn from the major collections. Ibn Rajab is Abdul Raḥmân ibn Aḥmad who died in Damascus in 795H (1393CE). Although famous for jurisprudence and his commentaries on *ḥadîth,* he also wrote *Laṭâif al-Ma'ârif* which describes the duties related to different times of the year. It deals with similar content and was used extensively during the translation process.

The reader will notice that some words have been left in their Arabic form. Examples of these are *ḥadîth* and *Jumu'a* (Friday congregational prayer). I felt this to be preferable in the case of certain terms that have become well known to non-Arabic speaking Muslims, and are either cumbersome when translated, or were felt to be so well known that the original Arabic word may be clearer than an obscure, but technically accurate, translation. Their explanations are included in a glossary at the end of the book.

The translation of Quranic verses is based on the translation of Abdullah Yusuf Ali with occasional modifications; such as changing the use of 'thee', 'ye' and 'thou' to 'you'.

This rendition of the text into English was based on the 1997 Dâr al-Kutub al-'Ilmiyya edition with cross-referencing to the 2003 Dâr Ibn Ḥazm edition. The cross-referencing of the *ḥadîth* in the footnotes is drawn from the two printed editions and my own research. Wherever possible, *ḥadîth* have been attributed to the better known collections of the famous scholars of *ḥadîth* including, where appropriate, the likes of Imâm al-Bukhâri and Imâm Muslim. Biographical details of these scholars and a brief introduction to their collections are included as appendices. This does not imply that the text before you is not valid in itself or is inferior to these collections. The intention and purpose are very different, and therefore Imâm al-Bayhaqî's use of *ḥadîth* applies criteria more appropriate to his intention.

It is well known that there are many categories and classifications of *ḥadîth.* Imâm al-Bayhaqî's intention in writing this book was for people to act in a way that would take best advantage of the blessings relating to specific times. Therefore, he does not go into detail about the strength of different chains of narration. Occasionally, he relates a *ḥadîth* that has serious weaknesses in its chain. He does not do this out of ignorance of the weakness, but for two important reasons: First, where the weaknesses are severe, he relates the *ḥadîth* to make sure people are aware of it; and second, to make sure that the discussion of the topic is complete. He then comments by stating that the *ḥadîth* is 'denounced' (*munkar*).

Where the weaknesses are not severe and the *ḥadîth* is acceptable for use in the situation, he does not give details. The acceptable use of weak *ḥadîth* can best be understood from the words of the great *ḥadîth* master, Imâm al-Nawawî who said:

> *'The scholars from among the jurists and narrators of* ḥadîth *have said that it is permitted and recommended to act upon weak* ḥadîth *in the case of supererogatory acts and acts where one hopes for extra reward (*targhîb*) or abstinence out of fear they might be wrong*

> (tarhîb) *as long as they are not rejected. As for rulings such as what is permitted and forbidden, trade, marriage, divorce, and other legal matters, one should not act except upon* ḥadîth *which have been authenticated as correct or sound.'*[4]

This book is all about blessings, excelling, and seeking the best. For this reason, the use of *ḥadîth* that do not necessarily meet the same standards for identifying the permitted and prohibited, or for determining rules of worship, is perfectly appropriate, as is the use of stories and anecdotes.

The Arabic title is *Faḍâ'il al-Awqât. Faḍâ'il* is the plural of *faḍîla,* which is usually translated as 'moral excellence', 'excellent quality', 'virtue' or, 'merit'. It is derived from the root *f-ḍ-l,* which means to 'go beyond', to 'excel' or to be 'excessive'. Those who act upon the contents of this book are seeking extra blessing, and are striving to get the most out of every moment in the best possible way. There is an implication of rank in the word *faḍîla*. The horse can never attain the *faḍîla* of the human being. Each 'time' of the year has its particular *faḍîla.* If we want to excel in our use of time and access the inherent *faḍîla* of time, this book will be of great benefit. It has been an honour to translate it.

With the intention of brevity, and hoping to make the text easier for English speaking readers, I have shortened the chains of transmission. This usually only includes the Companion who narrates the *ḥadîth.*

I recall the *ḥadîth* lessons of my teacher, Syed Muḥammad bin 'Alawi al-Mâlikî, and the way in which he introduced the Companion who related the *ḥadîth.* Following his method, and that of the great commentators on *ḥadîth*, I have attempted to make a few biographical notes on each of the Companions, and where appropriate, on important scholars from later generations. The biographical notes are drawn from two main sources: *al-Isâba fi Tamyîz al-Saḥâba* of Ibn Ḥajr and *Kitâb al-Thiqât* of Ibn Ḥibbân.

Arabic names are usually subject to declension depending on their role in the sentence, for example Abû Bakr becomes Abâ Bakr and Abî Bakr. To avoid any confusion, I have opted to ignore declension and always use the nominative case, which in this example is Abû Bakr.

I pray that Allah does not consider any of my alterations poor etiquette, and that He forgives every mistake I may have made during the translation process.

---

[4] Imâm al-Nawawî, *Kitâb al-Adhkâr*, Beirut, 2005 p36.

I do not claim any expertise in *ḥadîth* studies or in any of the related disciplines; nor in Arabic or translation, but I have a deep love for Imâm al-Bayhaqî and for this book in particular. I desperately wanted to share this gem with my fellow spiritual aspirants. I ask you to pardon any mistakes that I have made, and to ask for my forgiveness. And by Allah is enabling success.

I turn to Allah begging Him to bless this work, and to preserve it from my misinterpretations, misunderstandings and mistakes. By Allah is enabling success.

About the Author

His name was Abû Bakr, Aḥmad ibn al-Ḥusayn al-Bayhaqî, known to his students as 'al-Faqîh Aḥmad'. He was born in the small town of Khusraugird near Bayhaq[5] in the region of Nishapur[6], which is in modern day North Eastern Iran, in the month of Sha'bân 384H, 994CE. He excelled in his studies as a child, and as a young man, learning from the likes of al-Sayyid Abul Ḥasan Muḥammad ibn Ḥusayn al-Ḥasîb. He continued his studies with the Shaykh's student, the famous al-Ḥâkim al-Naysabûrî. In total, al-Bayhaqî had more than a hundred teachers in Central Asia, Baghdad, and later, in the two Holy Cities of Makkah and Madina.

He is credited with over a thousand titles, most of them scholarly compilations of *ḥadîth,* sayings of the Prophet ﷺ and the wisdom of the early scholars. Some deal purely with jurisprudence like the *al-Ṣunan al-Kubrâ,* others with ascetic discipline such as *Kitâb al-Zuhd* and *al-'Araba'ûn al-Ṣughrâ,* and others on the wide range of Islamic Sciences he excelled in, including Creed, History, and language. An abridged version of his massive collection *The Seventy Seven Branches of Faith* was translated into English by Abdul Hakim Murad, and published by The Quilliam press in 1990.

He was a jurist specialising in the school of al-Shâfi'î[7]. It is related that Abû Ma'la al-Juwaynî said: "There is no Shâfi' scholar except that he is indebted to al-Shâfi'î other than Abû Bakr al-Bayhaqî. For indeed, al-Shâfi'î is indebted to him for his authoring of texts which support his school."[8] It has been reported that al-Dhahabî added: "Abû Ma'la was right. It is as such. If al-Bayhaqî had wanted to establish a juristic school (*madhab*) himself he could have done so because of the vastness of his knowledge and his awareness of divergent interpretations."[9]

---

[5] The town of Bayhaq is now known as Sabsevar. It is approximately 220 km west of Mashad in North Eastern Iran.

[6] Nishabur or Nishapur are the usual modern transliterations for the name of the region referred to here. In both Arabic and Persian, the name is Nayshâbûr or Nayshâpûr

[7] Muḥammad bin 'Idrîs al-Shâfi' (d. 204H, 820CE) was the founder of the Shâfi' school of jurisprudence which is one of the four main Sunni schools of law.

[8] Introduction to *Kitâb al-'Arba'ûn al-Sughrâ,* Dâr al-Kutub al-'Arabî: Beirut, 1988, p7.

[9] Ibid.

Imâm al-Bayhaqî was a righteous ascetic man. He fasted the perpetual fast (that is, every day except the days of 'Eid during which fasting is prohibited) for the last thirty years of his life.

He died on the 10th of Jumâdi al-Awwal 458H, 1066CE in Nishapur where he was teaching, and was buried in his native Khusraugird.

May Allah shower his soul with mercy and benefit us by his vast knowledge and inner secrets.

About the Translator

Abdul Aziz Ahmed was born and educated in England. He trained as a primary school teacher but has taught at all levels from Nursery to University. Although he does not claim to be a scholar of the Islamic sciences, he has been fortunate enough to attend the classes of some of the greatest scholars of the previous generation including al-Ḥabîb Aḥmad Mashûr al-Ḥaddâd, al-Ḥabîb 'Abdul Qâdir al-Saggaf, and al-Syed Muḥammad bin 'Alawî al-Mâlikî. He studied under them during his stay in Jeddah.

In recent years, his teachers and guides have included al-Ḥabîb Ḥasan al-Attâs, Shaykh Afeefuddin al-Jailani and Shaykh Muhammad bin Yaḥya al-Ninowy. The latter two acted as formal consultees during the translation of this text.

His Arabic studies have included both traditional and modern routes. He studied through the University of South Africa (UNISA), and traditionally with several teachers including Shaykh Mahmud Galal, with whom he studied Arabic grammar texts in London, and from whom he received a written *ijâza* (completion certificate).

Abdul Aziz has translated several books from Arabic including *The Essentials of Islam* (*al-Risâlat al-Jâmiah)* of Aḥmad bin Zayn al-Ḥabashî, the *Book of Worship* and the *Book of Taqwa* by Imâm al-Ḥaddâd, the *Forty Ḥadîth on the Quran* by Mulla 'Ali al-Qari, and *Removal of Distress* (*Jaliyatul Kadr*) by Imâm al-Barzanjî. He has written a commentary on Imâm al-Ramli's *Riyâdatul Ṣibyân,* which was published under the title *Educating Children,* as well as articles and books on social inclusion and education. Among his other writings are *Living With Blindness* and *The Umra Diaries.* Abdul Aziz has a regular progamme on IKIM radio in Malaysia, and has travelled widely as a teacher and lecturer on Islam, social issues and education.

Abdul Azîz has a special love for Imâm al-Bayhaqî. He received *ijâza,* permission to teach, his *Branches of Faith* from both al-Ḥabib Aḥmad Mashûr al-Haddad in Jeddah in 1992 and Shaykh Muhammad Yaqubi in Glasgow in 2007.

He currently lives in Scotland with his wife and young son.

Transliteration of Arabic

ا	a or â, when following a consonant thereby acting as a *madd* (prolongation of preceding vowel sound)
ب	b
ت	t
ث	th
ج	j
ح	ḥ
خ	kh
د	d
ذ	dh
ر	r
ز	z
س	s
ش	sh
ص	ṣ
ض	ḍ
ط	ṭ
ظ	ẓ
ع	ʻ (*ayn*)
غ	gh
ف	f
ق	q
ك	k
ل	l
م	m
ن	n
ة and ه	h
و	w or û when following a consonant thereby acting as a *madd* (prolongation of preceding vowel sound)
ي	y or î when following a consonant thereby acting as a *madd* (prolongation of preceding vowel sound)
أ, ؤ and ئ	ʻ (*hamza*)

In the Name of Allah, Most Gracious, Most Merciful

And in Him is my trust

Chapter One
The Blessings of the Month of Rajab

Abdul Aziz Ahmed comments:
The Islamic calendar, like the Gregorian calendar, has twelve months. The main difference is that the Islamic calendar is based on the cycles of the moon rather than the cycles of the sun. As the lunar year is eleven days shorter than the solar year, the Arabic/Islamic months do not correspond directly to the Gregorian ones that have come to prevalence in the West. The first of the Islamic months is Muḥarram and the last is Dhûl Ḥijja. The months in order are:

Muḥarram
Ṣafar
Rabî' al-Awwal
Rabî' al-Thâni
Jumâdi al-Awwal
Jumâdi al-Thâni
Rajab
Sha'bân
Ramaḍân
Shawwâl
Dhûl Qa'da
Dhûl Ḥijja

The text we have before us does not start with the first month of the year. Perhaps the reason al-Bayhaqî begins with Rajab is because it is one of the four sacred months mentioned in the Quran. This concept is discussed by the Imâm in this and subsequent chapters. Of the four months, three are consecutive and Rajab stands alone, leading some scholars to identify it as the most sacred of the four.

Abdul Ḥamîd Qudus in his book *Kanz al-Najâḥ wa al-Surûr* said:

> *"Know that Rajab is a month of great blessing. Worship in it has majestic reward, especially fasting, the seeking of forgiveness and repentance from burdensome acts (of disobedience). It is recommended to supplicate during the first night (of the month), and supplications will (certainly) be answered. He*[10] ﷺ *said: 'There are five nights when supplications will not be rejected. (They are) the first night of Rajab, the night that is midway through Sha'bân, the evening preceding Friday, the night following the end of the fast (of Ramaḍân) and the night of the Sacrifice (which is the Eid associated with the Pilgrimage).' This* ḥadîth *was related by al-Suyûṭî in his book called* Al-Jâmi *from Ibn Asâkir on the authority of Abû Umâma, may Allah be pleased with him." (*Kanz al-Najâḥ wa al-Surûr p 46)

He says: *"The scholars say that Rajab is the month of seeking forgiveness (istighfâr), Sha'bân is the month of Prayer upon the Prophet ﷺ and Ramaḍân is the month of the Qurân."*

It is during this month that the Qibla was changed from Jerusalem to Makkah, and on the 27th of Rajab, shortly before the Prophet's migration to Makkah, he was taken on the celebrated night journey to Jerusalem after which he ascended to the Heavens where the ritual prayer known as the *ṣalah* was made compulsory.

'Abdul Ḥamîd Qudus mentions that 'Ali, may Allah be pleased with him, used to go into retreat on four special nights of the year, during which he would focus solely on worship. These were the first night of Rajab, the nights preceding the two Eid days, and the fifteenth of Sha'bân.

There are several famous supplications associated with the first night of Rajab. Although not directly from the Prophet ﷺ they are attributed to the masters of the spiritual path including 'Abdul Qâdir al-Jaylânî. It can be found in his book al-Ghunya, and is quoted by 'Abdul Ḥamîd Qudus. It is included as an appendix. The

---

[10] The reader will notice the symbol ﷺ, which is known as a "ligature" in the field of typography, throughout this work either in reference to, or immediately following the name of our Beloved Prophet Muhammad ﷺ. It reads, *Ṣalla Allahu 'Alayhi wa Sallam*, which means *"May the peace and blessings of Allah be upon him."* This practice of sending peace and blessings upon him is based on the verse in The Qur'an, *"Verily! Allah and His angels shower blessings on the Prophet. O ye who believe! Ask blessings on him and salute him with a worthy salutation."* (33:56) Moreover, the Prophet ﷺ promised that, *"Whoever sends blessings upon me once, Allah (SWT) will send blessings upon him tenfold, and will erase ten sins from him, and will raise him ten degrees in status."* Reported in al-Nasâ'î [Vol. 2, Book 13, Hadith 1298] *(Editor)*

son of Imâm al-Ḥaddâd, Syed Ḥasan bin 'Abdullah al-Ḥaddâd, compiled a litany of prayers for forgiveness which is often referred to as *Istighfâr Rajab, The Prayer of Seeking Forgiveness in Rajab,* which is commonly recited in many parts of the Muslim world.

Some have recommended a prayer called *Ṣalât al-Raghâ'ib* be read on the first Friday of Rajab, but Abdul Ḥamîd Qudus warns against it saying it is an innovation, and it would be better to pray the well-established prayer of *Ṣalât al-Awâbîn* or the *Ṣalât al-Tasbîh,* which have been described in the books of *ḥadîth*. And Allah knows best.

Know that the month of Rajab is among the Sacred Months about which Allah, the Mighty and Majestic, has said:

﴿إِنَّ عِدَّةَ الشُّهُورِ عِندَ اللهِ اثْنَا عَشَرَ شَهْرًا فِي كِتَابِ اللهِ يَوْمَ خَلَقَ

السَّمَاوَاتِ وَالأَرْضَ مِنْهَآ أَرْبَعَةٌ حُرُمٌ ذَلِكَ الدِّينُ الْقَيِّمُ

فَلاَ تَظْلِمُواْ فِيهِنَّ أَنفُسَكُمْ﴾

The number of months in the sight of Allah is twelve (in a year) - so ordained by Him the day He created the heavens and the earth. Of them, four are sacred. That is the straight usage. So wrong not yourselves therein.

(al-Tauba, 9:36)

Narration 1:

It has been reported[11] on the authority[12] of Abû Bakra,[13] that the Prophet ﷺ said: *"Indeed time rotates in its current form as it has done since the day Allah created the heavens and the earth. The year has twelve months. Four are sacred. Three of them are consecutive: Dhûl Qa'da, Dhûl Ḥijja, Muḥarram; and Rajab, which is the month of Muḍr,[14] between Jumâdi and Sha'bân."* [15]

Narration 2:

It has been reported on the authority of Abû Talḥa[16], that Ibn Abbâs[17] said about the verse *"The number of months in the sight of Allah is twelve (in a year) - so ordained by Him the day He created the heavens and the earth. Of them, four are sacred. That is the straight usage. So wrong not yourselves therein." (al-Tauba, 9:36)*

---

[11] *Ruwiya,* the passive form of the verb *Rawâ* (*to report, transmit*). This form is used often to identify weak *ḥadîth*, because it hints to a lack of certainty in either the chain or text. *(Editor)*

[12] Literally *'An Abî Bakra* (from/on the authority of Abû Bakra). This phrase is used frequently in *ḥadîth* transmission to indicate whom the person reportedly heard or transmitted the narration from. "Authority" here *does not* mean the religious authority and status of a *Ṣaḥâbî,* as the term is used in all stages of a chain, including weak and even fabricated ḥadîths. *(Editor)*

[13] Abû Bakra is Nâfi' ibn al-Ḥârith (although it is also recorded that his father was called Masrûḥ) al-Thaqafî. He was born in Ṭâif, joined the Prophet ﷺ in Madina, and died in Basra in 59H (678CE). He was famous for his recitation of Quran and as a narrator of *ḥadîth*, fifty-seven of which can be found in the books of Muslim and al-Bukhârî.

[14] Muḍar is the clan of the Prophet Muhammad ﷺ. They considered the month of Rajab to be sacred, whereas some other Arab clans mentioned different months in addition to the three months of Ḥajj agreed upon by all the Arab tribes of the time.

[15] Related by al-Bukhârî (6/83), Muslim (*ḥadîth* number 1689), Aḥmad (5/37) Abû Dawûd (*ḥadîth* number 1947).

[16] Abû Ṭalḥa, Zayd ibn Sahl al-Khazrajî, was a famous Companion of the Prophet ﷺ and one of the most noted horsemen and archers. He was chosen to be at the Prophet's side at the battles of Badr, 'Uḥud, and Khandaq. He died in 34H (654CE), aged 70, in Madina.

[17] 'Abdullah ibn 'Abbâs was the cousin of the Prophet ﷺ. He was recognised by fellow Companions as one of the greatest scholars of their generation, and was one of the most prolific narrators of *ḥadîth,* relating 1660 in total. He died in Tâ'if in 68H (687CE).

"'Do not wrong yourselves therein' means 'in any of them,' but then the four months are emphasised as they are sacred. Their sanctity is immense and therefore wrongdoing in them is immense, as is the reward in them for righteous actions."

And the Shaykh[18], may Allah show him mercy, said: "The people in the time preceding Islam used to honour these sacred months, especially the month of Rajab and they would not fight each other during any of them."

Narration 3

Mahdî ibn Maymûn[19] said: *"I heard Abû Rajâ' al-'Utâradî*[20] *say, 'During the time of Jâhiliyya, when the month of Rajab entered, we would say, "The Iron Remover has come." We would not place iron in our arrows nor in our bows. We would remove them and throw them away (indicating that they would not engage in battle).'"* [21]

---

[18] The reader will find the saying *"The Shaykh said"* throughout this work. This is actually referring to Imam Al-Bayhaqî himself, and the phrase was most likely added by one of his students, who received and copied the book from the Imam directly. This was common amongst copiests to differentiate the author's words from those of others, especially the texts of *ḥadîth*. *(Editor)*

[19] Mahdi bin Maymûn was a Kurdish scholar of the third generation. He heard ḥadîth from several people, including Abû Rajâ' al-'Utâradî who had heard from a number of Companions including 'Aisha, 'Umar ibn al-Khattab, and 'Ali ibn Abû Tâlib, may Allah be pleased with them all. He died in Basra in 172H (788CE).

[20] He is 'Imrân bin Malḥan, Abû Rajâ' al-'Utâradî who was born eleven years before the migration of the Prophet ﷺ to Madina and lived to the age of 117. He is counted in *al-Isâba* as a Companion, although he did not relate *ḥadîth* directly from the Prophet but did so from several other Companions.

[21] Related by al-Bukhârî (Book 59, *ḥadîth* 661).

Narration 4

Bayân said: "I heard Qays ibn Abû Ḥâzim[22] mention Rajab and he said, *"We used to call it the Deaf One (meaning the sound of fighting cannot be heard in that month) during the time of Jâhiliyya (the time before the Prophecy of Muḥammad ﷺ) because of its sanctity and high esteem with us."'*

The Shaykh, may Allah be pleased with him, said that Rajab was called the "*Deaf One*" because the clamour of arms could not be heard in it. *Ḥadîth* have been related in this regard but with weak chains.

Narration 5

Among them is what has been related by 'Aisha,[23] may Allah be pleased with her, who said that she heard the Messenger of Allah ﷺ say: *"Indeed Rajab is the Month of Allah, and it is called The Deaf One. The people of Jâhiliyya used to make idle their weapons and lay them down; so people would be safe and the roads would be safe, and people would not fear one another until it ended."*

The Shaykh, may Allah be pleased with him, said: "And what is related in this *ḥadîth* is well known among the scholars of history. It used to be like that in the early years of Islam. They would not fight (during these months)

---

[22] According to Shaykh Muhammad al-Ninowy this is not Qays ibn Abû Ḥâzim, the Bedouin Companion given specific protection by the Prophet ﷺ according to the Arab tradition as referred to in *al-Isâba*. He said he is a *Tâbî,* Follower. Bayân is unknown to him but he noted that this *ḥadîth* includes in its chain of narrators Aḥmad bin 'Abdul Jabbâr al-'Uṭâridî, who he said "is weak and is only accepted in the narration of the *Sîrah*, Prophetic Lifestory." And Allah knows best.

[23] 'Aisha bint Abû Bakr (see note 433) was the wife of the Prophet ﷺ which is why she is referred to here as the 'Mother of the Faithful'. She was known for her great knowledge, wisdom and closeness to the Prophet, upon him be ﷺ. She was born nine years before the Hijra to Madina and died there on 17th Ramaḍân 57H (677CE). The Prophet ﷺ told the Companions that one third of knowledge can be taken from her. She related 1210 *ḥadîth*.

and then Allah, the Exalted, gave permission to fight the polytheists at any time, but the sanctity of the Sacred Months remained effectual in terms of additional reward and burden (for wrongdoing) during them, to the extent that Allah the Exalted specified that during these months, wrongdoing is forbidden. For this reason, al-Shâfi'î was very harsh about the payment of blood money for someone killed mistakenly during the Sacred Months. If wrongdoing during these months carries a greater burden, then goodness during it has greater reward. And the following has been related about fasting in these months:

Narration 6

On the authority of Mujîba al-Bâhiliya from her uncle or her father[24] that he came to the Messenger of Allah ﷺ and then left, returning a year later. His state and appearance had changed. He said, "Do you know me, O Messenger of Allah?"

"Make yourself known," he said.

"I am al-Bâhilî. I came to you last year," he said.

"What has happened to change you so? You used to have such a handsome form," he said.

"Since departing from you, I have not eaten food except during the night," he said.

And so the Messenger of Allah ﷺ said: *"You have tortured yourself."* Then he said, *"Fast the month of Steadfastness (that is, the month of Ramaḍân) and one day each month."*

"Give me more, for I am strong," he said.

"Fast two days," he said.

"Give me more, for I am strong," he said.

[24] He is 'Abdullah ibn Ḥârith al-Bâhili, a Companion of the Prophet ﷺ.

"Fast three days," he said.

"Give me more, for I am strong," he said.

"Fast from the Sacred (months) and leave (some days). Fast from the Sacred (months) and leave (some days). Fast from the Sacred (months) and leave (some days)."

(As he said it) he indicated with three of his fingers, closing them and then unfolding them.[25]

The Shaykh, may Allah be pleased with him, said: "The Messenger of Allah ﷺ established in this statement the preference of fasting during the Sacred Months but leaving a few days (so as not to fast it in the same way one would fast Ramaḍân). This is how the Messenger of Allah ﷺ used to fast during these months."[26]

Narration 7

Uthmân ibn Ḥakîm said: "I asked Sa'îd ibn Jubayr[27] about fasting during the month of Rajab. He said that Ibn Abbâs told him that the Messenger of Allah ﷺ used to fast sometimes so much of it that we thought he fasted it all and other times he would fast so little that we thought he did not fast any of it."[28]

---

[25] Related by Abû Dawûd (2/810) and Ibn Mâjah (1/544).

[26] There are two chains of narration for this *ḥadîth.* The Dar al-Kutub edition counts them as two separate *ḥadîth* and from here on the numbering between the editions differs. The second chain is as follows: "Abû 'Abdullah al-Ḥâfiẓ informed us that Abû al-'Abbâs Muḥammad bin Ya'qûb told us that Yaḥyâ bin Abû Ṭâlib that 'Abdul Wahâb bin 'Aṭâ told us that Sa'îd al-Jurayrî said..."

[27] Sa'îd ibn Jubayr was a well-known *Tâbi'î,* Follower, who related *ḥadîth* from Ibn 'Abbâs and 'Umar among others. He was well known for his intense worship and as a scholar, jurist and judge. He was executed by Ḥajjâj bin Yûsuf in Kufa in 95H (713CE).

[28] Related by Muslim (2/811), Abû Dawûd (3/811), al-Nasâ'î (4/199) and Ibn Mâjah (1/546).

And he[29] said: There are many Prophetic Traditions about the blessings of fasting in Rajab some of which have weaknesses in their chains of narration. Among them are the following:

Narration 8

Mûsâ ibn 'Imrân said that Anas ibn Mâlik[30] said: "The Messenger of Allah ﷺ said, '*Indeed, in the Garden there is a river called Rajab. It is whiter than milk and sweeter than honey. Whoever fasts a day of the month of Rajab, Allah will allow him to drink from that river.*'"

Narration 9

On the authority of 'Abdul 'Azîz bin Sa'îd[31] from his father who said that the Messenger of Allah ﷺ said: "*Whoever, fasts a day from the month of Rajab, it is as if he fasted the whole year. Whoever fasts seven days, seven doors of Hell will be locked against him. Whoever fasts eight days, eight doors of the Garden will be opened for him. Whoever fasts ten days, will not ask Allah, the Mighty and Majestic, for anything except that he will be given what he asks for. Whoever fasts fifteen days, a caller will call from the sky, 'Surely what has preceded is forgiven and so return to your action, your wrong actions have been turned into rewards. Whoever increases, Allah will increase him.' It was in Rajab that Noah's Ark was carried (over*

[29] *Imam al-Bayhaqî*, as mentioned previously. *(Editor)*

[30] Anas ibn Mâlik was the servant of the Prophet ﷺ and therefore grew up in his household. He was given to the Prophet ﷺ by his mother when they both embraced Islam shortly after the Prophet's arrival in Madina. After the death of the Prophet ﷺ he moved to Syria and then to Basra where he was the last Companion to die there. He died in 93H (711CE), and related 1280 *ḥadîth*.

[31] 'Abdul 'Azîz bin Sa'îd bin Sa'd bin 'Ubâda was one of the Followers (*Tâbi'în*) who related *ḥadîth* from his father. According to some, this particular *ḥadîth* was related from his grandfather. And Allah knows best.

the water). Noah fasted and ordered those with him to fast. The Ark rode the seas for six months until ten days had passed from the month of Muḥarram."[32]

Narration 10

On the authority of Anas ibn Mâlik[33], the Messenger of Allah ﷺ said: "*The elect of all months is Rajab. It is the Month of Allah, the Mighty and Majestic. Whoever esteems the month of Rajab has indeed esteemed the command of Allah. Whoever honours the command of Allah, He will enter him into the Blessed Gardens and grant for him his greatest pleasure. Sha'bân is my month. Whoever honour the month of Sha'bân has esteemed my command, and whoever honour my affair I will be his flagbearer*[34] *and treasure on the Day of Standing. The Month of Ramaḍân is the month of my nation. Whoever recognises its sanctity and does not desecrate it, and fasts its days and stands in prayer during its night, and protects their limbs will leave from Ramaḍân with no wrong action about which Allah will ask him.*" This *ḥadîth* is denounced[35] completely.

Narration 11

Salmân al-Fârisî[36] said that the Messenger of Allah ﷺ said: "*In Rajab is a (special) day and a night that if one fasts the day and stands in prayer in the night,*

---

32 Parts of this *ḥadîth* are found in Ibn Ḥajr's *Tibyân al-'Ajâib* (*ḥadîth* number 45).

33 See note 30.

34 *Faraṭ* is from the verb 'to overflow' or 'hasten forward' or 'be excessive'. In the context of this *ḥadîth,* it implies 'one precedes to the watering hole' or 'overflowing treasure'. And Allah knows best.

35 *Munkar* means denounced or weak. This is usually because one of the narrators is known for having a poor memory or the text clearly contradicts a stronger *ḥadîth*. And Allah knows best.

36 Salmân al-Fârisî was born into a Persian, fire-worshipping family, but converted to Christianity, seeking the truth in various monasteries of Iraq and Syria before being sold into slavery and ending up in Madina. He recognised the Prophet ﷺ from the scriptures he

it will be as if he fasted for a hundred years and stood in prayer for a hundred years. It is the 27th of Rajab. On it, the Messenger ﷺ was sent." It has been related with other chains of narration too.

Narration 12

It is related on the authority of Anas[37] that the Messenger of Allah ﷺ said: *"In Rajab is a night during which the worker of good deeds will receive the rewards of a hundred years and that night is the 27th of Rajab. Whoever performs twelve prayer cycles* (raka'ât) *in which he reads the Opening Chapter of the Quran and another chapter and reads the* tashahud[38] *and completes each (couple of prayer cycles) with the salutation (that ends the prayer) and then he says* 'subḥan_Allâh wal_ḥamdullilâh wa lâ ilâha il_Allâh wa_llâhu akbar' *(Transcendent is Allah, all praise is for Allah, there is no god but Allah and Allah is greatest,) a hundred times and seeks forgiveness a hundred times and prays upon the Prophet ﷺ a hundred times, and then supplicates for himself that which he wishes from the affairs of his temporal life and his everlasting life, and then fasts the next day, surely Allah will answer all his supplications, except if he has supplicated for disobedience."*[39]

The Shaykh, may Allah be pleased with him, said that the chain of narration is not as exemplary as the previous one. (Much) has been related about the desirability of supplication during the Sacred Months of which Rajab is one. A good *ḥadîth* in this regard is the following:

---

had studied previously and embraced Islam, and was bought and freed by the Prophet ﷺ He died in Madina in 36H (656CE).

[37] See note 30.

[38] The *tashahud* is the part of the prayer that is read while sitting in the second and final prayer cycles. What is meant by "praying the *tashahud* in every second prayer cycle along with the salutation" is completing them as six sets of two prayer cycles (*raka'tayn*).

[39] Parts of this are related by al-Suyûṭî in *Durr al-Manthûr* (3/235) and Ibn Ḥajr in *Tibyân al-Ajâib* (*ḥadîth* number 58).

Narration 13

Ibn 'Abbâs[40], may Allah be pleased with him, said: "While we were sitting with 'Umar ibn al- Khaṭṭâb[41], may Allah be pleased with him, on a day his administration was being presented to him, a blind disabled man passed by, burdening his guide (because of his limping).[42] On seeing him and his strange state, 'Umar said, 'Who knows this man?'

A man from the company said, "He is a man from Banî Ṣabghâ', Burayq cursed him."

'What is Burayq?' he said.

"A man from Yemen," he said.

'Is he here?' he said.

"Yes," he said. He was brought to 'Umar.

'What is the situation with you and what is Banî Ṣabghâ?' He said.

"Banî Ṣabghâ were twelve men. We used to argue in the times before Islam. They used to take my money and insult my honour. I pleaded with them and implored them by Allah and ties of kinship (to stop), but they rejected (my pleas). I was patient for some time, until the Sacred Month came and then I supplicated against them and I said:

O Allah, I ask you with the prayer of the one who strives
Destroy Banî Ṣabghâ all but one of them
Then strike the foot and leave him disabled
And blind, so when he moves, his guide becomes burdened

---

40 See note 17.

41 'Umar ibn al-Khaṭṭâb was a close Companion of the Prophet ﷺ and the second ruler after him. He was the first to be called 'Commander of the Faithful'. His predecessor, Abû Bakr was called the 'khalîfa' meaning 'representative' of the Messenger. Initially, he was a fierce opponent of Islam but Allah guided him after the Prophet ﷺ made a special supplication that Islam be strengthened by him. As a ruler he was known to take special care of widows, the blind, and the disabled, personally providing support and help. He related 539 *ḥadîth.*

42 The wording was taken from a version edited by Adnan Abdul Raḥmân al-Qaysī and the explanation was provided by Shaykh Afeefuddin al-Jaylani.

A year had not passed when all but one of them had died. This is the person you can see (before you). His guide is burdened whenever he moves."

'*Subḥânallâh*! (Transcendent is Allah!), indeed in this is a lesson and something to marvel at,' said 'Umar.

And to this, another man from the company said, "O Commander of the Faithful, shall I tell you something even more amazing than this?"

'Indeed, yes!' he said.

"There were some men from Khuzâ'a who were neighbours to a particular man. They cut off family ties and showed very poor neighbourliness. He beseeched them by Allah and their family ties to free him of the reprehensible things (they were doing to him). They refused. He was patient for a while until the Sacred Month came, and then he supplicated against them:

> O Allah! Lord of the one who feels safe and the one who fears
> Who hears the calls of voices carried through the air
> Indeed Khuzâ'a are fond of assembling
> But they give not rights, nor equal share
> Gather their progeny,
> And those of close ties and discourse
> Gather them in the depths of every quake!"

He said: "While they were attending a well to draw water, some of them were in the well and others above it. It collapsed and became their grave until the Final Hour."

'*Subḥânallâh*! (Transcendent is Allah!), indeed in this is a lesson and something to marvel at,' said 'Umar.

Another man from among the people said: "O Commander of the Faithful, shall I tell you something even more amazing than this?"

'Indeed, yes!' he said.

"There was a man from Hudhayl who inherited all the wealth of his sub-clan, as there was no one left among (that sub-clan) except him. He gathered a lot of wealth and went to a group of his clansmen called Banî Mu'amal. He wanted to live in their neighbourhood but they prevented him from doing so and stopped him from doing as he wished. This was because they were jealous of him because of his wealth and they wanted a share of his riches. They got together and took his wealth and insulted his honour. He implored them by Allah and the ties of kinship to be fair and to stop doing such reprehensible acts to him. They refused. One man among them called Rabâḥ or Rayâḥ spoke to them saying, 'O Banî Mu'amal! Your cousin has chosen to be your neighbour rather than any other (neighbourhood) so show good neighbourliness.' They rejected (his pleas). He was patient with them for a while until the Sacred Month, and then he supplicated against them, saying:

O Allah! Free me of Banû Mu'amal
Throw a fetter upon their napes
From a boulder or a huge army
All but Rabâh for he did not do (what they did)

He said that on that day they were descending to the foot of the mountain when a boulder descended from the mountain. It crushed everything it passed. It passed their homes and pulverised them in one go, all but the house of Rabâḥ, which was saved."

'*Subḥânallâh*! (Transcendent is Allah!), indeed in this is a lesson and something to marvel at,' said 'Umar.

Another man from among the people said: "O Commander of the Faithful, shall I tell you something even more amazing than this?"
'Indeed, yes!' he said.

"There was a man from Bani Juhayna who became a neighbour of people from Bani Ḍamra during the time before Islam. There was a man from Bani Ḍamra called Raysha who showed animosity towards him. He slaughtered his camel. (The man) complained to his people about it and they said 'we have abandoned him, wait and we will kill him'. When he saw that, he still did not desist. (The man) waited until the Sacred Month and then supplicated against him:

Sanction to Raysha of Damra
    That Allah set in motion his destiny
If he were to continue to take and slaugther
    Taking them from the valley
With a sharp, harsh blade
    O Allah! If you punish, take him
And make him a lesson before the people
    That he is eaten for all to behold

Allah caused a decimating disease to consume his limbs and he died less than a year later."
'*Subḥânallâh*! (Transcendent is Allah!),' said 'Umar. 'Indeed in this is a lesson and something to marvel at. It was that Allah used to do such things to people during the times before Islam. Some would be struck by (the prayers) of others but when Allah brought Islam, He delayed such punishment until the Day of Resurrection. That is why Allah said:

(إِنَّ يَوْمَ الْفَصْلِ مِيقَاتُهُمْ أَجْمَعِينَ)

Verily the Day of Sorting Out is the time appointed for all of them.

(al-Dukhân, 44:40)

(بَلِ السَّاعَةُ مَوْعِدُهُمْ وَالسَّاعَةُ أَدْهَى وَأَمَرُّ)

Nay, the Hour (of Judgment) is the time promised them (for their full recompense). And that Hour will be most grievous and most bitter.

(al-Qamar, 54:46)

And He said:

(وَلَوْ يُؤَاخِذُ اللَّهُ النَّاسَ بِمَا كَسَبُوا مَا تَرَكَ عَلَى ظَهْرِهَا مِن دَابَّةٍ وَلَكِن يُؤَخِّرُهُمْ إِلَى أَجَلٍ مُّسَمًّى)

If Allah were to punish men according to what they deserve, He would not leave on the back of the (earth) a single living creature, but He gives them respite for a stated term.'"

(al-Fâtir, 35:45)

And the Shaykh, may Allah be pleased with him, said: "This *ḥadîth* was also related by Muḥammad bin Isḥâq bin Yasâr, from what he heard from 'Ikrima on the authority of 'Ibn Abbâs, but without the references to Banî Ḍamra, and that strengthens the narration of Ibn Lahi'a.

It has also been narrated on the authority of Nuṣayr ibn Abû al-'Ashath. He said: ''Umar swore an oath and looked to the face of the blind man' and then he mentioned (the rest of the *ḥadîth*)."

And the Shaykh, may Allah be pleased with him, said: "There have been many narrations about supplication with the beginning of Rajab, but they are not strong *ḥadîth*."[43]

---

[43] There is some difference between the two published editions. The ones quoted above are from the Dar al-Kutub edition. The Dar Ibn Hazm edition mentions the following slightly different lines of poetry.

O Allah! Lord of the one who feels safe and the one who fears
Hearing the voices of those whose calls are carried on air
Indeed Khuzâ'a have gathered to oppress
And to not give me my right or my equal share
Gather their beloved all but the one who was kind
Between the evil company and their well
Gather them in the depths of every quake

Later in the narration it mentions Rumaytha rather than Raysha. Shaykh Muhammad al-Ninowy says the version given above is more accurate as Rumaytha is normally a female name. The poetry differs there also with the following lines found in the Dar Ibn Hazm edition.

Is it true of Rumaytha from Ḍamra
That Allah will ease forward his destiny?
If he continues with the camels and cattle
To attack in the valley
With a harsh sharp blade
O Allah! If there is a dawn for me after this
Show before my eyes, his limbs
Being eaten until he finds his grave

And Allah knows best.

Narration 14

Anas[44] said that the Messenger of Allah ﷺ used to say as the month of Rajab entered, "*Allahumma bârik lanâ fî Rajab wa Sha'bân wa ballighnâ Ramaḍân. O Allah! Bless us in Rajab and Sha'bân, and may we reach Ramaḍân.*" He also used to say, "*The night preceding Friday is the evening of blazing light, and the day of Friday is the day of shining brightness.*"[45]

Narration 15

It has been reported on the authority of Ibn 'Abbâs that the Messenger of Allah ﷺ forbade fasting the whole of Rajab.[46]

This is how Dawûd bin 'Aṭâ' related it, yet he is not a strong (narrator), and we have already narrated a tradition on the authority of Ibn 'Abbâs about the action of the Prophet ﷺ (regarding fasting the whole of Rajab). His action has (here) been changed into a prohibition. If it is correct, it needs to be interpreted as (the Prophet ﷺ) distancing himself (from the recommendation to fast the whole of Rajab and thereby equating it with the month of Ramaḍân). The meaning is as has been mentioned by al-Shâfi'î in the old school of thought.[47] He said: "*It is disliked that a man fasts a month in its entirety in the way that we fast the month of Ramaḍân.*" And *ḥadîth* are required in support of this position, and they are as follows:

---

[44] See note 30.

[45] Related by Aḥmad (1/259).

[46] Related by Ibn Majâh (1/444).

[47] Imam al-Shafi'î issued legal rulings from a relatively early age. Towards the end of his life, after settling in Egypt, his methodology was refined even further, and subsequently some of his older rulings were changed. The older rulings, which were kept by his students he had left behind in Iraq, became known as the old school of thought. His newer opinions were taught to his students in Egypt and became known as the new school.

Narration 16

'Aisha[48], the Mother of the Believers, may Allah be pleased with her, said that the Messenger of Allah ﷺ used to fast so much that we said he was always fasting, and sometimes he would not fast to the extent that we would say he never did (additional) fasts. However, I never saw him fast a whole month except the month of Ramaḍân. I did not see him fast in any month more than he did in Sha'bân.[49]

Al-Shâfi'î said, *"that is (he would miss) a day or so,"* and he said, *"he only showed dislike (for fasting a whole month) so that the ignorant one would not think it was an obligation. Otherwise if one fasted it, it would be fine."* So al-Shâfi'î (firstly) explains that it is disliked (*makrûh*), but then says that if one did it, it would be fine, because the general knowledge among the Muslims is that there is no obligation in the foundation of Islamic law to fast other than Ramaḍân (and this was the point of the prohibition), and (in doing so) he clarifies what is meant by 'reprehensible' (*makrûh*) in this case. And Allah knows best.

Narration 17

'Âmir bin Shabal said he heard Abû Qalâba[50] say, *"In the Garden is a palace for those who fast (the month of) Rajab."*

The Shaykh, may Allah be pleased with him, said: "Abû Qalâba was one of the great Followers (*Tâbi'în*) from among the second generation, and he would not have said something like that except if he had heard it from someone above him."

---

[48] See note 23.

[49] Related by al-Bukhârî (2/244) and Aḥmad (6/107. 153 and 242).

[50] Abû Qalâba is 'Abdullah bin Zayd al-Jarmî who related *ḥadith* from many Companions including Abû Hurayra and al-Nu'mân ibn Bashîr. He was born in Basra, died in Syria in 104H (722CE), and was known as a scholarly jurist.

Chapter Two
The Blessings of Sha'bân

Abdul Aziz Ahmed comments:
Sha'bân is the eighth month of the Islamic Calendar. Its name is derived from the roots Sh-'a'-b which means 'to gather, assemble or rally' or alternatively it could have the opposite meaning of 'to scatter or disperse.' It is thought that its name is taken from the second meaning, and historically it was the month in which people would separate themselves from each other and disperse in search of water. This was when the months were associated with the solar calendar and Sha'bân was approximately equivalent to July. It is also thought to imply that they would disperse in hunting parties after the restrictions of the Sacred Month of Rajab were lifted as they moved from the seventh to the eighth month of the year. And Allah knows best.

Abdul Ḥamîd Qudus in his book *Kanz al-Najâḥ wa al-Surûr* said:

> *'Know that the noble month of Sha'bân is one of the mighty months. It is a month famed for its blessing and abundant good. Repentance in it is among the greatest of the righteous gains and acts of obedience in it are among the most profitable trades. Allah made it one of the racetracks of time. He granted safety to those who turn back to Him in it. Those who accustom themselves to striving in it, succeed in Ramaḍân. It is the month of the Prophet, may Allah the Exalted send prayers upon him, as we have mentioned from the* ḥadîth *that states, 'and Sha'bân is my month'. In it, the moon was miraculously split for the Messenger ﷺ. It is the month of sending prayers on the Prophet as has been mentioned in* Tuḥfat al-Ikhwân. *And so always pray upon him abundantly O my brothers, especially in the month of your Prophet, Sha'bân. On the night that falls midway through it, the life spans of the slaves are divided, and proximity and distance are determined.'* (Kanz al-Najâḥ wa al-Surûr p.53)

Narration 18

Abû Salama[51] said he said: "I asked 'Aisha[52], may Allah be pleased with her, about the fasting of the Messenger of Allah ﷺ. She said, *'He used to fast so much that we said he was always fasting, and sometimes he would not fast to the extent that we would say he never did (additional) fasts. I did not see him fast in any month more than he did in Sha'bân. He would fast almost all of it.'*"[53] Al-Shâfi'î, may Allah show him mercy, related it and said of Sha'bân, *"that he fasted it all or all but a little."*

Abû Bakr bin Abû Shayba also related it on the authority of Sufyân and said, *"that he fasted it all or all but a little."*

Narration 19

It is related by Mu'âwiya bin Ṣâliḥ that 'Abdullah ibn Qays heard 'Aisha[54], may Allah be pleased with her say: *"The most beloved month to the Messenger of Allah ﷺ for fasting is Sha'bân and then to join it to Ramaḍân."*[55]

---

[51] This is Abû Salama, Abdullah bin Abdul Raĥmân, one of the *Tâb'iîn*. The Prophet ﷺ sent Abdul Raĥmân bin 'Awf to call the people of Bani Kalb and to marry one of their noblewomen. Abû Salama was born of that marriage. He heard *ĥadîth* from many of the major Companions. He died in Madina in 94H (712CE).

[52] See note 23.

[53] Related by Muslim (2/811), al-Nasâi (4/200-201) and Aḥmad (6/39 and 108).

[54] See note 23.

[55] Related by Abû Dawûd (2/812), al-Nasâi (4/199) and Aḥmad (6/188).

Narration 20

It has been reported on the authority of Anas ibn Mâlik,[56] that it was said, "O Messenger of Allah, which fast is best?"
"The fast of Sha'bân honouring Ramaḍân," he said.
"And which charity is best?" He said.
"Charity in Ramaḍân," he said.[57]

Narration 21

Usâma bin Zayd[58] said: "I said, 'O Messenger of Allah, indeed I see you fast a month in a way I do not see you fast any other month.'
"Which month is that?" He said.
'Sha'bân,' I said.
"Sha'bân is between Rajab and the month of Ramaḍân. People forget about it. The actions of the servant are raised in it and I would love that my actions are not raised other than while I am fasting.""[59]
And Ibn Abû 'Uwais related it on the authority of Abû Ghaṣn, Thâbit bin Qays al-Ghifârî on the authority of Abu Sa'îd al-Maqbarî on the authority of Usâma bin Zayd from the Prophet ﷺ.

---

[56] See note 30.
[57] Related by al-Tirmidhî (3/51).
[58] 'Usama's father, Zayd ibn al-Ḥaritha was kidnapped and sold into slavery, eventually ending up in the household of the Prophet ﷺ After his father had found him, he chose to stay in the Prophetic household rather than return to his blood family. He married the lady who looked after the Prophet ﷺ when his own mother died. 'Usama was born of this marriage and grew to be a great warrior and respected and much loved Companion. He was born 7 years before the Hijra to Madina and died in the year 54H (674 CE) in Madina.
[59] Related by al-Nasâi (4/201) Abû Dawûd (*ḥadîth* number 2436) and Aḥmad (5/201).

Chapter Three
Blessings of the Fifteenth of Sha'bân

Abdul Aziz Ahmed comments:
Laylatul Niṣf min Sha'ban literally means the night which is in the middle of Sha'bân but is throughout this chapter translated as 'the fifteenth of Sha'bân'.
Abdul Ḥamîd Qudus in his book *Kanz al-Najâḥ wa al-Surûr* said:

> *The night that is midway through Sha'bân has many names and having many names indicates the high status of the thing being named. Al-Fashnî mentions most of them in his book* al-Tuḥfa *and with each name the wisdom behind it being attributed to that particular name. And after it, he provides a ḥadîth or tradition about it, and so look at it, and you will see amazing things. And of the names he mentions are* al-Laylat al-Mubâraka, *The Blessed Night,* al-Laylat al-Barâ'a, *the Night of Freedom (from the Fire),* al-Laylat al-Qisma, *The Night of Distribution and al-Laylat al-Ijâba, the Night of Answering (to supplication). He said it has been related on the authority of Ibn 'Umar who said: "There are five nights on which supplication will not be rejected. They are the night preceding Friday, the first night of Rajab, the night midway through Sha'bân, the Night of Power and the nights preceding the two Eid days."* (Kanz al-Najaḥ p55-56)

Narration 22

It has been reported on the authority of Mu'âdh bin Jabal[60] that the Prophet ﷺ said: *"Allah, the Exalted, looks over His creation on the fifteenth night of Sha'bân and forgives all creation, except the one who attributes partners to Him or one who shows enmity (towards the Religion and its people)."*[61]
The Shaykh said, "it was also said on the authority of Makḥûl."

Narration 23

It has been reported on the authority of Abû Tha'laba al-Khushanî[62] that the Prophet ﷺ said: *"On the fifteenth night of Sha'bân, Allah the Exalted looks over His creation and forgives the believers, and allows the disbelievers to continue (without punishing them) and leaves the people of spite to their spite so that they leave Him."*[63]

---

[60] Muadh bin Jabal embraced Islam when he was eighteen years old and went on to attend all the battles that the Messenger ﷺ attended. He was known for his good looks, bravery, generosity and intellect. He was sent as an envoy to the Yemen to teach its inhabitants about Islam and to judge between them in their affairs. He related 157 *ḥadîth*. He died during the plague, which swept through what is now modern day Jordan, in the year 18H (639CE).

[61] The word used in this *ḥadîth* is *mashâḥin* which is derived from the verb *shâḥana* which means "he bore rancour" or "treated another with rancour", therefore the *mashâhin* is "one who regards or treats another with rancour". According to Lane's Lexicon it has the technical definition of *"the schismatic innovator in Religion, or one who has rancour in his heart towards the Companions, or he who forsakes the institutes or rule and usage of his Prophet, who speaks against his people or who sheds their blood."* The *ḥadîth* forms part of a *ḥadîth* related by Aḥmad (2/176) and al-Mundhirî (2/119).

[62] Abû Tha'laba was Jurthûm bin Nâshir. He attended the Oath of Allegiance known as the Bayatul Ridwân. He prayed to die in his prayer, which was accepted. He died praying in his mosque in Syria in 95H (713 CE). He related 40 *ḥadîth.*

[63] The *ḥadîth* forms part of a *ḥadîth* related by al-Mundhirî (2/119).

And al-Ḥajâj bin Arṭa' related it on the authority of Makḥûl on the authority of Kathîr bin Murra al-Ḥadramî[64] from the Prophet ﷺ.
And al-Ḥasan ibn al-Ḥasan on the authority of Makḥûl, where it stops (That is, it is not attributed to the Prophet ﷺ.)

Narration 24

And 'Ali ibn 'Abû Ṭâlib[65] said that the Messenger of Allah ﷺ said: *"When the fifteenth night of Sha'bân comes, stand its night (in prayer) and fast its day, for surely Allah the Exalted has said: 'Is there any seeker of forgiveness so that I can forgive him? Is there any seeker of provision, so that I can provide for him? Is there anyone asking for something so that I can give it to him? It will be like that until the rise of dawn.'"* [66]

Narration 25

It has been reported on the authority of 'Uthmân ibn Abû al-'Âṣ[67] that the Prophet ﷺ said: *"On the fifteenth night of Sha'bân a caller calls, 'Is there any seeker of forgiveness whom I can forgive? Is there any asker whom I can give to?' For*

---

[64] He was better known as Abû Shajrah, and considered by some to be one of the Companions, although he only relates *ḥadîth* from other Companions, including Muadh ibn Jabal. Most consider him to be a *Tâb'î*, Follower. They say he met more than 70 Companions in Syria. And Allah knows best. He spent much of his life in Syria, and is buried in Homs.

[65] 'Ali ibn Abû Ṭâlib was the cousin and son-in-law of the Messenger ﷺ. He grew up in his household, and was among the first to embrace Islam. He was ten years old at the time. He accompanied the Prophet ﷺ in every battle except Tabuk. He was the fourth ruler after the Messenger, and was martyred in the city of Kufa on the 21st of Ramadan, 40H (661 CE).

[66] Related by Ibn Mâjah (1/444).

[67] Uthmân bin Abû al-Âs bin Nawfal was a Qurayshite Companion whose father died as a disbeliever at the Battle of Badr.

surely, no one asks except that he is given, other than the adulteress and the one who attributes partners to Allah." [68]

Narration 26

It has been reported on the authority of 'Urwah ibn Zubair that 'Aisha[69], may Allah be pleased with her, said: "*On the fifteenth night of Sha'bân, the Messenger of Allah ﷺ gently withdrew from our blanket.*" She then said, "*And by Allah, our blanket was not made of woven silk nor raw silk or old cotton or flax or wool.*"

"Praised is Allah! Then what was it made of?" we said.

"*Its thread was of wool and its filling was of camel hair,*" she said.

"I was afraid that he (was leaving me) to go to one of his other wives, so I got up to ensure he would not leave the house, and my feet came across his and (I realised) he was in prostration, and so I memorised his words. He said:

> *'Sajada laka sawâdi wa khayâli. Wa âmana laka fu'âdi wa abû'u laka bi_ni'ami wa_'atarifu bi_dhunûbi al-'aẓîma. Ẓalamtu nafsi faghfirli, innahu lâ yaghfiru_dhunûba illa anta. A'ûdhu bi 'afwika min 'uqûbatika wa a'ûdhu biraḥmatika min naqmatika wa a'ûdhu biriḍâka min sakhaṭika wa a'ûdhu bika minka. Lâ 'uḥṣi thanâ'an 'alayka. Anta kamâ athnayta 'ala nafsika.'*
>
> *The inner core of my heart and my spirit have prostrated to You. My mind has believed in You, and I come to You in recognition of the blessings (bestowed upon me) and recognising my mighty sins. I have*

---

[68] The *ḥadîth* forms part of a *ḥadîth* related by al-Mundhirî (2/119) and by al-Dhahabî in al-Mizân (*ḥadîth* number 20024).

[69] See note 23.

wrongedmyself and so I ask forgiveness (of You) for my sins for surely no one can forgive sins other than You. I seek refuge in Your pardon from Your punishment. I seek refuge in Your mercy from Your vengeance. I seek refuge in Your pleasure from Your wrath. I seek refuge in You from You. I am unable to praise You, except in the way You have praised Your Self.

He continued to pray standing and sitting until morning," she said. "Morning came and his feet were swollen. I touched them and said, 'By you, my father and my mother! You have tired yourself. Has not Allah pardoned your sins that you have done and not done?'

And he said: *"Indeed, yes, O 'Aisha! Should I not therefore be a grateful servant? Do you know what this night contains?"*

'What does it contain, O Messenger of Allah?' I said.

"In it, every birth of one of the children of Adam for that year is recorded. And in it, every one of the children of Adam who will die is recorded. And in it, their actions are raised up. And in it, their provisions descend." And then he said, *'Nobody enters the Garden except by the Mercy of Allah.'*

"And not even you, O Messenger of Allah?" I said.

He placed his hand upon his crown and said: 'Indeed no, not even me! It is only that Allah has enveloped me in His Mercy.' He said this three times."[70]

---

[70] Related by al-Aqîlî in *al-Du'afâ al-Kabîr* (1/116).

Narration 27

It has been reported on the authority of Abû Rajâ' al-'Utâradî[71] that Anas ibn Mâlik[72] said: "The Prophet ﷺ sent me to the house of 'Aisha, may Allah be pleased with her, on an errand. I said to her, 'Be quick, as I left the Messenger of Allah ﷺ talking to them about the night of the fifteenth of Sha'bân.'

"O dear Anas! Sit and I will tell you about the night of the fifteenth of Sha'bân. That night was my night with the Messenger of Allah ﷺ. The Prophet ﷺ came to me and joined me under the blanket. I woke during the night and did not find him. I went around all the rooms of his wives and did not find him. I then thought that perhaps he had gone to Mâriya, the Copt, and so I left (to find out) and I passed by the Mosque and my foot bumped into him while he was prostrating. And he was saying:

سَجَدَ لَكَ سَوَادِي وَخَيَالِي، وآمَنَ بِكَ فُؤَادِي، وَهٰذِهِ يَدِي جَنَيْتُ بِهَا عَلىٰ نَفْسِي، فَيَا عَظِيمُ هَلْ يَغْفِرُ الذَّنْبَ الْعَظِيْمَ إِلَّا الرَّبُّ الْعَظِيْمُ ، فَاغْفِرْ لِي الذَّنْبَ الْعَظِيْمَ

'Sajada laka sawâdi wa khayâli. Wa âmana bika fu'âdi wa hâdhihi yadi janaytu bihâ 'ala nafsî fa yâ 'Aẓîm! Hal yaghfir al-dhanb al-aẓîm illa rabb_ulaẓîm? Faghfirli al-dhanb al-aẓîm.'

The inner core of my heart and my spirit have prostrated to you. My mind has believed in You. And this is my hand, I have harvested (wrong actions) by it against my own self. So O Mighty One, who can forgive great sin except the Great Lord, and so forgive me the great sins.

---

[71] See note 20.
[72] See note 30.

And then he raised his head and said:

اللَّهُمَّ هَبْ لِي قَلْبًا تَقِيًّا نَقِيًّا مِنَ الشَّرِّ، بَرِيّاً لَا كَافِرًا وَلَا شَقِيًّا

Allahumma hab lî qalban taqiyyan naqiyyan min al-sharr bariyyan lâ kâfiran wa lâ shaqiyyan

"O Allah! Bestow me with a righteous heart free of evil, devoid of ungratefulness and not wretched."

Then he returned to his prostration and he said:

أَقُولُ لَكَ كَمَا قَالَ أَخِيْ دَاودُ عَلَيهِ السَّلَامُ: أُعَفِّرُ وَجْهِيَ فِي التُّرَابِ لِسَيِّدِي، وَحُقَّ لِوَجْهِ سَيِّدِي أَنْ تُعَفَّرَ الْوُجُوهُ لِوَجْهِهِ

'Aqûlu laka kamâ qâla akhî Dâwûd 'alayhi_salâmu 'u'affir wajhî fi_turâb li sayyidî wa ḥuqqa li wajhi sayyidî an tu'affara al_wujûhu li_wajhihi

'I say to you what my brother David ﷺ said, "I cover my face with dust for my Master, for it is deserving for the Face of my Master that faces are made dusty before His Face."'

Then he raised his head and I said to him: "By my father and my mother you are in one valley and I am in another."[73]
And he said, *'O Humayra![74] You know this is the fifteenth night of Sha'bân. Indeed on this night Allah frees people from the Fire to the amount of the hair of the herds of (the tribe) of Kalb.'*

---

[73] An expression used to describe how she viewed her spiritual state in comparison to that of the Prophet ﷺ. *(Editor)*

"What is the significance of the hairs of the herds of the tribe of Kalb?" I said.
He said, *'There was no tribe with more animals than them. On this night, the only ones (not to be forgiven) are six: The one persistent in drinking alcohol; one who neglects the rights of his parents; one who is persistent in adultery; one who breaks ties (with fellow Muslims); one who makes idols; and the slanderer.* '"

Narration 28

It has been reported on the authority of 'Aisha, may Allah be pleased with her, who said: "The Prophet ﷺ disappeared one night and so I went out to look for him. He was in the Baq'î Cemetery with his head raised to the sky. He said, *'O 'Aisha, do you fear that Allah and His Messenger will treat you unfairly?'*
"I wouldn't do that, but I thought that you might have gone to one of your other wives," I said.
And he said, *'Indeed Allah, the Mighty and Majestic, descends to the lowest heaven on the fifteenth of Sha'bân and forgives more (people) than the hairs of the herds of the tribe of Kalb.'"* [75]

---

[74] This was a pet name that the Prophet ﷺ had for 'Aisha.
[75] Related by al-Tirmidhî (3/116) and Ibn Majâh (1/444).

Narration 29

'Abdul Raḥmân ibn 'Azrab said that he heard Abû Mûsâ al-Ash'arî[76] say: "I heard the Messenger of Allah ﷺ say, *'Our Lord descends to the lowest heaven on the fifteenth of Sha'bân and forgives the denizens of the earth except for one who attributes partners or one who shows enmity (towards the Religion and its people.)'"* [77]

And the Shaykh, may Allah show him mercy, said, "I heard Abû 'Abdullah al-Ḥâfiẓ say, 'I heard Abû Muḥammad Aḥmad bin 'Abdullah al-Muznî say that the *ḥadîth* about the descent has been well established on the authority of the Messenger of Allah ﷺ from various correct (sources), and what has been narrated confirms the words of the Exalted: "*And your Lord comes, and His angels, rank upon rank.*"' [78] '*The descent*' and '*The coming*' are two attributes that cannot be used as attributes of Allah if they imply movement or changing from one state to another. Rather they are attributes of Allah which have no likeness (to human action), and He is Exalted beyond what those who deny His attributes and what the anthropomorphists say."

---

[76] Abû Mûsâ's name was 'Abdullah bin Qays. He was from the Yemeni tribe known as the 'Asharis. After hearing of the Prophet ﷺ he came to Makkah to join him but returned when the persecution of Muslims became so extreme that many of them were forced to migrate to Ethiopia. He spread the word of Islam in Yemen before joining the Prophet ﷺ in Madina some years later. He was a well-known emissary of the Prophet ﷺ as well as the Khalifs that followed him. He was renowned as a warrior, scholar, ascetic, and reciter of Quran. He died in Makkah in 52H (673CE), after staying in Basra for a while.

[77] For explanation of the word *mashâḥin* see note 61.

[78] Al-Fajr 89:22.

Chapter Four
The Blessings of the Month of Ramaḍân

Abdul Aziz Ahmed comments:

Ramaḍân is the ninth month of the Islamic year. Its name is derived from the root letters r-m-ḍ, which means "he had his feet burnt by the vehement heat of the sun", or in the case of the earth, "it was heated vehemently by the sun." It is understood that the names were related to the times when the solar calendar was adopted. Ramaḍân corresponded to the hottest month of the year. Others believe it is called Ramaḍân because it burns away the sins of the one who fasts in it. There is a tradition attributed to Mujâhid, which says it is one of the names of Allah and that is why it cannot have a plural, but this is denounced as weak by al-Bayhaqî and others. And Allah knows best.

Allah the Exalted said:

(يَا أَيُّهَا الَّذِينَ آمَنُواْ كُتِبَ عَلَيْكُمُ الصِّيَامُ كَمَا كُتِبَ عَلَى الَّذِينَ مِن قَبْلِكُمْ
لَعَلَّكُمْ تَتَّقُونَ ۝ أَيَّامًا مَّعْدُودَاتٍ فَمَن كَانَ مِنكُم مَّرِيضًا أَوْ عَلَى سَفَرٍ
فَعِدَّةٌ مِّنْ أَيَّامٍ أُخَرَ وَعَلَى الَّذِينَ يُطِيقُونَهُ فِدْيَةٌ طَعَامُ مِسْكِينٍ فَمَن تَطَوَّعَ
خَيْرًا فَهُوَ خَيْرٌ لَّهُ وَأَن تَصُومُواْ خَيْرٌ لَّكُمْ إِن كُنتُمْ تَعْلَمُونَ ۝ شَهْرُ
رَمَضَانَ الَّذِيَ أُنزِلَ فِيهِ الْقُرْآنُ هُدًى لِّلنَّاسِ وَبَيِّنَاتٍ مِّنَ الْهُدَى وَالْفُرْقَانِ فَمَن
شَهِدَ مِنكُمُ الشَّهْرَ فَلْيَصُمْهُ)

"O you who believe! Fasting is prescribed to you as it was prescribed to those before you, that you may (learn) self-restraint.

Fasting is for a fixed number of days; but if any of you is ill, or on a journey, the prescribed number (should be made up) from days later. For those who cannot do it (with hardship), is a ransom, the feeding of one that is indigent. But he that will give more, of his own free will, it is better for him. And it is better for you that you fast, if you only knew.

Ramaḍân is the month in which was sent down the Quran, as a guide to mankind, also clear signs for guidance and judgment (between right and wrong). So every one of you who is present (at his home) during that month should spend it in fasting.

(al-Baqara 2:183-85)

Narration 30

It has been reported on the authority of 'Amr bin Murra who said: "I heard Ibn Abû Layla[79] say that our companions told us that when the Messenger of Allah ﷺ came to Madina he ordered them to fast three days. Then the (command to fast in) Ramaḍân was sent down and some people were not used to fasting. Fasting was very difficult for them. Those who were unable to fast, fed a poor person. And then the verse *'So every one of you who is present (at his home) during that month should spend it in fasting'* was revealed, and there was licence granted to the sick and the traveller, and (the others) were ordered to fast. Our companions told us that if a man, after breaking his fast, slept before eating, he would not eat even in the morning (meaning they would have started their fast by falling asleep. On one occasion) 'Umar came desiring his wife and she said she had already slept (implying that she had started her fast). As he thought she was using this as an excuse, he still approached her. A man from the Ansâr came and wanted food. They said, "Wait until we have heated some food," but he slept (before it was prepared). And when the morning came, the following verse was revealed:

﴿أُحِلَّ لَكُمْ لَيْلَةَ الصِّيَامِ الرَّفَثُ إِلَى نِسَآئِكُمْ﴾

'Permitted to you, on the night of the fasts, is the approach to your wives.'"
(al-Baqara 2:187)

---

[79] 'Amr bin Murra was a second or third generation scholar of Kufa who died in 116H. Abû Layla al-Anṣârî was a Companion who fought at the battle of Uḥud and heard directly from the Prophet ﷺ as well as from other Companions. His name was 'Amr bin Balîl but was best known as Abû Layla. It is likely that 'Amr bin Murra heard this from his son 'Abdul Raḥmân bin Abû Layla who was his teacher. And Allah knows best.

The Shaykh, may Allah show him mercy, said: "When the fast of Ramaḍân became a compulsion on every individual, it became one of the pillars of Islam, and in that respect are the following *(ḥadîth)*:

Narration 31

Ṭâwûs[80] said: "A man came to Ibn 'Umar[81] and said, 'O Abû Abdul Raḥmân! Do you not go out to battle?' And he said, "I have indeed heard the Messenger of Allah ﷺ say, 'Islam is built on five (pillars), bearing witness that there is no god but Allah, establishing the prayer, giving the Zakât, the Ḥajj and fasting in Ramaḍân.'" [82]

And he said, may Allah be pleased with him, that many *ḥadîth* have come from the Messenger of Allah ﷺ concerning the blessings of the month of Ramaḍân and the blessing of fasting in it. Among them are the following:

---

[80] Tawûs bin Kaysân, a Yemeni *Tâb'î,* Follower, who related *ḥadîth* from many Companions including Ibn 'Abbâs and Ibn 'Umar. He died 106H (724CE).

[81] 'Abdullah was the son of 'Umar ibn al-Khaṭṭâb (see note 41). He embraced Islam with him while very young. He was one of the main jurists from among the Companions, and famed for his worship, good character and knowledge. He performed over 1000 minor pilgrimages ('Umra) and 60 pilgrimages. He freed over 100 slaves, and on one occasion was given 20,000 gold dinars, which he distributed immediately to his students. He related 1630 *ḥadîth* before he was poisoned and died in 74H in Makkah.

[82] Related by al-Bukharî (1/8), Muslim (Book of Faith, 20 and 21), al-Tirmidhî (*ḥadîth* 2609), al-Nasâ'î (8/107) and Aḥmad (2/26, 93 and 120).

Narration 32

It has been reported on the authority of Ibn Abû Anas that his father told him that Abû Hurayra[83] said the Messenger of Allah ﷺ said: *"When Ramaḍân comes the Gates of the Garden are opened, the Gates of Hell are locked and the devils are chained."* [84]

Narration 33

Abû Hurayra said that the Messenger of Allah said: *"On the first night of Ramaḍân the devils and their rebellious minions from among the Jinn[85] are shackled, the Gates of the Fire are locked, and not one of the doors will be left open; the Gates of the Heavens are opened, and not one of them will be closed. A caller will call, 'O desirer of good come forward and O desirer of evil be distant! And Allah has those whom He frees from the Fire.'"* [86]

And Abû Kurayb adds on the authority of Abû Bakr bin 'Ayyâsh that *"that is every night."*

Narration 34

It has been reported on the authority of Abû Hurayra[87] that the Messenger of Allah ﷺ gave glad tidings to his Companions and said: *"Ramaḍân has come to you. A blessed month has come to you. Allah has prescribed fasting for you in it. The Gates of the Gardens are opened during it. The Gates of Hell are locked during it.*

---

[83] Abû Hurayra's name was 'Abdul Raḥmân bin Ṣakhr, but was best known by the nickname given to him by the Prophet ﷺ He was once seen carrying a kitten in the sleeve of his shirt, after which he was known as Abû Hurayra, "father of the kitten". As the leader of the group of poor Muslims who lived in the Mosque, he had close access to the Prophet ﷺ and as a result became one of the most prolific narrators of *ḥadîth.*

[84] Related by al-Bukharî (2/32), Muslim (Fasting 1), al-Nasâ'î (4/128) and Aḥmad (2/357).

[85] *Jinn* are creatures created from fire. They, like humans, have discretion and are legally responsible for their actions. Therefore some of them are good and others evil.

[86] Related by al-Tirmidhî (3/66) and Ibn Mâjah (1/526).

[87] See note 83.

The devils are chained in it. In it is a night that is greater than a thousand months. Whoever is denied its good is truly denied." [88]

And he, may Allah be pleased with him, said concerning the shackling of the devils in Ramaḍân, that the intended meaning is that it was specifically during the days of the Prophet ﷺ. What is intended are the devils who listen (to what is being recited) but are not seen. He said, "rebellious devils?" (And he explained) that it was because the month of Ramaḍân is the time of the descending of the Quran to the lowest heaven, and its protection (during the descent) was by shooting stars as Allah has said (that they are), *"(For beauty) and for guarding against all obstinate rebellious evil spirits."*[89] And the "shackling" in the month of Ramaḍân is the ultimate in protection. And Allah knows best.

It is possible that what is meant (concerning the schackling of the devils) is in *its days and those that follow it.* Its meaning is that the devils are not as focused on spoiling people in the month of Ramaḍân as they are during other months, because most Muslims are busy with breaking their desires through their fasting, recitation of Quran, and other forms of worship. And Allah knows best. And there are other (*ḥadîth*) which point to this meaning, among them are the following:

Narration 35

Abû Hurayra[90] said that the Messenger of Allah said: *"My nation was given five qualities in the month of Ramaḍân that were not given to any nation before them. The mouth odour of the fasting person is sweeter with Allah than the smell of musk. The angels seek forgiveness for them until they break their fast. Allah embellishes His Garden every day, then He says (to the angels), 'My fasting servants hasten to*

[88] Related by al-Nasâ'î (4/129) and Aḥmad (2/230,385 and 425).
[89] Ṣaffât, 37:7.
[90] See note 83.

throw off the burdens and difficulties, and have become like you.' The devils are shackled, and they do not work tirelessly (to distract them) as they do in other months. They are forgiven on the last night." It was said, "Is that the Night of Power?"

"No," he said. *"It is that everyone that has worked should be paid his wage once he has completed his work."* [91]

Narration 36

Abû Basra said: "I heard Jâbir ibn 'Abdullah[92] say that the Messenger of Allah said, *'My nation have been given five things in Ramaḍân that no Prophet before me has been given. As for the first, when it is the first night of Ramaḍân, Allah, the Mighty and Majestic, looks at them and whoever Allah looks at, He will never punish him. As for the second, it is that the mouth odour of the person who has fasted until the afternoon is sweeter with Allah than the smell of musk. As for the third, the angels will seek forgiveness for them every night. As for the fourth, it is that Allah the Mighty and Majestic orders His Garden saying to it, "Prepare and adorn yourself for My slaves. They are about to take a rest from the temporal world for My abode and My benevolence." As for the fifth, it is that on the last night, all of them are forgiven.'* A man said (to the Messenger ﷺ): "Is it the Night of Power?" And he said, *'No, do you not see those who work? When they have finished their work they take their wages.'"*

---

[91] Related by Aḥmad (2/292) and al-Mundhirî (2/91).

[92] Jâbir ibn 'Abdullah witnessed the second pledge of 'Aqaba along with his father who had witnessed the first pledge and went on to be martyred at 'Uhud. Jâbir did not attend that battle as he was told to take care of his seven sisters. He died by the banks of the Tigris in 78H (693CE) aged 94. He related 1540 *ḥadîth*.

Narration 37

It has been reported on the authority of Salmân[93] that the Messenger of Allah ﷺ addressed us in a sermon on the last day of Sha'bân and said: *"O People! Indeed you have come under the shade of a mighty month. In it, is a night that is better than a thousand months. Allah made fasting its days a compulsion and standing in prayer in its nights a supererogatory worship. Whoever draws close with a portion of goodness in it, it will be like fulfilling a duty in any other month. And whoever fulfils a duty in it, it will be like fulfilling seventy duties in any other month. It is the month of steadfastness. And the reward for steadfastness is the Garden. It is the month of charity, and the provisions of the believer are increased in it. Whoever feeds a fasting person will be forgiven for all his sins, will have freed his neck from the Fire, and will have the reward of the person he fed without diminishing anything from his reward."*

They said, "O Messenger of Allah, not all of us have the means to feed a fasting person."

He said: *"Allah, the Majestic and Mighty, gives this reward to whoever feeds a fasting person with a taste of milk, or a date, or a gulp of water; and whoever satiates a fasting person, Allah will allow him to drink from my basin a drink that will satisfy him until he enters the Garden. It is a month, the beginning of which is mercy, the middle of which is forgiveness, and the end of which is freedom from the Fire. Allah will forgive whoever reduces the duties of his slave and will free his neck from the Fire. Be abundant in four things, two of which lead to your Lord's pleasure, and two things that you cannot do without. As for the two things that will lead to the pleasure of your Lord, it is your bearing witness that there is no god but Allah and your seeking of His forgiveness. As for the things that you cannot do without, it is your asking Allah for the Garden and your seeking refuge with Him from the Fire."*

[93] See note 36.

And others have narrated it on the authority of ‘Ali ibn Ḥajr and in the beginning he said, *“Indeed you have come under the shade of a mighty month, a blessed month.”*

Narration 38

Abû Sa’îd al-Zâhid told us that Abû ‘Amr bin Maṭar told us that Ja’far bin Aḥmad bin Nasr al-Ḥâfiẓ told us that ‘Ali ibn Ḥajr told us the (same *ḥadîth*), and he mentioned his chain of narrators.

Narration 39

It is related on the authority of Abû Hurayra[94] that the Messenger of Allah said: *“Whoever fasts the month of Ramaḍân in faith and contentment will have his previous sins forgiven.”*[95]

And al-Ḥamîdi related it on the authority of Sufyân concerning fasting Ramaḍân and standing in prayer on the Night of Power.

And likewise, it was related by Yaḥya ibn Abû Kathîr on the authority of Abû Salama.

---

[94] See note 83.

[95] Related by Ibn Mâjah (1/526) and Aḥmad (2/232, 375 and 483).

Narration 40

Abû Hurayra[96] said: *"I heard the Messenger of Allah ﷺ say about Ramaḍân that whoever establishes it in faith and contentment will have his previous sins forgiven."* [97]

And this is how (it is related by) 'Uqayl bin Khâlid and others on the authority of Ibn Shihâb. It was also related by Muḥammad bin 'Amr on the authority of Abû Salama concerning both fasting and standing as follows:

Narration 41

It has been reported on the authority of Abû Hurayra that the Prophet ﷺ said: *"Whoever fasts the month of Ramaḍân and stands in prayer in faith and contentment will have the sins previously committed forgiven; and whoever stands in prayer on the night of Power in faith and contentment will have all sins of the past forgiven."* [98]

---

[96] See note 83.

[97] Related by al-Bukharî (2/252), Muslim (1/524), al-Tirmidhî (3/181), Abû Dawûd (2/103), al-Nasâ'î (4/156) and Aḥmad (2/281, 486 and 529).

[98] Related by al-Bukharî (2/253), Muslim (1/523), al-Tirmidhî (*ḥadîth* number 683), Abû Dawûd (2/103), Ibn Mâjah (1 *ḥadîth* number 1326) and Aḥmad (2/503).

Narration 42

It has been reported on the authority of Abû Salama bin 'Abdul Raḥmân ibn 'Awf[99] on the authority of his father that the Prophet ﷺ said: *"Surely Allah the Mighty and Majestic made the fasting of Ramaḍân compulsory; and I made standing in prayer during its nights my way* (sunnah)*, and so it will be for the one who fasts in faith, contentment, and certainty a recompense for what has happened in the past"* or as he said.[100]

Abû 'Abdullah al-Ḥâfiẓ informed us (with a chain which mentioned) that Naḍr ibn Shaybân mentioned his chain which Muḥammad bin 'Umar and others related (to him) on the authority of Abû Salama from Abû Hurayra which is better authenticated.

Narration 43

Abû Sa'îd al-Khudrî[101] said that the Messenger of Allah said: *"On the first night of Ramaḍân, the doors of the sky are opened and none of them will be shut until the last night of Ramaḍân. There will be no believing slave who prays during one of its nights except that Allah writes for him one thousand five hundred rewards. With*

---

[99] 'Abdul Raḥmân bin 'Awf was originally called 'Abdul 'Amr, but the Messenger ﷺ changed his name after he embraced Islam. He was one of the first to become Muslim and part of the first group of migrants to Ethiopia. He was rich and generous and fought valiantly at the battles of Badr and 'Uḥud. On one occasion, he provided 1500 camels for the Muslim army and at the death of the Prophet ﷺ provided money for his widows, as he had done for the widows of those martyred at Badr. He died in Madina in 31H (652 CE) aged 72. This *ḥadîth* is related by his son Abû Salama who is also known as 'Abdullah or Ashgar. It is also said his name was Ismâîl. He died in Madina in 94H (712 CE). And Allah knows best.

[100] Related by Ibn Mâjah, al-Nasâ'î (1/421) and Aḥmad (1/191).

[101] His name was Sa'd, but better known by his nickname Abû Sa'îd and his family name al-Khudrî, which is either based on one of his grandfathers Khudra bin 'Awf or the Anṣârî clan of Khudra. His father was Mâlik bin Sinân who died at the battle of 'Uḥud and lapped up the blood of the Prophet ﷺ after he was injured. To this, the Prophet ﷺ described him as one of the People of the Garden. Sa'd was left as a young orphan and grew up as one of the People of the Bench who lived in the Mosque. He went on to attend 12 battles with the Prophet ﷺ and to relate 1170 *ḥadîth* before dying in Madina aged 93 years in 74H (693 CE).

every prostration He will build for him a home of rubies in the Garden that will have sixty thousand doors, each leading to a golden palace crafted with rubies. When he fasts the first day of Ramaḍân he would have been forgiven all sins committed up to that day; and whoever witnesses the month of Ramaḍân, seventy thousand angels will seek forgiveness for him every day from the Morning Prayer until the veil disappears. For every prostration he prostrates in the month of Ramaḍân during the night or day, he will have a tree (planted in the Garden so tall that) a rider could ride for five hundred years in its shade." [102]

Narration 44

Abû 'Abdullah al-Ḥâfiẓ informed us (with his chain) on the authority of Muḥammad bin Marwân with his chain, which mentioned something similar, except that he said, "*seventy thousand doors*" instead of sixty, and he added, "*that he will have for every day of the month of Ramaḍân that he fasts a place with doors of gold,*" and he said in the end, "*a hundred years.*"

Narration 45

It has been reported on the authority of Ibn 'Umar[103] that the Prophet ﷺ said: "*The Garden is adorned for Ramaḍân from the beginning of the year to the following year. On the first day of Ramaḍân a breeze blows from under the Throne to the part of the Garden where the Ḥouris (reside), and they will say, 'O Lord prepare for us from amongst Your slaves, spouses who will be pleasing to our eyes, and [for whom] we will be pleasing to theirs.'*" [104]

---

[102] This can be found in Suyûtî's *Durr al-Manthûr* (1/186).
[103] See note 81.
[104] This can be found in Miskhât al-Masâbîḥ (*ḥadîth* number 1967)

Narration 46

It has been reported on the authority of Nâfʾî bin Barda that Abû Mas'ûd al-Ghifarî [105] said, "I heard the Messenger of Allah ﷺ say on the day that the moon of Ramaḍân was sighted, *'If the servants knew what was bestowed upon my nation in Ramaḍân, they would have wished the whole year was Ramaḍân.'*

A man from the tribe of Khuzâ'a said, "O Prophet of Allah, tell us."

So he said, *'The Garden is embellished for Ramaḍân from the beginning of the year to the following year. On the first day of Ramaḍân, a breeze blows from below the Throne. The leaves of the Garden flap (in the wind), and the Ḥouris look at that and say 'O Lord prepare for us from amongst Your slaves during this month, spouses who will be pleasing to our eyes, and for whom we will be pleasing to theirs.' There is no servant who fasts a day of Ramaḍân except that he will be married to a spouse from among the Ḥouris in a tent made of a hollowed out pearl as described in the verse, "Companions restrained (as to their glances), in (goodly) pavilions."[106] Each bride will have seventy cloaks, and each cloak will be of a different colour and will give off seventy thousand unique types of perfume. Each bride will have seventy thousand handmaidens to tend to her needs. Each handmaiden will have a golden plate each with (a different) type of food of which the first taste will be different to the last. Each bride will have seventy beds of precious jewels crafted with pearls, on each bed will be seventy sheets of silk, and above each sheet will be a bridal canopy and each spouse will be given the like made of rubies crafted with pearls upon which will be two golden bracelets. This is for each day he fasts in Ramaḍân, and this is beside the other good actions he does.'"*

In another gathering, he said:

---

[105] I am unsure if this is 'Uqba ibn 'Amr also known as Abû Mas'ûd al-Badrî who was the youngest person to witness the second oath at 'Aqaba who died in Madina in 40H or Abû Mas'ûd al-Anṣâri about which little is known or perhaps a different Companion not included in the sources I have accessed. And Allah knows best.

[106] Al-Raḥmân, 55:72.

Narration 47

It has been reported on the authority of Abû Hurayra[107] that the Messenger of Allah ﷺ used to say: *"The five daily prayers, the Jumu'a Prayer to the next Jumu'a Prayer, and Ramaḍân to Ramaḍân are atonement for that which is between them as long as the major sins are avoided."* [108]

And the Shaykh, may Allah be pleased with him, said that (there have been other *ḥadîth*) that have been narrated in different forms by Abû Hurayra that clarify which major sins count as the exceptions referred to in this narration.

Narration 48

Abû Hurayra said that the Messenger of Allah ﷺ said: *"The prescribed prayer wipes out what occurred since the prescribed prayer before it. The Jumu'a Prayer wipes out that which occurred since the Jumu'a Prayer before it, and the Month to the Month - meaning the month of Ramaḍân - is an atonement for that which is between them except for three: ascribing partners to Allah, abandoning my Way, and betraying a handshake."*

Abu Hurayra said, "We understood that this was said because of a specific occurrence, so I said, 'O Messenger of Allah, as for ascribing partners to Allah, we understand this, but what of *abandoning my way* and *betraying a handshake?*'"

He said, *"Giving your allegiance to a man,[109] then you break your oath and fight (against) him with your sword. And as for 'abandoning my Way' it is leaving the Community."* [110]

---

[107] See note 83.
[108] Related by Muslim (1/209) and Aḥmad (2/400).
[109] Such as a ruler, Caliph, etc. *(Editor)*
[110] Related by Aḥmad (2/229 and 506).

And the Shaykh, may Allah be pleased with him, said there have been other *ḥadîth* related (implying that) avoiding the major sins means avoiding the association of partners with Him. And among them are the following:

Narration 49

It has been reported on the authority of Anas ibn Mâlik[111] who said that as the month of Ramaḍân approached, the Messenger of Allah said: *"Blessed is Allah! What is it that approaches you? And what is it you approach?"*

And 'Umar ibn al-Khaṭṭâb, may Allah be pleased with him, said, "May my father and mother be ransomed for you, revelation has come down or an enemy has approached?"

He said, *"No, but it is the month of Ramaḍân. Allah, the Exalted, forgives all the people of this Qibla*[112] *on its first night."*

He said that there was a man among the people who shook his head and said, "*Bakhin*! *Bakhin*!"[113]

So the Prophet ﷺ said to him, *"It is as if your chest became constricted by what I said?"*[114]

The man said, "No, By Allah! No, O Messenger of Allah! Rather it is that I remembered the hypocrite."

So the Prophet ﷺ said, *"The hypocrite is a disbeliever, and the disbelievers have no portion of this."*

---

[111] See note 30.

[112] The *Qibla* is the prayer direction, that is, towards Makkah. The Muslim nation are called the people of the *Qibla,* and one of the criteria for being part of that nation is that one prays in that direction.

[113] A phrase used as an exclamation, or to show happiness about something, similar to "Excellent!" or "Bravo!"

[114] In spite of the man's initial statement, the Prophet ﷺ must have seen something in the man's expression that suggested otherwise. And Allah knows best. *(Editor)*

Narration 50

Abû 'Umâma[115] said that the Messenger of Allah ﷺ said: "*Surely Allah the Mighty and Majestic with every breaking of the fast has those whom He frees (from the Fire).*"[116]

The Shaykh, may Allah be pleased with him, said this *ḥadîth* does not specify the number of those He frees from the Fire. However, it has been related in another *ḥadîth:*

Narration 51

It has been reported on the authority of 'Abdullah ibn Mas'ûd[117] that the Messenger of Allah ﷺ said: "*On the first night of Ramaḍân, the gates of the Heavens are opened, and not one of the gates will be closed during the whole month. The gates of Hell are locked, and not one of them will be opened during the whole month. The insolent ones from among the jinn*[118] *are shackled. A caller from the sky calls out each night until the morning breaks, 'O desirer of good, fulfil (your desire), and receive glad tidings! O desirer of evil, be distant and look on! Is there one who seeks forgiveness so that he may be forgiven? Is there a repentant wishing to turn so*

---

[115] Abû Umâma's real name was As'ad bin Sahl bin Ḥanîf, and he was born two years before the death of the Prophet ﷺ He was named by the Prophet ﷺ after his maternal grandfather, As'ad bin Zurâra, who played an important role in preparing the Madinite people for the arrival of the Messenger ﷺ This, and all other *ḥadîth* related by him, are not direct from the Prophet, due to his young age at the time. He related *ḥadîth* from many of the major Companions including 'Umar, 'Uthmân, his father, and Zayd ibn Thâbit. He died in 100H (718 CE) in Kufa.

[116] Related by Aḥmad (5/256).

[117] 'Abdullah bin Masûd was the sixth person to embrace Islam after witnessing a miracle where the Prophet ﷺ milked a baby ewe. He went on to be the first person to recite Quran publically, and was very close to the Prophet ﷺ He was known as the "Keeper of the Secret of the Prophet," looking after his shoes and waking him from sleep. The Messenger ﷺ used to honour and respect him. 'Abdullah was so close to the Quran and the Messenger that he would say there is no verse of Quran that he did not know when and where it was revealed. He related 848 *ḥadîth*. He died 32H or 33H (658 CE).

[118] See note 85.

that he can be turned to (in acceptance)? Is there a supplicant hoping to be answered? Is there an asker who wishes his plea to be answered? For Allah has, with every breaking of the fast in Ramaḍân, sixty thousand whom He frees from the Fire. And when the month comes to an end on the Day of Fast Breaking, He frees the number he freed during the month, thirty times sixty thousand."

Narration 52

Al-Ḥasan[119] said that the Messenger of Allah ﷺ said: *"Indeed, Allah has sixty thousand He frees from the Fire every night of Ramaḍân. And when it is the last night, He frees the number that has already (been freed)."* And this is how it has been related in the *ḥadîth mursal* (that is, one that omits the Companion).

And he said, may Allah be pleased with him, that what is intended by the number mentioned here, according to our scholars, is a vast amount without actually being that specific number. And Allah knows best.

[119] Al-Ḥasan is Ḥasan bin Abû al-Ḥasan al-Baṣrî. His father was Yasâr the freed slave of Zayd bin Thâbit al-Anṣârî, and his mother was the freed slave of the Prophet's wife, Umm Salama. As a result of this, he was born in the house of the Prophet ρ a few years before the end of the rule of 'Umar ibn al-Khaṭṭâb. He was called *the Crown of the Followers*. He met over 120 Companions, and was known as a scholarly ascetic, much loved by the whole Muslim nation. He died in 110H (728 CE) in Basra.

Chapter Five
Regarding the One Who Is Aware of the Limits of This Month and Preserves Its Duties[120]

Narration 53

Aṭâ ibn Yasâr told ‘Abdullah bin Qurayṭ that he heard Abû Sa’îd al-Khudrî[121] say: “I heard the Messenger of Allah ﷺ say *‘Whoever fasts Ramaḍân, and knows its limits and preserves them in the way they should be preserved, all that preceded will be covered up.’*” [122]

Narration 54

Abû Hurayra[123] said that the Messenger of Allah ﷺ said: *“The month of Ramaḍân has shaded you. (I swear) with the oath of the Messenger of Allah, no month has passed the Muslims that has been better for them (than it). (I swear) with the oath of the Messenger of Allah, no month has passed the hypocrites that has been worse for them (than it). Indeed, Allah has recorded the reward and the extra actions even before (the month) has entered. Its burdens (of sin) and misery (for the hypocrites) have been written even before it has arrived. That is because provision has been promised to the believer for worship, and the neglect of the Muslims and prying into their private matters has been promised for the hypocrites. It is part of the spoils of war for the believer that he gains when overpowering the wrong doer (in the spiritual battle)”.* And in another narration it says, *“it is booty for the*

---

[120] This is not a separate chapter in the Dar al-Kutub edition.
[121] See note 101
[122] Related by Aḥmad (3/55).
[123] See note 83.

believer and disobedience for the wrong doer," meaning the month of Ramaḍân.[124]

Narration 55

It has been reported on the authority of Abû Hurayra[125] that the Messenger of Allah ﷺ ascended the pulpit (*mimbar*). He said, *"Âmin! Âmin! Âmin!"*
It was said to him, "O Messenger of Allah! Why did you do that?"
He said, *"Jibrâil (the angel Gabriel), upon him be peace, said, 'Abased be the nose of the slave who, when Ramaḍân enters, is not forgiven.' To that I said, "Âmin!" And then he said, 'Abased be the nose of the slave who, when your name is mentioned, he does not pray upon you.' To that I said, "Âmin!" And then he said, 'Abased be the nose of the slave whose parents or one of them reaches old age, and he doesn't enter the Garden (by looking after them).' To that I said, "Âmin!""* [126]

---

[124] This narration is related by al-Bayhaqî in Sunan al-Kubrâ (4/304).
[125] See note 83.
[126] Related by Aḥmad (2/254) and al-Tirmidhi (5/550).

Narration 56

It has been reported on the authority of Abû Hurayra[127] that the Prophet ﷺ said: *"If the fasting person does not abandon false testimony and acting according to it, and ignorance[128]; then Allah does not have any need[129] of him giving up his food and drink."* [130]

Narration 57

It has been reported on the authority of Abû Ṣâliḥ al-Zayyât that he heard Abû Hurayra say that the Messenger of Allah ﷺ said: *"(Allah, the Exalted, said,) 'All the actions of the children of Adam are for himself except fasting, for that is for Me. And I will reward (him) for it.' Fasting is a shield. And so if the day comes for one of you to fast, do not speak ill on that day and do not shout, and if someone insults you or tries to fight you, one should say, "I am a person who is fasting." I swear by the one in whose Hands is the soul of Muḥammad, the odour from the mouth of the fasting person is sweeter with Allah on the Day of Resurrection than the smell of musk. The fasting person will have two joys that he will delight in. When he breaks*

---

[127] See note 83.

[128] Imam al-Sindi said in his *Hashiya* of *Sunan Abu Dawud* (1/517), "Meaning the characteristics and conditions of the ignorant... and all sins are deeds done with ignorance." Imam al-San'ânî said in *Subul al-Salâm* (1/567), "Ignorance, meaning shamefulness, foolishness (*al-safah*)." This is in keeping with Allah's saying in the Quran, *"Do you lustfully approach men instead of women? Nay, you engage in acts of sheer ignorance." (27:55)* Shaykh al-Sha'râwî said in his commentary of this verse, "*Al-Jahl* (literally ignorance) as used here is not the opposite of knowledge, but rather means shamelessness (*al-safah*)." *(Editor)*

[129] Our scholars have mentioned this is a metaphor for a lack of acceptance from Allah, as Allah is not in need of anything to begin with. See Al-'Aynî's 'Umdat al-Qârî (22/130), Dâr Ihyâ al-Turâth, Beirut. *(Editor)*

[130] Related by al-Bukhârî (2/228), al-Tirmidhî (3/87), Abû Dawûd (2/767), Ibn Mâjah (1/539) and Aḥmad (2/252 and 505).

his fast, he will delight in the breaking of his fast, and when he meets his Lord he will delight at his fasting." [131]

Narration 58

Abû 'Ubayda bin al-Jarrâḥ[132] said: "I heard the Messenger of Allah ﷺ say, *'The fast is a shield as long as it is not pierced.'"* [133]

Narration 59

It has been reported on the authority of Abû Sa'îd al-Maqburî that Abû Hurayra heard the Prophet ﷺ say: *"Perhaps the portion of the one who stands in prayer is (only) sleeplessness, and perhaps the portion of the one who fasts is (only) hunger and thirst."* [134]

Narration 60

It has been reported on the authority of al-Sha'bî[135] that 'Ali, may Allah be pleased with him, used to deliver a sermon when Ramaḍân came, then he

---

[131] Related by al-Bukhârî (2/227), Muslim (2/907), al-Tirmidhî (3/87), al-Nasâ'î (4/163) and Aḥmad (2/273 and 516).

[132] Abû 'Ubayda was 'Âmir bin Abdullah ibn al-Jarrâḥ, one of the earliest Muslims, and one of the ten promised the Garden by the Prophet ﷺ He was a skilled and trusted solider, fighting in all the major battles, dying of the plague at Imwas near Jerusalem while on a military expedition. The Prophet ﷺ said of him that every nation has its "trustworthy one" (*amîn*), and the trustworthy one of this nation is Abû 'Ubayda.

[133] Related by al-Nasâ'î (4/167 and 168) and Aḥmad (1/195-196).

[134] Related by Ibn Mâjah (1/539) and Aḥmad (2/373).

[135] Al-Sha'bî was one of the leading *tâbi'în,* followers. His name was Âmir ibn Sharâhil al-Sha'bî, and he related *ḥadîth* from various Companions including 'Ali ibn Abû Ṭâlib and Sa'îd ibn Abû Waqqâs. He died in Kufa in 104H (722 CE).

would say: *"This is the blessed month in which Allah has made fasting compulsory, but he did not make standing in prayer compulsory. So one must be cautious of saying, 'I will fast if so and so fasts, and I will not fast if so and so does not fast.' Be aware that fasting is not the abandonment of food and drink, but it is (staying away) from lies, falsehood, and frivolity. Do not bring the fast forward (through following speculation), but rather when you have seen the new moon, fast.*

And when you see the (next) new moon end the fast. If the (new moon) is obscured, complete the number (of days of the month which are thirty when the moon has not been sighted)." He used to say that after the Morning Prayer and after the Afternoon Prayer.

He said, "Huthaym told us on the authority of Mujâhid,[136] on the authority of al-Sha'bî, on the authority of Masrûq, that 'Umar, may Allah be pleased with him, used to say the same."

And the Shaykh, may Allah show him mercy, said that this is how the Commanders of the Faithful, 'Umar ibn al-Khaṭṭâb and 'Ali, may Allah be pleased with them both[137], used to deliver their sermons about keeping the fast free of lies, falsehood, and frivolity. And we have conveyed this meaning from the Prophet ﷺ

Narration 61

Abû Hurayra said that the Messenger of Allah ﷺ said: *"The fast is not abstinence from food and drink alone. The fast is (abstinence) from frivolity and obscenity. So if someone comes to try to engage you in abusive discourse, or acts ignorantly towards you say, 'indeed I am fasting!'"*

---

[136] Mujâhid bin Jâbir is one of the most prominent Followers *(tâbi'în)*. He was born in Makkah in 21H and died there in 104H, and related knowledge from many major Companions including 'Ali ibn Abû Ṭâlib, Sa'îd ibn Abû Waqqâs, and Ibn 'Abbâs.

[137] See notes 41 and 65.

Narration 62

It has been reported on the authority of Sulaymân bin Mûsâ[138] that Jâbir ibn 'Abdullah[139] said: *"If you fast, make your hearing, sight, and tongue fast from lies and the forbidden, and do not harm your servant; and there should be a dignity and tranquillity about you on the day you fast, and don't make your fasting and non-fasting days the same."*

Narration 63

It has been reported on the authority of Abû Ṣâliḥ al-Ḥanafî from his brother Ṭalîq bin Qays that Abû Dharr[140] said: *"If you fast, protect yourself (from doing bad) as best you can."* So when Ṭalîq used to fast, he would not go out except to the Prayer.

---

[138] Sulaymân bin Mûsâ al-Asadî, a *Tâbi'î* (Follower) who lived and died in Damascus in 115H (733CE).

[139] See note 92.

[140] Abu Dharr was from the tribe of al-Ghifâr, and was a monotheist before the advent of Islam. On hearing about the message of Muhammad ﷺ he sent his brother to find out more before eventually making his own way to Makkah to embrace Islam. He is credited with being the first person to use the greeting *"al-salaamu 'alaykum"*. After embracing Islam, he was told to return to his tribe whose strategic role was ensuring or hampering trade between Makkah and Syria. Some years later, the whole tribe became Muslim and received a special supplication, which played on their name al-Ghifâr which is connected to the name al-Ghaffâr, the all-Forgiving. Abu Dharr was known for his righteousness and disregard for worldly affairs. He died in seclusion just outside Madina in 21H (652CE), and related 281 *ḥadîth*.

Narration 64

It has been reported on the authority of Abû al-Bahktarî[141] that there was a woman in the time of the Prophet ﷺ who was fasting, but was cursing. And so he said to her, *"you are not fasting."* She stopped cursing, and then he ﷺ said, *"now you are fasting."*

Narration 65

It has been reported on the authority of Layth that Mujâhid[142] said: *"There are two things which, if you can stay away from them, you will be safe: Backbiting and lies."*

The Shaykh, may Allah be pleased with him, said that just as you should stay away from that which is not appropriate to the fast, you should also strive hard during Ramaḍân as best you can, and that is why it has been related that:

Narration 66

It has been reported on the authority of Muṭṭalib bin 'Abdullah that 'Aisha[143], the wife of the Prophet ﷺ said: *"When the month of Ramaḍân entered, the Messenger of Allah ﷺ used to tie his wrap[144] and not go to his bed until it was over."*

---

[141] Sa'îd bin Fayrûz al-Kalbî was a *Tâbi'î* (Follower) who lived and died in Kufa in 83H (703CE). He narrated *ḥadîth* from major Companions including Ibn 'Abbâs and Ibn 'Umar.

[142] See note 136.

[143] See note 23.

[144] This phrase is similar to the English phrase, *"roll up one's sleeves,"* and means that he became more intense and focused on the task at hand, which in this case was worship. And Allah knows best.

Narration 67

It has been reported on the authority of 'Aṭâ ibn Abû Rabâḥ[145] that 'Aisha, the wife of the Prophet ﷺ said: "When the month of Ramaḍân entered, the Messenger of Allah's colour ﷺ would change, his prayers would increase, he would immerse himself in supplication, and he would be deeply concerned about it."

Narration 68

'Umar ibn al-Khaṭṭâb[146] said: *"I heard the Messenger of Allah ﷺ say, 'The one who remembers Allah in Ramaḍân is forgiven, and the one who asks Allah will not (have his plea) unheeded.'"*

---

[145] 'Aṭâ ibn Abû Rabâḥ was a famous *Tâbi'î* (Follower) who was born in the Yemen of Nubian descent, and became a well-respected commentator on Quran and jurist, acting as Mufti in Makkah where he died in 115H (733CE). He related *ḥadîth* from major Companions including Ibn 'Abbâs.

[146] See note 41.

Narration 69

It has been reported on the authority of al-Ẓuhri on the authority of ‘Ubaydullah ibn ‘Abdullah ibn ‘Utba, that Ibn ‘Abbâs said that when the month of Ramaḍân entered, the Messenger of Allah ﷺ would free all prisoners and give to whoever asked.

And the Shaykh, may Allah be pleased with him, said Abû Bakr al-Hudhalî likewise related it from al-Ẓuhri, and it is only the great transmitters who related (*ḥadîth*) from al-Ẓuhri.[147]

Narration 70

It has been reported on the authority of ‘Ubaydullah ibn ‘Abdullah that Ibn ‘Abbâs said the Messenger of Allah ﷺ was the most generous of people in giving goodness. He was at his most generous during Ramaḍân when he would meet Jibril (Gabriel) ﷺ each night until Ramaḍân ended. The Prophet ﷺ would go over the Quran (with him). When Jibril, peace be upon him, would meet him ﷺ, he would be more generous in giving out goodness than the wind sent (to bring rain).[148]

And the Shaykh, may Allah be pleased with him, said: “And we have already shown in the Chapter on Sha’bân the *ḥadîth* of Ṣadaqa ibn Mûsâ, on the authority of Thâbit ibn Anas, who said that it was said: ‘O Messenger of Allah! Which charity is best?’

“*Charity in Ramaḍân*,” he said.”

---

[147] Al-Zuhri is Muḥammad bin Muslim, a first generation scholar who related *ḥadîth* from a number of Companions including Ibn ‘Umar and Anas ibn Mâlik. Born in 51H (671CE) in Madina, he was considered one of the most learned of his generation, specialising in legal rulings and *ḥadîth*. Many of his students took written notes providing the oldest written copies of *ḥadîth*. He died in Ramaḍân 124H (741 CE).

[148] Related by al-Bukhârî (1/4), Muslim (4/1803) and al-Nasâ’î (4/125).

Narration 71

Zayd ibn Khâlid al-Juhnî[149] said that the Messenger of Allah ﷺ said: "*Whoever feeds a fasting person will have the reward of the one who acted (that is, he will be given the same reward as the fasting person) without reducing the reward of the fasting person in any way. Whoever prepares a soldier for battle or takes care of his family in his absence will have the like of his reward without decreasing his reward in any way.*" [150]

Narration 72

On the authority of Sa'îd ibn Musayyib[151] who related that Sulaymân said that the Messenger of Allah said: "*Whoever feeds a fasting person in Ramaḍân from legitimate means, the angels pray for him for all the nights of Ramaḍân, and Jibrâil (Gabriel), peace be upon him, will shake his hand. Whoever's hand Jibrâil shakes, his heart will become soft and his tears plentiful.*"

A man said, "O Messenger of Allah, what if he does not have the means?"

"*Then just a pinch of food,*" he said.

"And what if he doesn't even have that?" he said.

"*Then a crumb of bread,*" he said.

"Have you not seen that there are those who do not even have that?"

"*Then a gulp of water,*" he said.

---

[149] Zayd bin Khâlid was present at the Treaty of Hudaybiya and the Conquest of Makkah, where he carried the flag of his tribe al-Juhâna. He died in Madina in 68H or 78H (688 or 698 CE).

[150] Related by al-Bukhârî (3/214), Muslim (3/1507), al-Tirmidhî (4/167), al-Nasâ'î (4/64), Ibn Mâjah (1/555) and Aḥmad (4/114).

[151] Sa'îd ibn Musayyib was one of the Seven Great Jurists of Madina. He was born during the reign of 'Umar and met many of the great Companions. He married the daughter of Abû Hurayra to be close to him and to learn from him. He died in Madina in 96H (715CE).

Chapter Six
On Striving During the Last Ten Days of Ramaḍân

Narration 73

It is related on the authority of Masrûq who said: *"I heard 'Aisha,*[152] *may Allah be pleased with her, say 'When the last ten nights of Ramaḍân entered, he would bring to life the nights, wake up his family, and tighten*[153] *his garment.'"* [154]

Narration 74

It has been reported on the authority of al-Aswad bin Yazîd that 'Aisha, may Allah be pleased with her, said: *"The Messenger of Allah ﷺ used to strive in the last ten (nights) of Ramaḍân in a way he did not strive in other times."* [155]

Narration 75

It has been reported on the authority of 'Âṣim bin Ḍamra that 'Ali[156], may Allah be pleased with him, said: *"The Prophet ﷺ when the last ten (nights) of Ramaḍân came, would roll up his garment*[157] *and stay away from women."*

---

[152] See note 23.
[153] See note 144.
[154] Related by al-Bukhârî (2/255), Muslim (2/832), Abû Dawûd (2/105), Ibn Mâjah (1/62) and Aḥmad (6/40-41).
[155] Related by Muslim (2/832) and Abû Ibn Mâjah.
[156] See note 65.
[157] See note 104.

Narration 76

It has been reported on the authority of Ubay ibn K'ab[158] that the Prophet ﷺ used to seclude himself (in the mosque)[159] during the last ten days of Ramaḍân. One year, he travelled and did not seclude himself. The following year he cut himself off for twenty days.[160]

---

[158] Ubay was one of the first people of Madinah to embrace Islam. He attended all the major battles. He was one of the few Companions to memorise the whole Quran by heart and was known to have committed it to writing. He served as a scribe for the Prophet ﷺ was an adviser to Abu Bakr and Umar, and was greatly respected by other Companions. He died in Madina in 32 AH (652CE).

[159] *I'tikâf* is the practice of secluding oneself off from the world, usually in a mosque, for a set period of time with the specific intention of worship. It is a common practice during the last days of Ramaḍân.

[160] Related by Abû Dawûd (2/230), Ibn Mâjah (1/562) and Aḥmad (5/141).

Chapter Seven
The Blessing of the Night of Power

Allah, the Mighty and Majestic said:

(بِسْمِ اللَّهِ الرَّحْمَٰنِ الرَّحِيْمِ)

(إِنَّآ أَنزَلْنَاهُ فِي لَيْلَةِ الْقَدْرِ)

(وَمَآ أَدْرَاكَ مَا لَيْلَةُ الْقَدْرِ)

(لَيْلَةُ الْقَدْرِ خَيْرٌ مِّنْ أَلْفِ شَهْرٍ)

(تَنَزَّلُ الْمَلَآئِكَةُ وَالرُّوحُ فِيهَا بِإِذْنِ رَبِّهِم مِّن كُلِّ أَمْرٍ)

(سَلَامٌ هِيَ حَتَّى مَطْلَعِ الْفَجْرِ)

In the name of Allah, Most Gracious, Most Merciful.

We have indeed revealed this (Message) in the Night of Power.

And what will explain to you what the night of power is?

The Night of Power is better than a thousand months.

Therein come down the angels and the Spirit by Allah's permission, on every errand.

Peace! This until the rise of morn!

(Al-Qadr, 97: 1-5)

Narration 77

It has been reported on the authority of Ibn Abû Najîḥ from Mujâhid that the Prophet ﷺ mentioned a man from Banî Isrâîl who carried weapons in the cause of Allah for a thousand months, and the Muslims were amazed at that. And then Allah sent down *"We have indeed revealed this (Message) in the Night of Power. And what will explain to you what the night of power is? The Night of Power is better than a thousand months."* (This taught them that the Night of Power) is better than the thousand months that that man carried weapons in the cause of Allah.

Narration 78

Al-Qa'nabî[161] told us about what he read to Mâlik[162] about what had reached him from the Messenger of Allah ﷺ that (he said) the lifespans of the people before him, or that of them that Allah wished (to show), were shown to him. It was as if the lifespans of his nation were shorter and did not reach the lifespans that the others reached in terms of (their) longevity. And so Allah gave him the Night of Power, which was better than a thousand months.[163]

---

[161] He is 'Abdullah ibn Maslama ibn Qa'nab, *Al-Qa'nabî.* He took the Muwaṭṭa from Imam Malik, later moving to Basra. Imam Muslim took from him, and he was the highest person (with the fewest people between him and the Prophet ﷺ) in his *Saḥîḥ*. He died in 121AH, May Allah have mercy upon him. See *Siyar* of Imam Al-Dhahabî (10/257). *(Editor)*

[162] Mâlik ibn Anas was the greatest scholar of Madina during the second century of Islam, and one of the four Imâms whose schools of jurisprudence are followed by the Sunni masses up until today. His collection of *ḥadîth* called *al-Muwaṭṭa* is one of the earliest sources of *ḥadîth* and was described by Imâm al-Shâfi'i as the most authentic book after the Quran. It is a source of law, as well as a description of the Madinan society during the generation immediately after the Prophet ﷺ. He was born in 93H (711CE) and died in 179H (795CE). He only left Madina once to make his pilgrimage, and he said that was only because it was compulsory otherwise, he would never have left the City of the Prophet ﷺ.

[163] Related by al-Ḥâkim in *al-Mustadrak* (2/28).

Narration 79

Yûsuf bin Mâzin said a man stood up (and addressed) al-Ḥasan bin 'Ali[164], may Allah be pleased with him, and said, "O you who turned the face of the believers dark!"[165] To which al-Ḥasan, may Allah be pleased with him, said: *"Do not scold me, may Allah show you mercy! Surely the Messenger of Allah had seen the Banî Umayya delivering sermons from their pulpit, one leader after the next, and this troubled him and so Allah sent down (the verses): 'To thee have We granted the Fount (of Abundance.)'*[166] *And that is a river in the Garden. And these verses were also sent down, "We have indeed revealed this (Message) in the Night of Power. And what will explain to you what the night of power is? The Night of Power is better than a thousand months." Banî Umayya would rule for that period, and we have counted that, and indeed it will not be increased or decreased."* [167]

---

[164] Al-Ḥasan bin 'Ali is the grandson of the Prophet ﷺ His father was 'Ali ibn Abû Tâlib (see note 65) and his mother was the daughter of the Prophet, Fâtima, may Allah be pleased with them both. He was born in Ramaḍân three years after the migration to Madina, and was martyred in 50H (670CE). The Prophet ﷺ took him on his shoulders one day and said, *"O Allah, I indeed love him so love him!"* and he also said, *"I love whoever loves him."* He was extremely generous, modest, and wise. He was a pious worshipper who walked from Madina to perform the Pilgrimage twenty five times. He received the allegiance of more than forty thousand people to make him the Khalîfa, but he gave this up in favour of Mu'âwiyya to avoid any further bloodshed and in doing so ensured peace and prosperity for the Muslims for a long period.

[165] This part of the *ḥadîth* does not appear in the Dar al-Kutub edition.

[166] Al-Kawthar 108:1.

[167] Related by al-Tirmidhi (5/444).

Narration 80

It has been reported on the authority of Abû Hurayra[168] that the Prophet ﷺ said: *"Whoever stands the Night of Power in faith and contentment will have the sins previously committed forgiven, and whoever fasts in Ramaḍân in faith and contentment will have all sins of the past forgiven."* [169]

The Shaykh, may Allah be pleased with him, said, 'The meaning of *The Night of Power* is that Allah the Exalted ordains to the angels everything that will occur at their hands from the management of the affairs of the children of Adam, including their lives and deaths, that will occur during the forthcoming year up to the next Night of Power. And within this entirety are the days of the life of the Prophet ﷺ including what revelation of Quran will be sent down during the forthcoming year. And Allah says in His description of this night, *'We sent it down during a Blessed Night.'* [170] This means "blessed for the Friends of Allah the Mighty and Majestic for indeed it has been made better than a thousand months." Bring it to life! Esteem it, as it deserves to be esteemed! Fill it with prayer and recitation of Quran and remembrance without any frivolity or triviality, and then he said, *'For We (ever) wish to warn (against Evil). In the (Night) is made distinct every affair of wisdom.'*[171] Meaning that "every affair is built upon wisdom and correctness." The meaning of '*made distinct*' is that 'everything is clarified so that what he gives to the angels for the year is destined according to a plan that encompasses them."

---

[168] See note 83.
[169] Related by al-Bukhârî (2/227), Muslim (1/523), al-Tirmidhi (3/67), Abû Dawûd (2/103), al-Nasâ'î (4/157) and Aḥmad (2/473, 503).
[170] Al-Dukhân 44:3.
[171] Al-Dukhân 44:3-4.

Narration 81

It has been reported on the authority of Sa'îd ibn Jubayr from Ibn 'Abbâs[172] that he said regarding the Words of the Exalted: *'We have indeed revealed this (Message) in the Night of Power,'* that Allah, the Mighty and Majestic, sent it down in one go on the Night of Power, meaning to the lowest heaven and it was then sent down in parts, like falling stars with Allah, the Mighty and Majestic, sending it down upon the Messenger of Allah ﷺ with one part following directly from other parts. And then he read, *"Those who reject Faith say, 'Why is not the Qur'an revealed to him all at once?' Thus (is it revealed), that We may strengthen thy heart thereby, and We have rehearsed it to you in slow, well-arranged stages, gradually."* [173]

Narration 82

It has been reported on the authority of Sa'îd ibn Jubayr from Ibn 'Abbâs that he said, "Surely you see a man walking in the market place, but his name is written among the dead," and then he read the verse, *"We sent it down during a Blessed Night. For We (ever) wish to warn (against Evil). In the (Night) is made distinct every affair of wisdom."* And he meant *The Night of Power*, for on that night the affairs of the temporal world for the coming year are distributed.

---

[172] See note 14.
[173] Al-Furqân 25:32.

Narration 83

It has been reported that Sa'îd told us on the authority of Qatâda regarding the Words of the Exalted, "*In the (Night) is made distinct every affair of wisdom,*" that he said, "He makes the affairs of the year distinct (on this night)."

Narration 84

It has been reported on the authority of Abû Mas'ûd al-Jurayrî that Abû Naḍra said, "*The affairs of the whole year, its tribulations, its comforts, and its livelihoods are 'made distinct' on the Night of Power until the same time the following year.*"

And the Shaykh, may Allah be pleased with him, said, "And the blessings of the Night of Power mentioned in the Quran will remain until the Day of Resurrection, and it is in every Ramaḍân according to the following evidence":

Narration 85

It has been reported on the authority of Mâlik ibn Marthad that his father said to Abû Dharr,[174] "Did you ask the Messenger of Allah ﷺ about the Night of Power?"

He said, "I used to ask him about it – meaning I was one of the most persistent in asking him about it - and I said, 'O Messenger of Allah, tell me about the Night of Power, is it the month of Ramaḍân or some other month?'"

And to that he said, *"No, indeed it is in Ramaḍân."*

And I said, "O Prophet of Allah, will you be like the other Prophets that when they passed away all the means of ascension ascend with them, or will it be here until the Day of Resurrection?"

And to that he said, *"No, indeed it is until the Day or Resurrection."*

And I said, "In which month is it?"

He said, *"It is in Ramaḍân, look for it among the last ten nights and during the first ten."* Then he told us some more things but then my inattentiveness made it incomprehensible and I asked him again, "can you tell me which ten nights it is in?"

He said, *"Look for it among the last ten nights and do not ask me about it again."*

Then he talked more and more, but then my inattentiveness made it incomprehensible and I said, "I swear an oath to you O Messenger of Allah, by the rights I have over you, tell me again in which ten it is."

He became angry in a way he had never done with me previously, or ever did again after that, and then he said, *"Look for it among the last ten nights and do not ask me about it again."* [175]

---

[174] See note 140.

[175] Related by Aḥmad (5/181).

Section on Encouragement to Seek It During the Last Ten Nights

Narration 86

It has been reported on the authority of al-Ẓuhri[176] from Sâlim ibn 'Abdullah,[177] that it reached his father that the Prophet ﷺ said, *"A man saw a dream that the Night of Power was in the last ten nights, and so the Messenger of Allah ﷺ said, 'I see that your dream has confirmed this, so seek it in the last ten nights.'"* [178]

And in another narration it adds on the authority of Sufyân, "seek it on the odd nights."

Narration 87

And we have narrated the *ḥadîth* of 'Aisha and others that the Prophet ﷺ said: *"Seek the Night of Power on the odd nights among the last ten of Ramaḍân."*

---

[176] See note 136.

[177] Sâlim bin 'Abdullah was the grandson of 'Umar ibn al-Khaṭṭâb and related many *ḥadîth* directly from his father, of whom it said he resembled in appearance and character. He died in Madina in 106H (725CE).

[178] Related by al-Bukhârî (2/254), Muslim (2/823), al-Tirmidhi (3/185) and Aḥmad (2/8).

Section on Encouragement to Seek It on the Twenty First and Twenty Third Night

Narration 88

Abû Sa'îd[179] said that the Messenger of Allah ﷺ one year, went into seclusion (*I'tikâf*) during the middle ten days Ramaḍân until the twenty first night, which was the night he would come out of seclusion, and he said: "*Whoever went into seclusion with me should go back into seclusion for the last ten. I saw the night but I was made to forget it. I saw myself prostrating in the morning upon water and clay, and so seek it during the last ten nights, and seek it during the odd nights.*" And Abû Sa'îd said, "It rained that night and the mosque had a palm roof and it leaked into the mosque." And Abû Sa'îd said, "I saw the Messenger of Allah ﷺ with my own eyes, and upon his forehead and nose were the traces of water and clay, and that night was the twenty first."[180]

And the Shaykh said, may Allah be pleased with him, 'Abdullah ibn 'Unays differed from this in that he said about this *ḥadîth* that it was the twenty third night, and that is as we have been informed in the following:

[179] See note 94.

[180] Related by al-Bukhârî (2/255 and 256), Muslim (2/824) and Abû Dawûd (2/109).

Narration 89

It has been reported on the authority of Abdullah ibn 'Unays[181] that the Messenger of Allah ﷺ said: *"I saw the Night of Power but then I was made to forget it. I saw myself prostrating upon water and clay in the morning."* And he said, "It rained on the twenty third night and the Messenger of Allah prayed with us and then left. Upon his forehead and nose were the traces of clay." And Abdullah ibn 'Unays used to say it was the twenty third.[182]

Narration 90

Yaḥyâ bin 'Ayyûb said, "Ibn al-Hâd told me that Abû Bakr bin Muḥammad bin 'Amr bin Ḥazm informed him that 'Abdul Raḥmân bin Ka'b bin Mâlik informed him that Abdullah ibn 'Unays said, 'We were in the desert steppe, and we said that if we were to go forward (to the City) with our families it would be burdensome for us, but if we left them behind it would leave them in difficulties.' He said, "So they sent me to the Messenger of Allah ﷺ and I was the youngest of them, and I mentioned to him what they had said, and he ordered me to (seek the Night of Power on the) twenty third night." And Ibn al-Hâd said that Muḥammad bin Ibrâhim used to exert himself (in worship) on that night."

---

[181] 'Abdullah bin 'Unays al-Juhnî was a Companion from among the Anṣâr who after embracing Islam destroyed the idols of his tribe Banû Salama. He was present at the Oath of Allegiance at 'Aqaba. He travelled to North Africa before dying in Syria in 54H (674CE).
[182] Related by Muslim (2/828) and Aḥmad (3/495).

Section on Encouragement to Seek It During the Last Seven Nights

Narration 91

On the authority of 'Uqba ibn Ḥurayth who heard Ibn 'Umar[183] say that the Prophet ﷺ said, *"Prepare for it in the last ten (nights), and if one of you is too weak or incapable don't be overcome (by your weakness) during the last seven."* [184]

Narration 92

It has been reported on the authority of Anas ibn Mâlik[185] from 'Ubâda ibn al-Ṣamit,[186] who said the Messenger of Allah came out to us wishing to inform us about the Night of Power. There were two men from among the Muslims trading insults with each other and the Messenger of Allah ﷺ said, *"Indeed I had come out to you and I had hoped to inform you about the Night of Power. There was an argument between so-and-so and so-and-so, and as a result, it was taken up and perhaps in that is goodness. So search for it in the last ten nights, on the fifth, seventh and ninth (of those ten)."* [187]

---

[183] See note 81.
[184] Related by Muslim (2/283), Abû Dawûd (2/11) and Aḥmad (2/62, 84 and 114).
[185] See note 30.
[186] 'Ubâda ibn al-Ṣâmit was one of the leaders of the Ansar at the Oath of Allegiance at 'Aqaba. He participated in all battles during the Prophet's lifetime, and went on to participate in the Conquest of Egypt. He was a prolific narrator of *ḥadîth* and many Companions also related from him. He was one of those who collected the verses of Quran during the time of the Prophet ﷺ and was sent to Syria during the time of 'Umar to teach them the Quran. He was known to be tall, strong, and handsome.
[187] Related by Bukhârî (1/18) and Aḥmad (5/313 -319).

Narration 93

It has been reported on the authority of Anas ibn Mâlik from 'Ubâda ibn al-Ṣamit, who said the Messenger of Allah said: *"I came out and wanted to inform you about the Night of Power but two men were trading insults with each other and it went from me, so seek it in the last ten nights, when there are seven remaining, nine remaining and five remaining (of the month)."*

Abû Bakr bin Muḥammad ibn Ḥasan al-Isfahâni informed us that 'Abdullah bin Ja'far told us that Yûnus ibn Ḥabîb told us that Abû Dawûd told us that Ḥamâd told us, and then he mentioned the above.

Narration 94

Likewise, it was related by Ayyûb, on the authority of 'Ikrima, on the authority of Ibn 'Abbâs[188] from the Prophet ﷺ with the meaning of both (narrations), and Abû Bakra Nufay'a narrates it in a fuller (narration).

---

[188] See note 14.

Narration 95

It has been reported on the authority of 'Abdul Raḥmân bin Jawshan from his father, who said the *Night of Power* was mentioned in front of Abû Bakra[189] and he said, "As for me, I do not seek it except in the last ten nights after the *ḥadîth* I heard from the Messenger of Allah ﷺ in which he said, *'Search for it during the last ten nights with ten remaining, seven remaining or five remaining or three remaining or one remaining.'*" Abû Bakra used to pray during the (first) twenty days as he did during the rest of the year but when the last ten entered, he exerted himself (greatly in worship).

The Shaykh, may Allah be pleased with him, said that it is implied that what is meant by *'nine remaining'* is that nine is the number of nights left in the month after the twenty had already passed. This is the same with the other numbers we have mentioned here. All of this brings us back to the point of seeking it on the odd nights of the last ten nights, as has been covered in the *ḥadîth* that have already been presented.

It might imply that what is meant is the second night of the last ten and the fourth of the last ten and so on to the end of the month. For this (is based on) the specific number remaining once that night was completed. And so one should also be careful to seek it on the even nights from the last ten, because if we count back from the end of the month it would encompass both odd and even numbers. This is indicated by what has been related by Abû Naḍra and Abû Sa'îd al-Khudrî.[190]

---

[189] See note 10.

[190] See note 94.

Narration 96

Ḥadîth with the same meaning as those reported above by 'Ubâda ibn Al-Ṣamit are reported by Abû Naḍra and Abû Sa'îd al-Khudrî in a more complete form, and then he said that Abû Naḍra said, "I said to Abû Sa'îd, 'Surely, you are the Companions of the Messenger of Allah ﷺ and you know more about these numbers than we do, so how do you count them?' He said, "True, we have a greater right than you in this respect. When twenty-one has passed, the night that follows it is the fifth." In another narration it is said, "when twenty-three has passed, the one that follows is the seventh, and if twenty-five has passed, then the one that follows is the fifth."

This clearly explains that it is among the odd nights if you count from the end and it is on the even if you count from the beginning (of the ten). And it is this interpretation that is related from Abû Dharr[191] in the most correct of the two narrations from him about the night prayer of the Prophet ﷺ and this affirms everything that we have related from these transmissions about seeking it in all of the last ten nights. It is related on the authority of 'Abdullah ibn Mas'ûd from the Prophet ﷺ as follows:

Narration 97

Ibn Mas'ûd[192] said, the Messenger of Allah ﷺ said to us: "*Seek it on the twenty seventh night of Ramaḍân, the twenty first night of Ramaḍân and the twenty third night of Ramaḍân,*" and then he was silent.[193]

---

[191] See note 140.
[192] See note 117.
[193] Related by Abû Dawûd (2/110).

Narration 98

'Ibrâhîm al-Nakh'aî related it on the authority of al-Aswad that he said that 'Abdullah ibn Mas'ûd said: *"Prepare for the Night of Power on the seventeenth, the morning of Badr or on the twenty-first or the twenty-third."*

Narration 99

And it is related that Zayd ibn Arqam was asked about the Night of Power and he said, *"It is the nineteenth and we do not have any doubt."* He said, *"Day of Testing, the Day of the meeting of the two forces."* [194]

This is as it has been related on the authority of the two of them about the nineteenth. The first narration is from Ibn Mas'ûd and it is the most strongly authenticated. It is well known among the war historians that the fighting at Badr took place on the seventeenth of the month of Ramaḍân, and I love to seek the Night of Power during its night (that is the night preceding it) and by Allah is enabling success.

---

[194] The verse referred to here is Al-Furqân 8:41. The ḥadîth is related by al-Bukhârî (3/91).

Section on Encouragement to Seek It on the Twenty Seventh Night

Narration 100

Abû al-Ḥusayn, 'Ali bin Muḥammad bin 'Abdullah bin Bishr informed us in Baghdad (of a chain of narrators linking him to) Sufyân ibn 'Uyayna (the following). We now change to another chain[195] where:

Narration 101

Sufyân told us that 'Abda bin Abû Lubâba and Âṣim bin Bahdala that they both heard Zirr bin Ḥubaysh say: "I said to Ubay ibn Ka'b[196], 'O Abû al-Mundhir, surely your brother Ibn Mas'ûd used to say that whoever stands in prayer all year will definitely get the Night of Power.'

And he said to this, "May Allah show you mercy, indeed what he wanted was that you did not become lazy. He knew it was in the month of Ramaḍân and that it was in the last ten nights and that it was actually the twenty seventh night." Then he swore an oath, 'there is no exception – it is the twenty seventh night.'"

He said, "We said, 'O Abû al-Mundhir, by what do you know this?'

He said, "By signs or indicators that the Messenger of Allah ﷺ informed us of. (Among them is that) the sun rises on that day with no rays emanating from it."" [197]

---

[195] A common way to mention two different chains of narration which a person (in this case Imam al-Bayhaqî) received directly from two different narrators, which both link back to the same person, and from him or her, back to the end of the chain (which is usually the Prophet ﷺ). In this case, Sufyân is that common person, and from him back to the Ibn Mas'ûd, the two chains are identical. *(Editor)*

[196] See note 158.

[197] Related by Muslim (1/252), al-Tirmidhî (3/160) and Abû Dawûd (2/106).

The wording of the *ḥadîth* of al-Ḥumaydî, and the *ḥadîth* of Sa'dân are abridged and do not mention the story of Ibn Mas'ûd.
There are two weak *ḥadîth* that describe the weather on the Night of Power. In one of them, it says it is a gentle pleasant night, not hot and not cold, and the sun rises with a little redness. And in the other *ḥadîth*, the same meaning is given.

Narration 102

It has been reported on the authority of Mu'âwiya bin Abû Sufyân[198] that the Prophet ﷺ (indicated) it was the twenty seventh of Ramaḍân.[199] And Abû Dawûd al-Tayâlasî related it, but stopped the narration with Mu'âwiya (without attributing it to the Prophet ﷺ).

Narration 103

It has been reported that Ma'mar told us on the authority of Qatâda and Âṣim that they both heard 'Ikrima say that Ibn 'Abbas[200], may Allah be pleased with both of them, said that 'Umar,[201] may Allah be pleased with him, called the Companions of the Messenger of Allah ﷺ and asked them about the *Night of Power.* There was consensus that it was in the last ten nights. (He said,) "And so I said to 'Umar, 'Indeed, I am more knowledgeable (than most), and I think I know which night it is.'

---

[198] Mu'âwiya was the son of Abû Sufyân, the onetime opponent of Islam who embraced Islam shortly before the Conquest of Makkah. Mu'âwiya was born five years before the advent of Islam, and went on to become the first ruler of the Ummayad Dynasty. He establishing the first Muslim navy, and establishing important state institutions and mosques. He died in 60H (680 CE).
[199] Related by Abû Dawûd (2/111).
[200] See note 14.
[201] See note 41.

He said, "And which night is it?"
He said, 'I said it is when seven nights of the last ten have passed or when seven nights of the last ten remain.'
He said, "And how do you know that?""
He said, "I said, 'Allah created the seven earths, and the seven heavens in seven days, and time rotates around seven, and a man was created to eat on seven, and to prostrate on seven limbs, and circumambulate (the Holy House as part of the pilgrimage), and to use seven stones.'
He said, 'You have understood this in a way we have not!'"
And the Shaykh, may Allah be pleased with him, indicates, but there is no certainty about it, that the Messenger of Allah knew it in the beginning, but was not granted permission to inform others of it so that people would not become complacent about its knowledge and fail to strive for it on other nights. And then he ﷺ was made to forget it as he was obliged to answer when asked about any affair of the Religion. What is indicated in these transmissions, and those with similar meanings, is that it rotates within the last ten nights, and in some years it might be on the twenty-first and in another year it might be on another night. This is because the preference of this night (over others) is only through its connection to the sending down of the Quran accompanied by the angels in it. And the descending of the angels is, by His permission, to greet the slaves of Allah, which can be on different nights, and so whatever night the angels descend to greet, (that is the night that) rewards for good actions are multiplied. And by Allah is enabling success.

Narration 104

It has been reported on the authority of 'Ikrima that Ibn 'Abbas, may Allah be pleased with both of them, said, "Once I was visited while I was sleeping in Ramaḍân. It was said to me, 'Indeed tonight is the Night of Power.' I stood up and I was in slumber, and so I held on to the ropes of the tent of the Prophet ﷺ and he was praying. I looked at which night it was and it was the twenty-third." And ('Ikrima) said that Ibn Abbâs said, "Indeed Shaytân (the Devil) rises with the sun every morning, except on the Night of Power, and that it rises on that day without any rays (appearing to emanate from it)."[202]

Narration 105

It has been reported on the authority of Mûsâ ibn 'Ubayda that Ayyûb bin Khâli said: "I was at sea and in a state of ritual impurity[203] on the twenty-third of Ramaḍân, so I washed in sea water and found it to be sweet and pure."

And the Shaykh, may Allah be pleased with him, said that this has also been found on the twenty-seventh and among the narrations are the following:

Narration 106

It has been reported on the authority of al-'Awza'î that 'Abda bin Abû Lubâba said, "I tasted seawater on the twenty-seventh of Ramaḍân and it tasted like fresh water."

Narration 107

Abû Sa'îd bin al-'Arâbî said, "I heard Abû Yaḥyâ bin Abû Masarra say, 'I was going around (the Ka'ba) on the twenty-seventh of Ramaḍân and I saw the angels going around the House in groups.'"

---

[202] Related by Aḥmad (1/255, 282).

[203] Meaning he required a ritual bath due to having sexual intercourse or ejaculation.

Narration 108

And he, may Allah be pleased with him said, "I heard Abû Sa'îd, 'Abdul Malik bin 'Uthmân al-Zâhid say, 'I heard Abû Muḥammad al-Miṣrî say when he was in Makka, "I was in seclusion in a mosque in Egypt and before me was Abu 'Ali al-La'kî, and so I rose from my sleep and saw the sky as if its doors had opened. In it the angels descended with remembrance of *la ilaha illallah* and *Allâhu Akbar* and I took note and said this is the Night of Power and it was the twenty-seventh of Ramaḍân."'"

And the Shaykh, may Allah be pleased with him, said there are *ḥadîth* that have been related about the month of Ramaḍân and the Night of Power, some of which are with chains of narration that are not known other than that they mention the descending of the angels. We can confirm the descending of the angels on the Night of Power and their greeting the believers ,and what we have mentioned in the *ḥadîth* about Sha'bân is also confirmed (in the following):

Narration 109

On the authority of one of our shaykhs called Abû al-Ḥasan, on the authority of al-Ḍaḥâk bin Muzâḥim from 'Abdullah ibn 'Abbâs[204] that he heard the Messenger of Allah ﷺ say: "Indeed the Garden is adorned and embellished from year to year for the arrival of Ramaḍân. When it is the first of Ramaḍân, a breeze blows from beneath the Throne. It is called al-Muthîra, and the leaves of the trees of the Garden shake. The orchestra of their tremor can be heard and the (sweet) rumbling they make is more beautiful than anything ever heard. The Ḥouris pull up their garments and rise to the highest points of the Garden and call, 'Is there any who proposes

[204] See note 14.

to Allah, the Mighty and Majestic, that we may marry him?' And then the Ḥouris say (to the Gatekeepers of the Garden) "O Riḍwân,[205] what is this night?" He answers them with the call 'labayk'[206] and then he says, "This is the first night of the month of Ramaḍân. The doors of the Garden are opened for those who are fasting from among the nation of Muḥammad ﷺ" He said, 'Allah, the Mighty and Majestic, says "O Ridwân! Open the doors of the Gardens, O Mâlik![207] Close the doors of Hell for those who fast from among the nation of Muḥammad ﷺ O Jibrîl (Gabriel)! Descend to the earth, and chain up the rebellious devils and shackle them with fetters, and throw them into the seas so that they cannot spoil the fast of the nation of Muḥammad, my beloved.' He, Mighty and Majestic, says every night during the month of Ramaḍân to a caller that he should call out three times, "Is there any asker whom I can give what they ask? Is there anyone turning to me in repentance that I can turn to him in acceptance? Is there anyone seeking forgiveness that I can forgive? Who gives the one who is full and the one who has nothing?" [208]

And Allah, the Mighty and Majestic, sets free from the Fire every breaking of the fast, a million people, all of whom deserved the Fire. And on the last day of the month of Ramaḍân, Allah frees the equivalent number of people that He had freed from the first to the last day. And when it is the Night of Power, Allah, the Mighty and Majestic commands Jibrîl to descend with a group of angels to the earth. With them is a green flag. They place the flag upon the Ka'ba. He has one hundred wings, including two wings that do not appear except on that night and he will expose them on that night, and

---

[205] Riḍwân is the name of the angel who guards the Gates of the Garden.

[206] This has an approximate meaning of 'at your service' and is the traditional call used in the pilgrimage.

[207] Mâlik is the name of the angel who guards the Gates of Hell.

[208] In the Dar Ibn Hazm edition it says *'man yaqriḍu_lmil'a ghary al-Mu'dimi wal-wâfî ghayra al-Ẓulmi'* and the Dar al-Kutub edition says, *'man yaqriḍ al-mala' ghayr al-Mu'dimi wal-wâfî ghayra al-maẓlûmi.'* I referred this to Shaykh Ninowy and he translated it as above pointing out that the use of the *qarḍ,* unlike *iṭâa* means giving but with conditions. And Allah knows best.

they will encompass the East and the West. Jibrîl, peace be upon him, will hasten the angels on this night and they will greet everyone who is standing in prayer, sitting or praying or remembering Allah on his side, and they say 'Amen' to their supplications until the dawn breaks. When the dawn breaks, Jibrîl calls, "O Angels! Time to go! Time to go!" And they will say, 'O Jibrîl, what will Allah do about the needs of the believers from among the nation of Muḥammad ﷺ?' And he will say, "Allah gazes upon them on this night and pardons them and forgives them, all but four.""

And we said, "O Messenger of Allah! Who are they?"

He said, "The one who persists in drinking alcohol, the one who disobeys his parents, the one who cuts ties of kinship, and the rebellious one."

We said, "O Messenger of Allah! Who is the rebellious one?"

He said, "The one who cuts off (from other Muslims out of hostility and animosity). [209]

And when the night of ending the (month) of the fast comes, it will be called the Night of Reward. And on the morning following the end of the fast comes, Allah sends angels to every city. They descend to the earth and stand at the mouths of every path and call – and everything that Allah created except for humankind and the Jinn[210] will hear, 'O Nation of Muḥammad! Go out to a Generous Lord who will give you plenty and pardon the mighty sin.' And when they go out to their prayer place, Allah, Mighty and Majestic, will say to the angels, "What is the wage for the one who has completed his work?"" He said, "The angels say, 'O our God and our Master! His wage is that he is paid his due.'

And He will say: "Truly I make you bear witness, O my Angels, that I have made My pleasure and My forgiveness the reward for their fasting and their standing in prayer during the month of Ramaḍân." He will say: 'O My slaves! Ask Me! For by My Might and My Majesty, not one (of you) will ask me

---

[209] *'Muṣârim'* is taken from the verb ṣ-r-m which in this form implies, according to Lane's Lexicon, 'affecting disunion' with someone or 'cutting off friendly or loving communion.'

[210] See note 85.

anything for your next world in your gathering, except that I will grant it, and (none will ask about) worldly matters, except that I will see to them. And by My Might, I will ease your difficulties as long as you are vigilant towards Me. By My Might, you will not be left unanswered and I will not leave you disgraced among the people of the ditches. So leave forgiven, for indeed you have pleased Me, and I am pleased with you.' And so the angels will be happy and take delight in what Allah the Mighty and Majestic has granted this nation when they end the month of Ramaḍân."

Narration 110

It is related on the authority of al-Aṣbagh that 'Ali,[211] may Allah be pleased with him, said, "We were encouraging 'Umar, may Allah be pleased with him, to establish the night prayer (in congregation). I informed him that above the seven heavens is a settlement[212] called 'the Settlement of Holiness', in which a group (of angels) called *al-Rawḥ* live. On the Night of Power, they ask their Lord permission to descend to the earth. They do not pass by anyone on the way (or come across someone) praying except that that person receives blessing from them."

And 'Umar said to him, "O Abû al-Ḥasan! Encourage the people to pray the night prayer so they can attain some of this blessing," and he ordered the people to establish the night prayer (in congregation).

And the Shaykh, may Allah be pleased with him, said, 'This chain only goes through 'Ubayd bin Isḥâq al-'Aṭṭâr, on the authority of Sayf bin 'Umar, and if it is correct then it supports what has been related (in the *ḥadîth*) before it, and informs us about the coming down of the angels and their greeting

[211] See note 65.

[212] *Ḥaḍîra* usually refers to a troop and this would normally translated as 'there is a troop (of angels) known as the Sacred Troop. However, the context implies it is the name of a place. And Allah knows best.

of the believers on the Night of Power, and this has already been made clear in the Book of Allah, the Exalted.

Narration 111

It has been reported on the authority of Ibn Isḥâq that al-Sha'bî said about His words, Mighty and Majestic is He! *"On every errand. Peace! This until the rise of morn!"* that, "it is the greeting of the people of the mosque by the angels on the Night of Power which continues up until the dawn."

Narration 112

And with his chain of transmission, Sa'îd ibn Manṣûr told us that 'Isa bin Yûnus told us that al-'Amash told us on the authority of Mujâhid who said that His words, "*Peace! This...*" means "*this* (night) is safe, and the Devil is not able to do any harm in it, and no harm occurs in it."

And the Shaykh, may Allah be pleased with him, said, "And Allah knows who comprehends the status of this night and establishes its rights. And by Allah is enabling success."

As for the supplications that have been transmitted for this night, they are (found in the following *ḥadîth*):

Narration 113

It has been reported on the authority of Yazîd ibn Hârun (who said) Kamas bin al-Ḥusayn told us on the authority of ‘Abdullah bin Burayda[213] that Aisha, may Allah be pleased with her, said to the Messenger of Allah ﷺ "If I were to come across the Night of Power, what should I say?
And he said, ‘Say:

اللَّهُمَّ إِنَّكَ عَفُوٌّ تُحِبُّ العَفْوَ فَاعْفُ عَنِّي

Allâhumma innaka ‘afuwwun tuḥibb al-‘Afwa fa’fu ‘anni
O Allah, Surely you are pardoning and love to pardon, so pardon me!’" [214]
And Yazîd added, "I know that he said it three times."

---

[213] See note 358.
[214] Related by Ibn Mâjah (2/1256) and Aḥmad (6/181, 182, 183 and 208).

Narration 114

Sa'îd ibn al-Jurayrî related on the authority of 'Abdullah bin Burayda that Aisha, may Allah be pleased with her, said to the Messenger of Allah ﷺ "O Messenger of Allah, if you see that I see the Night of Power, what should I ask my Lord and (what prayer should I use to) supplicate my Lord?
And he said, 'Say:

اللَّهُمَّ إِنَّكَ عَفُوٌّ تُحِبُّ العَفْوَ فاعْفُ عنِّي

Allâhumma innaka 'afuwwun tuḥibb al-'Afwa fa'fu 'anni
O Allah, Surely you are pardoning and love to pardon, so pardon me!'"

Al-Imâm Abû Ṭâlib informed us that Abû al-'Abbâs al-Asam told us that Yaḥyâ ibn Abû Ṭâlib said that 'Ali bin Âṣim told us that al-Jurayrî told us, and then he mentioned (the above *ḥadîth*).
And the Shaykh, may Allah be pleased with him, said that the asking for pardon from Allah is recommended at all times, especially on the Night of Power.

Narration 115

It has been reported that Abû 'Uthmân, Sa'îd bin 'Ismâ'îl often used to say in his gathering and other occasions, "*Your Pardon! O You who pardons! Your Pardon! In life Your Pardon! In death Your Pardon! In the grave, Your Pardon! At the resurrection, Your Pardon! At the reading of the account, Your Pardon! On the Traverse, Your Pardon! At the Scales, Your Pardon! And in all states, Your Pardon! O You who pardons, Your Pardon!*" And Abû 'Amr said he saw Abû 'Uthmân in a dream a few days after he had passed away and it was said to him, "What benefited you from the actions of the temporal world?" And he said, "My saying *Your Pardon! Your Pardon!*"

Narration 116

It has been reported on the authority of Muḥammad bin Ḥujâda that Anas said that the Prophet ﷺ said: *"Whoever prays the Maghrib and 'Ishâ prayers in congregation until the month of Ramaḍân has ended has attained a good portion of the Night of Power."*

Narration 117

And we have related on the authority of Abû al-Ḥusnâ on the authority of Abû Hurayra that the Prophet ﷺ said, *"Whoever prays the 'Ishâ prayer in congregation in Ramaḍân has indeed got the Night of Power."*

Narration 118

It has been reported that al-Qa'nabî told us from what he had read to Mâlik what had reached him from Sa'îd ibn al-Musayyib that he used to say, *"Whoever attends the 'Ishâ prayer on the Night of Power has taken his portion of it."*

Chapter Eight

The *Tarâwîḥ* Prayer in the Month of *Ramaḍân*

Narration 119

It is related on the authority of 'Aisha[215], the wife of the Prophet ﷺ that one night the Messenger of Allah ﷺ went out to pray in the mosque and some people prayed with him. The next night he did the same, and the (number of people who prayed with him) was large. Then they gathered (in anticipation) on the third and fourth night, but the Messenger of Allah ﷺ did not go out. In the morning he said: "*I saw what you did and the only thing that prevented me from coming out (to pray with you) was that I feared it would be made compulsory upon you.*" And that was in Ramaḍân.[216]

Narration 120

It is related on the authority of Abû Hurayra, may Allah be pleased with him, that the Messenger of Allah ﷺ used to want to establish the night prayer of Ramaḍân without ordering them to do it as a compulsion, and so he would say: "*Whoever stands the nights of Ramaḍân in faith and contentment will have his previous sins forgiven.*" The Messenger of Allah ﷺ passed away and the situation was like that, and it continued like that in the time of Abû Bakr until the beginning of the reign of 'Umar.[217]

---

[215] See note 23.

[216] Related by al-Bukhârî (2/251), Muslim (1/524), al-Nasâ'î (3/203) and Abû Dawûd (2/104).

[217] Related by al-Bukhârî (2/251 and 252), Muslim (1/523), al-Tirmidhî (3/181 and 182), al-Nasâ'î (4/157) and Abû Dawûd (2/102 and 103) and Aḥmad (2/281 and 529).

Narration 121

It has been reported on the authority of 'Abdul Raḥmân bin 'Abdun al-Qârî[218] who said, "I went out one night during Ramaḍân with 'Umar ibn al-Khaṭṭâb,[219] may Allah be pleased with him, to the mosque. People were praying in scattered groups. A man would be praying on his own and another man might be praying with a small group. And so 'Umar said, 'I swear by Allah that if I gathered all these people to pray behind one reciter this would be much better.' He was determined (to implement this), and so he gathered them all behind Ubay ibn Ka'b."[220] Then he said, "I went out with him the following night and the people were praying behind their reciter and 'Umar said, 'What a blessed innovation this is. (But) that which you miss while you sleep is better than this.' What he meant was the last part of the night as the people (gathered to pray) during the beginning of the night."[221]

And the Shaykh, may Allah be pleased with him, said that this is what prevented 'Umar ibn al-Khaṭṭâb (going further and instructing them to establish the prayer in the last part of the night). If (establishing the *tarawîḥ*) was an innovation, it was a praiseworthy innovation, because it did not contradict what had already been established in the time of the Prophet ﷺ For we have already related that they prayed it with the Messenger of Allah ﷺ for some nights and the Messenger of Allah ﷺ only stopped it being prayed (regularly) in congregation out of fear that (in doing so) it would become compulsory upon them. With the passing of the Messenger of Allah, the Religion was completed and the obligations finalised. 'Umar ibn al-Khaṭṭâb did not fear what the Messenger of Allah ﷺ

---

[218] It was said that 'Abdul Raḥmân ibn 'Abdun al-Qâri came to the Prophet ﷺ with his brother when they were both very young. The Messenger ﷺ wiped his hand over the head of the young boys and supplicated for them. He died in Madina in 88H (707CE).

[219] See note 41.

[220] See note 158.

[221] Related by al-Bukhârî (2/252).

feared, and therefore thought gathering them behind one reciter was best. And so he ordered them to do that. In this, he was a guide to a matter about which the Commander of the Faithful, ‘Ali ibn Abû Ṭâlib said, “We did not deem it an exaggeration that tranquillity[222] was spoken on the tongue of ‘Umar.”

And the Shaykh, may Allah be pleased with him, said that we have related (*ḥadîṭh*) which show that the Prophet ﷺ saw some Companions praying behind Ubay ibn Ka’b[223] in Ramaḍân and he praised that. Among them are:

Narration 122

It has been reported on the authority of Ibn al-Hâdi that Tha’laba bin Abû al-Mâlik al-Quraẓî[224] told him that the Messenger of Allah ﷺ went out one night in Ramaḍân and saw people in an area of the mosque praying and he said, *“What are they doing?”* Someone said, “O Messenger of Allah, they are people who have no one amongst them who knows the Quran and Ubay bin Ka’b[225] is reading with them and they pray behind him.” And he said, *“Indeed, they have done something excellent,”* or *“They are indeed correct,”* and he did not show any dislike for what they had done, and Ibn Wahb said some (in the chain) added a few words that are not found in other (narrations).

---

[222] *Al-Sakîna,* translated literally as *calmness,tranquillity*. Scholars have understood the term to indicate a number of things, including a type of inspiration that Allah gives to his servants to help them. Imam al-Nawawi said, “The preferred meaning is a type of Allah’s creation which contains certainty, mercy, and with it, the Angels. Yet Allah knows best.” See his commentary on Sahih Muslim (6/82). *(Editor)*

[223] See note 158.

[224] There is difference of opinion about whether Tha’laba was actually a Companion. His father came from the Yemen and married a lady from Bani Qurayza, bringing her back to the Yemen, where Tha’laba was born. He returned to Madina and related *ḥadîth* from several Companions, but it is disputed whether he actually met the Prophet ﷺ And Allah knows best.

[225] See note 158.

Narration 123

Something similar has been reported on the authority of al-'Alâ ibn 'Abdul Raḥmân from his father from Abû Hurayra,[226] and in it is an indication that the Tarâwîḥ prayer in congregation is preferred for those who have not memorised the Quran. As for those who have memorised the Quran, Ibn 'Umar considers it best for them to pray alone. And for those who hold this opinion, their evidence is as follows:

Narration 124

It has been reported on the authority of Busr bin Sa'îd that Zayd ibn Thâbit[227] said that the Messenger of Allah ﷺ built an enclosure in the mosque using a straw mat. The Messenger of Allah ﷺ used to come out and pray in it. He said that men used to follow him, and when they saw him praying they would pray behind him, following his prayer. They used to do this every night until one night the Messenger of Allah ﷺ did not come out to them. They raised their voices and knocked at his door until the Messenger of Allah ﷺ came out to them and he was angry. He said to them: *"O People! As long as you were doing what you were doing, I thought it would be*

---

[226] See note 83.

[227] Zayd ibn Thâbit was one of the Companions who commited the whole Quran to memory. During the time of the first Khalifa, Abû Bakr (see note 433), a large number of Companions who had memorised the whole Quran were killed at the Battle of Yamama, and it was thought best to collect the Quran into one document. Zayd was given the task of collecting all parchments and pieces of bone and leather upon which the Quran was written as it was revealed into one place, and then to start writing it into a document. He knew the responsibility apparently saying, "if Abû Bakr were to order me to move a mountain it would have been easier." There are differences of opinion about when he died, but Abû Hurayra is reported to have said he died the same day as Ibn 'Abbâs (see note 14). And Allah knows best.

made an obligation. So pray in your homes for surely the best prayer of a person is in his home except for the prescribed ones." [228]

And we have related in a *ḥadîth* of Abu Dharr[229] (in which it is reported that) the Prophet ﷺ said: *"Indeed, if a person prays with the Imâm and then leaves, written for him will be (the reward of praying) the remainder of the night."* [230]

And the majority of the Companions went with what 'Umar ibn al-Khaṭṭâb did regarding the gathering of people (to pray) behind one reciter.

Narration 125

Abû 'Abdullah al-Thaqafî told us that Arfaja' al-Thaqafî said that 'Ali ibn Abû Ṭalib,[231] may Allah be pleased with him, ordered the people to stand in prayer (for *Tarâwîḥ*) in the month of Ramaḍân, and he appointed an Imâm for the men and an Imâm for the women, and I was the Imâm for the women.

---

[228] Related by al-Bukhârî (1/187), Muslim (1/539), al-Tirmidhî (3/312), al-Nasâ'î (3/197) and Abû Dawûd (2/145).
[229] See note 140.
[230] Related by al-Tirmidhî (3/169), al-Nasâ'î (3/83), Ibn Mâjah (1/420) and Abû Dawûd (2/105).
[231] See note 65.

Chapter Nine

The Number of Prayer Cycles in the Night Prayer During the Time of ‘Umar

Narration 126

It has been reported that al-Qa’nabî informed us from what he read to Mâlik, on the authority of Muḥammad bin Yûsuf, son of the sister of al-Sâ’ib, from al-Sâ’ib that ‘Umar, may Allah be pleased with him, ordered Ubay bin Ka’b[232] and Tamîm al-Dâri[233] to lead the people in eleven *raka’ât* (prayer cycles). The reciter used to read from the chapters containing around one hundred verses. We used to lean on staffs because the standing (during the recitation) was so long, and we would not leave until near to dawn.

This is how it has been related in this narration, and it is consistent with the narration of ‘Aisha,[234] may Allah be pleased with her, concerning the number of *raka’ât* (prayer cycles) that the Prophet ﷺ prayed in the month of Ramaḍân and at other times. And ‘Umar ibn al-Khaṭṭâb[235], may Allah be pleased with him, used to order this number for a period, and then it was as follows:

---

[232] See note 158.

[233] Tamîm al-Dârî converted from Christianity in 9H. He was quick to memorise the Quran, sometimes reciting it in its entirety in one raka’a (prayer cycle). On other occasions, he would spend the whole night reciting one verse over and over again. When he arrived in Madina, he carried a candle with him as he entered the mosque and the Prophet ﷺ said *"you have illumined our mosque, may Allah illumine you in this world and the next."* The Prophet ﷺ related *ḥadîth* from him concerning matters of the antichrist confirming they were true. He is the only human that he explicitly related from. After the death of ‘Uthmân ibn ‘Affân, he returned to Syria, later dying in Jerusalem in 40H (660CE).

[234] See note 23.

[235] See note 41.

Narration 127

It has been reported on the authority of Yazîd bin Khaṣîfa that al-Sâib bin Yazîd said that they used to pray twenty *raka'ât* (prayer cycles) during Ramaḍân in the time of 'Umar ibn al-Khaṭṭâb. They used to read from the chapters of the Quran that contain around two hundred verses, and they used to lean on their staffs in the time of 'Uthmân ibn 'Affân[236] because of the intensity of the standing.

And the Shaykh, may Allah be pleased with him, said that Yazîd bin Rumân related this meaning on the authority of 'Umar ibn al-Khaṭṭâb.

And we related on the authority of Shutayr bin Shakl, who was one of the companions of 'Ali, may Allah be pleased with him, that he used to lead them in the month of Ramaḍân in twenty *raka'ât* (prayer cycles), and then they would pray the *witr* prayer with three *raka'ât* (prayer cycles).

It has been reported on the authority of Suwayd bin Ghafla that he used to lead them in Ramaḍân, and he prayed five *Tarâwîḥ* prayers praying twenty *raka'ât* (prayer cycles).

And we have related on the authority of 'Uthmân al-Nahdî that 'Umar ibn al-Khaṭṭâb, may Allah be pleased with him, invited three reciters and asked them to recite (that is, to lead the people in the prayer). He ordered the fastest of the three reciters to read thirty verses for the people during (the night prayer) of Ramaḍân. He ordered the middle paced of the three to recite twenty-five verses, and he ordered the slowest of the three to recite twenty verses for the people.

---

[236] 'Uthmân ibn 'Affân was a wealthy Makkan businessman who was one of the first to embrace Islam. He was extremely generous, giving all his wealth away several times. He married two of the Prophet's daughters, Ruqayya, and after her death, Umm Kulthûm. For this reason, he had the nickname Dhû Nurayn, the possessor of two lights. He went on to become the third ruler after the Prophet ﷺ. He was very humble and was often seen sleeping alone in the mosque with no guards or entourage, and used to ride a mule with his son behind him. During that time, the first full written copies of the Quran were produced, and for this reason he is also called Jâmi Ayâtul Quran, *The Gatherer of the Verses of the Quran*. He was murdered while reading Quran in 35H (655 CE).

Narration 128

It has been reported that al-Qa'nabî informed us from what he read to Mâlik on the authority of Dawûd ibn al-Ḥaṣîn that he heard 'Abdul Raḥmân bin Hurmuz al-A'raj say, "I have not come across people except that they cursed disbelief in Ramaḍân. And the reciter (who led the prayer) used to stand in prayer reciting from the chapter (entitled) *al-Baqara,* and if he stood (to pray for) twelve *raka'ât* (prayer cycles), he would recite less."

Narration 129

And it has been reported with this chain of narrators on the authority of Mâlik that 'Abdullah bin Abû Bakr[237] said, "I heard my father say that we used to leave the prayer in Ramaḍân, and we would rush our servant to prepare the food out of fear that the dawn (would break very soon)."

Narration 130

And it has been reported with this chain of narrators on the authority of Mâlik on the authority of Hishâm bin 'Urwa from his father that Dhakwân, who used to be a slave of 'Aisha, the wife of the Prophet ﷺ and who was freed by her after that, used to lead the prayer for her in Ramaḍân.

---

[237] He is 'Abdullah bin Abu Bakr ibn Muḥammad ibn 'Amr ibn Ḥazm Al-Ansârî, Al-Madanî, Al-Qâḍî, and he died 135AH in Madina. He was a great scholar who relates many ḥadîth. He related ḥadîth from Anas, and scholars such as al-Thawrî, Ibn 'Uyayna, and others, and he related ḥadîth both to and from al-Zuhrî and Mâlik. His father, Abu Bakr ibn Muḥammad, was a scholar and judge during 'Umar ibn 'Abdul-'Azîz's governorship of Madina, then was appointed governor of Madina when 'Umar became the Khalîfa. He died 120AH in Madina. See al-Ṭabaqât al-Kubrâ (1/126). *(Editor)*

Narration 131

It has been reported that al-Ḥakm ibn Abân said that al-'Ikrima said that 'Aisha, may Allah be pleased with her, said, "We used to get the young boys from the school to lead the prayer for us in Ramaḍân, and we used to make *Qaliyya* and *Khushkananj*[238] for them."

[238] *Khushkananj* is bread made from wheat flour. Sesame seed oil is added to the dough. This is a word adopted into the Arabic language. And *Qaliyya* is a dish made of camel meat and liver. And Allah knows best.

Chapter Ten
The Prohibition of Preceding the Month of Ramaḍân With a Day or Two of Fasting

Narration 132

It is related on the authority of Abû Hurayra[239] that the Prophet ﷺ said: *"None of you should fast a day or two before Ramaḍân, except someone who regularly fasts that particular day. In this case, he can fast that day (as he normally would)."* [240]

Narration 133

Muḥammad bin Ḥunayn informed 'Amr ibn Dînâr that he heard Ibn 'Abbâs[241] say, "I am amazed at those who fast before Ramaḍân. The Messenger of Allah ﷺ said, *'If you see the new moon then fast. And when you see (the next new moon), end (the month of) fasting, and if it is obscured from you, count thirty days.'"* [242]

And we related that 'Ammâr bin Yâsir said, "Whoever fasts the Day of Doubt[243] has disobeyed Abû al-Qâsim ﷺ."[244]

---

[239] See note 83.

[240] Related by al-Bukhârî (1/230), Muslim (2/762), al-Tirmidhî (3/69), al-Nasâ'î (4/149) Ibn Mâjah (1/528) and Abû Dawûd (2/75).

[241] See note 17.

[242] Related by al-Bukhârî (2/229), Muslim (2/862), al-Nasâ'î (4/135,), Abû Dawûd (2/145) and Ibn Mâjah (1/530).

[243] That is the day before the new moon has clearly been sighted and the last month has not completed thirty days.

[244] This is a title given to the Prophet Muhammad ﷺ.

And we have related the prohibition of fasting the Day of Doubt on the authority of 'Umar ibn al-Khaṭṭâb, 'Ali ibn Abû Ṭâlib, Ibn Mas'ûd, Ibn 'Umar, Ibn 'Abbâs, Anas ibn Mâlik, and Ḥudhaifa bin Yamân, may Allah be pleased with them all.

Chapter Eleven
The Intention of Fasting

Narration 134

It has been reported on the authority of Ibn ‘Umar from Ḥafṣa[245] that the Messenger of Allah ﷺ said: *“Whoever did not think about fasting[246] the night before he does, has no fast.”* [247]

And the Shaykh said, ‘Yaḥya bin Ayyûb related the same meaning[248] as did Lahiy’a on the authority of ‘Abdullah bin Abû Bakr from Ibn Shihâb.

And this has been related about the compulsory fast, but as for the supererogatory fasts this is not the case, for it is permitted to start the day without the intention to fast based on the following:

---

[245] Ḥafṣa was the daughter of ‘Umar ibn al-Khaṭṭâb (see note 41). The angel Jibril (Gabriel) appeared to the Prophet ﷺ after her first husband died from wounds suffered at the battle of Badr and told him that “Ḥafṣa often fasts and worships abundantly and that she will be your wife in the Garden.” With that he ﷺ proposed to her. It was in her house that all the parts of the Quran were deposited after being collected by Zayd ibn Thâbit (see note 214), and it was there that the first full copies of Quran were written by the command of the *Khalifa,* Uthmân ibn ‘Affân (see note 223). She died in 41H or 45H (661 or 665CE) in Madina.

[246] *Bayyata* means to build something at night, to contrive a plan during the night or reflect upon it during the night. The *ḥadîth* indicates that the intention should be made prior to the fast beginning at dawn.

[247] Related by al-Nasâ’î (4/197).

[248] Related by al-Tirmidhî (3/108) and Abû Dawûd (2/823).

Narration 135

It has been reported on the authority of Ya'la bin 'Ubayd who told us that 'Aisha bint Ṭalḥa[249] said that the Messenger of Allah ﷺ said to 'Aisha, the Mother of the Believers, *"Do you have anything for us to eat this morning?"*
"We have nothing to eat this morning," she said.
"Then, in that case, I am fasting"
Then 'Aisha came to him and said, "O Messenger of Allah, we have been given a gift and I saved it for you."
"And what is it?" He said.
"*Ḥays*," she said.[250]
"I was fasting this morning," he said. He then brought it closer to him and ate a date from it.[251]
And this is the wording of Ya'la. And in the narration of Sufyân and others on the authority of 'Aisha bint Ṭalḥa from 'Aisha, the Mother of the Believers, from the Prophet ﷺ. The meaning is the same but the wording is different.

---

[249] 'Aisha bint Talḥa bin 'Ubaydullah was a second generation Follower who received knowledge from her parents, Talḥa and Umm Kulthûm, the daughter of Abu Bakr al-Siddiq (see note 433), who died shortly before her birth, as well as her aunt 'Aisha, the Mother of the Believers (see note 23). She died in Madina in 110H (728 CE).
[250] "Dates mixed with clarified butter, then kneaded vehemently or rubbed together until the stones fall from the curd," according to Lane's Lexicon.
[251] Related by Muslim (2/808), al-Tirmidhî (3/111), al-Nasâ'î (4/194), Abû Dawûd (2/824) and Aḥmad (6/49).

Chapter Twelve

The Preference of the Morning Meal

Narration 136

'Abdullah bin Ṣuhayb said, "I heard Anas bin Mâlik say that the Messenger of Allah, ﷺ said: *'Eat the dawn meal, for surely in the meal before dawn is a blessing.'"* [252]

Narration 137

It has been reported on the authority of Abû al-Qays that 'Amr ibn al-'Âs[253] said that the Messenger of Allah ﷺ said, *"The difference between our fast and the fast of the People of The Book is the eating of the dawn meal."* [254]

---

[252] Related by al-Bukhârî (2/232), Muslim (2/880), al-Tirmidhî (3/88), al-Nasâ'î (4/141), Abû Dawûd (2/824) and Aḥmad (2/99, 210, 229,243, 258 and 281).

[253] 'Amr ibn al-Âs was the father of Abû Muḥammad, 'Abdullah (see note 248). He embraced Islam shortly before the Conquest of Makkah, and had a special place with the Prophet ﷺ because of the love he had for his son. The seeds of his conversion were noticed when he was sent to Abyssinia to convince the Negus to send back the Muslims who had taken refuge there. He went on to be a military commander and diplomat, being sent to the Kings of Oman to call them to Islam, and to Egypt and Syria to lead the conquering armies there during the time of 'Umar ibn al-Khaṭṭâb. He died in 43H (664 CE) in Egypt.

[254] Related by Muslim (2/880-81), al-Tirmidhî (3/89), al-Nasâ'î (4/146), Abû Dawûd (2/858) and Aḥmad (4/202).

Chapter Thirteen

The Preference of Hastening to Break the Fast and Delaying the Morning Meal

Narration 138

It has been reported on the authority of Ḥâzim bin Dînâr from Sahl ibn Sa'd[255] that the Messenger of Allah ﷺ said: *"This nation will continue to be in a good state as long as they hasten to break their fast (as soon as the fast ends)."* [256]

Narration 139

Ibn 'Abbas[257] said that the Messenger of Allah ﷺ said: *"We, the Prophets, were ordered to hasten the breaking of our fasts, to delay eating our dawn meal, and to place our right hands over our left in prayer."*

The Shaykh, may Allah be pleased with him, said it is only preferred to delay the dawn meal as long as one knows there remains (sufficient) night left. And it is only preferred to hasten the breaking of the fast once it is known that the sun has actually set. For there have been harsh (warnings) given to those who break their fast before the sun has set, and among them are:

---

[255] Sahl was the son of Sa'd bin Mâlik who after preparing to attend the battle of Badr, died en route. He was originally called Huzn (meaning sadness) but the Messenger ﷺ renamed him Sahl (meaning ease). He was the last Companion to die in Madina in 88H (707 CE) or 91H (710 CE) aged one hundred. He related 188 *ḥadîth*.

[256] Related by al-Bukhârî (1/241), Muslim (2/881) and al-Tirmidhî (3/82).

[257] See note 17.

Narration 140

Abu 'Umâma al-Bâhilî[258] said: "I heard the Messenger of Allah ﷺ say, '*While I was sleeping, two men came to me and took me by the upper arm to a rocky mountain, and they said to me "climb!" and I said to them, 'I am unable to.' And they said, "We will make it easy for you." I climbed until I reached the peak of the mountain when I heard a loud sound and I said, 'What was that sound?' They said that it was the screaming of the people of the Fire. And then they took me away and I was (soon) with a people who were hanging by their hamstrings with their jaws broken. Pouring from their jaws was blood. I asked, "Who are they?" They said, 'They are those who used to break their fasts before the time their fast (should) end.''*"

[258] He is Abû 'Umâma Ṣuday ibn 'Ajlân al-Bâhili, a Companion of the Prophet, upon him be peace, who died in Homs in Syria in 81H (700CE) and related 250 *ḥadîth* from the Prophet, upon him be peace.

Chapter Fourteen
On What Is Preferred for Breaking One's Fast

Narration 141

Salmân bin 'Âmir al-Ḍabiy[259] said: *"If one of you breaks their fast, he should do so with dates if he finds them, and if he does not then with water, for water is purifying."* [260]

[259] Salmân bin 'Âmir bin 'Aws al-Ḍabiy was an old man during the time of the Prophet ﷺ, and lived until the *khilâfa* of Mu'awiya. He related *ḥadîth* to his daughter and grandson in Basra where he lived and died.

[260] Related by al-Tirmidhî (3/78-79), Ibn Mâjah (1/542), Abû Dawûd (2/865) and Aḥmad (4/17-19 and 213-215).

Chapter Fifteen

On the Preference of Supplication at the Time of Breaking One's Fast

Narration 142

'Abdullah ibn Abu Mulayka said that he heard 'Abdullah ibn 'Amr[261] say, "I heard the Messenger of Allah ﷺ say, *'The fasting person has a supplication at the time of breaking his fast that will not be rejected.'*" [262]

---

[261] 'Abdullah was the son of 'Amr ibn al-Âs (see note 240) but embraced Islam before him, and was always preferred of his father and others because of his great knowledge, spiritual excellence, and worship. He was known to read Quran intensely in tears to the extent people said he cried blood. He fasted the days and prayed all night, and preferred not to marry but did so on the order of the Prophetﷺ He conquered many lands including Egypt, where he stayed with his father until his father's death, after which he moved to Syria where he died in 63H (682 CE) aged 99 years old, although it is also said he died in Egypt. He related 700 *ḥadîth*.

[262] This *ḥadîth* is mentioned by al-Nawawî in Kitâb al-Adhkâr *ḥadîth* number 183.

Narration 143

It has been reported on the authority of Mu'âdh bin Zuhra that it reached him that the Messenger of Allah ﷺ used to say when he broke his fast:

اللَّهُمَّ لَكَ صُمْتُ وَعَلَىٰ رِزْقِكَ أَفْطَرْتُ

"O Allah, for You, I have fasted, and with Your provision, I break my fast."

And the Shaykh, may Allah be pleased with him, said: "And al-Thawrî related it on the authority of Ḥuṣayn on the authority of a man who related on the authority of Mu'âdh except that he said:

الحَمْدُ لِلَّهِ الَّذِي أَعَانَنِي فَصُمْتُ، وَرَزَقَنِي فَأَفْطَرْتُ

'All praise due to Allah who helped me and therefore I was able to fast and He provided for me so I broke my fast.'"

And we related on the authority of Ibn 'Umar that he used to say when breaking his fast:

يَا وَاسِعَ الْمَغْفِرَةِ اغْفِرْ لِي

"O Generous in forgiveness, forgive me!"

Chapter Sixteen
The Blessing of 'Eid

Narration 144

Ḥumayd ibn al-Ṭawîl and Anas Ibn Mâlik both said that the Messenger of Allah ﷺ came to Madina and they had two days in which they used to have merriment. The Messenger of Allah ﷺ said: *"Indeed Allah, the Mighty and Majestic, has exchanged these two days with two days which are better than them - al-Fiṭr and al-Aḍḥâ (that is, the Eid that follows the month of Ramaḍân and the Eid associated with the Ḥajj)."* [263]

And al-Ḥasan had additional wording, "He ﷺ said, *'as for the Day of al-Fiṭr, it is the day of prayer,'* and he (al-Hasan) said 'what is meant by (charity[264]) is a Ṣâ'a."[265] *"And on the Day of Aḍḥâ it is prayer and the rite,"* meaning your sacrificial slaughter."

---

[263] Related by al-Nasâ'î (3/179), Ibn Mâjah (1/542), Abû Dawûd (1/675) and Aḥmad (3/103, 187, 235 and 250).

[264] In this passage, the *ḥadîth* refers to the words *sadaqa* (charity), Zakât al-Fitr, and the *Zakât of Ramaḍân* interchangeably. I have tried to use the phrase *Zakât al-Fiṭr* wherever possible, as the subtleties of the different Arabic phrases are lost in translation and may cause confusion. And Allah knows best.

[265] Scholars agree that a *Ṣâ'a* is equal to four units of another measure called a *Mudd*, although there is some scholarly debate about the exact measure of a *Mudd*. A Mudd literally means a "cupped handful" (both hands cupped together), but refers in Islamic terms to the capacity of the "the Prophet Muhammad's ﷺ cupped handsful of barley". In modern measurements a *Ṣâ'a* is equivalent to about 3150gms. And Allah knows best.

And the Shaykh, may Allah be pleased with him, said, as for the discussion of the *Day of Aḍḥâ,* we deal with this amply in the section on the month of Dhûl Ḥijja. As for the *Day of al-Fiṭr*, its origin is found in the Words of the Blessed and Exalted:

(قَدْ أَفْلَحَ مَن تَزَكَّى)

(وَذَكَرَ اسْمَ رَبِّهِ فَصَلَّى)

But those will prosper who purify themselves,
And glorify the name of their Guardian-Lord, and (lift their hearts) in prayer.
(al-'Âlâ 87:14-15)

It has been related in some of the books of exegesis that, *"but those will prosper who purify themselves"* means by the *Zakâtul Fiṭr* and *"and glorify the name of their Guardian-Lord, and (lift their hearts) in prayer"'*means with the 'Eid prayer.

Narration 145

It has been reported by Kathîr ibn 'Abdullah bin 'Amr ibn 'Awf al-Muzni from his father, from his grandfather, that the Messenger of Allah ﷺ was asked about the verses, *"but those will prosper who purify themselves, And glorify the name of their Guardian-Lord, and (lift their hearts) in prayer."* He said, *"It is* Zakât al-Fiṭr."

And the Shaykh, may Allah be pleased with him said, "We have related on the authority of Ibn 'Umar that this verse came down regarding the *Zakât* of Ramaḍân."

And on the authority of Abû 'Âliya, he said, *"but those will prosper who purify themselves"* means one gives *Zakât al-Fiṭr* and then one prays.

Narration 146

Ja'far bin Burqân said that a letter came from 'Umar ibn 'Abdul Azîz saying, "Give your *Zakât al-Fiṭr*" before the Prayer. *'But those will prosper who purify themselves, and glorify the name of their Guardian-Lord, and (lift their hearts) in prayer.'* And say as your father Adam said, *"Our Lord! We have wronged our own souls: If You forgive us not and bestow not upon us Your Mercy, we shall certainly be lost."*[266] And say what Nuh (Noah) ﷺ said, *"O my Lord! I do seek refuge with You, lest I ask You for that of which I have no knowledge. And unless You forgive me and have Mercy on me, I should indeed be lost.'*[267] And say what Ibrâhîm (Abraham) ﷺ said, *"And who, I hope, will forgive me my faults on the Day of Judgment."* [268] And say what Mûsâ (Moses) ﷺ said, *''O my Lord! I have indeed wronged my soul! Do You then forgive me!' So (Allah) forgave him: for He is the Oft-Forgiving, Most Merciful.'* [269] And say what Dhû al-Nûn (Jonah) ﷺ said, *"There is no god but You. Glory to You: I was indeed wrong!"* [270] And I saw what was read (mentioned) that whoever does not have the means to give charity should fast and he meant – and Allah knows best – after 'Eid."

Narration 147

It has been reported on the authority of 'Ikrima that Ibn 'Abbâs[271] said: "The Messenger of Allah made *Zakât al-Fiṭr* a compulsion which cleanses the fasting person from any frivolity or vile speech, and as a means of feeding the poor. Whoever pays it before the prayer, it will be accepted as *Zakât*,

---

[266] Al-'Arâf, 7:23.
[267] Hûd, 11:47.
[268] Al-Shu'arâ, 26:82.
[269] Al-Qaṣaṣ, 28:16
[270] Al-Anbiyâ, 21:87.
[271] See note 17.

whoever pays it after the Prayer will have it counted as a general charity."[272]

Narration 148

It has been reported from Nâfi' from 'Abdullah ibn 'Umar[273] that the Messenger of Allah ﷺ made the *Zakât al-Fiṭr* of Ramaḍân a compulsion upon every soul from among the Muslims, whether free or a slave, whether a man or a woman, or an adult or a child. It should be a *Ṣâ'a* of dates or a *Ṣâ'a* of barley.[274]

And the Shaykh, may Allah be pleased with him, said, "We have related this *ḥadîth* in another form on the authority of 'Abdullah bin Tha'laba[275] from the Prophet ﷺ regarding the *Zakât of al-Fiṭr*. In addition (he says), 'Rich or poor, as for the rich, Allah will purify him by it, and as for the poor, Allah will give him back more than he gave.'"

Narration 149

'Abdul Razzâq told us that he was informed by someone who heard Ibn al-Baylamâni say on the authority of his father, that Ibn 'Umar said: "There are five nights on which supplications will not be rejected. They are, the eve of Friday, the first night of Rajab, the fifteenth of Sha'bân, and the two nights of the 'Eid."

---

[272] Related by Abû Dawûd (2/262) and Ibn Mâjah (1/585).

[273] See note 81.

[274] Related by al-Bukhârî (3/138), Muslim (2/687), al-Tirmidhî (3/61), and Abû Dawûd (2/263).

[275] 'Abdullah bin Tha'laba was an Anṣârî Companion who fought at the Battles of Badr and 'Uḥud. His date of death is not known, and he left no children.

Narration 150

It has been reported on the authority of Khâlid bin Ma'dân that Abû al-Dardâ[276] said: "Whoever stands in prayer to Allah in contentment during the nights preceding the two 'Eids, his heart will not die when other hearts die." [277]

And al-Shâfi'î, may Allah show him mercy said, "It has reached us that he used to say that supplication will be answered on five nights," and then he mentioned what was related in the *ḥadîth* of Ibn 'Umar.

Narration 151

It is with this chain of transmission that Al-Shâfi'î, may Allah show him mercy, informed us that Ibrâhîm bin Muḥammad said, "I saw the elders from among the elite of the people of Madina appearing in the Mosque of the Prophet ﷺ on the nights of the two 'Eids, and they would supplicate and remember Allah until a good hour had passed."

And Al-Shâfi'î, may Allah show him mercy, said, "I approve of all that has been said about these two nights, as long as one does not consider them obligatory."

And Al-Shâfi'î, may Allah show him mercy, said, "I love that the Imam glorifies Allah with the words 'Allâhu akbar' after the Maghrib, 'Ishâ and Subḥ[278] prayers, and between each of them, and while setting off (in the morning) until one reaches the place of prayer on the day of the 'Eid al-Fiṭr.

---

[276] Abû al-Dardâ's name was either 'Amr or 'Uwaymir but was best known by the nickname Abû al-Dardâ. He embraced Islam on the day of the Battle of Badr, and went on to fight at 'Uhud and most subsequent battles. He was asked by 'Umar (see note 41) to be the Governor of Syria. He refused, but agreed to settle there to teach the new converts the Quran and the rules of the Religion. He died there in 32H (653 CE).

[277] Related by Ibn Mâjah (1/568).

[278] These are the compulsory prayers that fall at sunset, at night, and between dawn and sunrise.

The proof for this is found in the Words of Allah, the Mighty and Majestic, *"to complete the prescribed period,"* meaning the month of Ramaḍân, and *'and to glorify Him in that He has guided you,'* meaning after its completion (glorify Him) for His guiding you."

Narration 152

Al-Shâfi'î, may Allah show him mercy, relates with his chain of transmission on the authority of Ibn 'Umar that he used to go out to the place of the 'Eid prayer on the day of al-*Fiṭr* when the sun rose, and he would glorify Allah until he got there, and then he would glorify Him until the Imâm sat down, and then he would stop the glorification.

Narration 153

It has been reported that 'Abdul Raḥmân bin Wahb said, "My uncle told us that 'Abdullah bin 'Umar said, on the authority of Nâfi' from 'Abdullah, that the Messenger of Allah ﷺ used to go out for the two 'Eid prayers with al-Faḍl bin al-Abbâs, 'Abdullah, al-Abbas, 'Ali, Ja'far, al-Ḥasan and al-Ḥusayn, 'Usamah bin Zayd and Zayd ibn al-Ḥaritha, and Ayman ibn Umm Ayman with his voice raised with glorification and recognition of Allah's unity,[279] taking one route to get to the Prayer place and a different route to return to his house.

[279] That is he would be saying *"Allâhu Akbar"* and *"La ilaha illAllah."*

Narration 154

It has been reported on the authority of 'Ubaydullah bin Abû Bakr bin Anas who said, "I heard Anas say that the Messenger of Allah ﷺ did not go out on the Day of 'Eid al-Fiṭr until he had eaten three, five, or seven dates, or an odd number more or less than that." [280]

Narration 155

It has been reported on the authority of Qatâda that Anas ibn Mâlik said that The Messenger of Allah ﷺ said: *"On the Night of Power, Jibrîl (Gabriel) descends among a group of angels who pray upon every slave (of Allah) that stands or sits remembering Allah. And when it is their 'Eid, that is the Eid of breaking their fasts, He boasts about them to the angels. He says, 'O My angels! What is the wage of the one who has completed his work?' "O our Lord! His wage is that he should be paid his reward." He says, 'O my angels! My male and female slaves have fulfilled the compulsion I had placed upon them, and now they hasten to Me in supplication. And so by My Power, My Majesty, My Generosity, My Highness, and My Lofty Station I will answer them.' And then He will say, "Return! For I have forgiven you, and turned your transgressions into good actions.""* And he said, *"And so they return forgiven."* [281]

Aṣram bin Ḥowsh al-Hamdhâni is unique in this chain of narrators. And we have related it in the long *ḥadîth* of the Night of Power.

And the following has been related on the authority of Ka'b al-Aḥbâr[282] about the blessing of the month of Ramaḍân, and about the coming out of the Muslims on the Day of Fiṭr to celebrate their 'Eid.

---

[280] Related by al-Bukhârî (2/3) and al-Tirmidhî (2/427).

[281] This is mentioned by al-Suyûṭî in *al-Durr al-Manthûr* (6/377).

[282] There is difference of opinion whether Ka'b al-Aḥbâr should be counted as a Companion. It is believed by some that he met the Prophet ﷺ in Madina, but did not embrace Islam until the time of 'Umar ibn al-Khaṭṭâb (see note 41). What is definite was that he was a Rabbi

Narration 156

On the authority of Hilâl bin 'Abdul Salâm al-Wazân that Ka'b al-Aḥbâr said, "Allah, the Exalted, revealed to Mûsâ (Moses) ﷺ 'Indeed, I have made the fast of the month of Ramaḍân compulsory upon my slaves. O Mûsâ! Whoever has established in his record of good deeds, ten Ramaḍâns is one of the *abdâl.*[283] Whoever has established in his record of good deeds, twenty Ramaḍâns is one of the *mukhbitîn.*[284] Whoever has established in his record of good deeds thirty Ramaḍâns is better with me than the martyrs. O Mûsâ! I have ordered the angels that carry the Throne to stop their worship when Ramaḍân comes, and that when those who fast in Ramaḍân supplicate, to say "Amen." For I have obligated myself to not reject the supplication of those who fast Ramaḍân. O Mûsâ! In Ramaḍân, I have inspired the heavens, the earth, the mountains, the birds, the animals, and the insects to seek forgiveness for those who fast (the month of) Ramaḍân. O Mûsâ! Find three

---

from the Yemen who, once he was convinced that the Prophet ﷺ matched the criteria described in his texts, believed in him. There is difference of opinion when this occurred. However, it is clear that he was Muslim during the time of 'Umar and 'Uthmân, as he played an advisory role in their administrations. Some of the *ḥadith* considered to be from Jewish sources are attributed to him. He died in Homs in 32H (652CE).

[283] In this context, it means a person of extremely high spiritual rank. The word a*bdâl* is the plural of *badîl,* according to Lane, and means 'those who are substituted'. It is believed that there is a special rank of believer that Allah has chosen as the means by which He sends His Mercy and through them and their prayers, Allah averts disasters from the Believers. It is based on a *ḥadîth* related by Imâm Aḥmad in his *Musnad* which says: "The people of Syria were mentioned in front of `Ali ibn Abi Talib while he was in Iraq, and they said. 'Curse them, O Commander of the Believers.' He replied, "No, I heard the Messenger of Allah say "The Substitutes (*al-abdâl*) are in Syria and they are forty men, every time one of them dies, Allah substitutes another in his place. By means of them, Allah brings down the rain, gives (Muslims) victory over their enemies, and averts punishment from the people of Syria."" And Allah knows best.

[284] The *mukhbitîn,* in this context, describes another spiritual rank. They are mentioned in the Quran where Allah says, *"and glad tidings to those who are humble,"* (al-Ḥajj 22:34). It comes from the roots *kh-b-t* meaning 'to become obscure,' and therefore the *mukhbitîn* according to Ibn 'Abbâs are "the humble ones," and according to Mujâhid are those who are at peace with Allah, and according to al-Nakha'î "the sincere ones." And Allah knows best.

people who are fasting the month of Ramaḍân. Pray with them. Eat and drink with them. For I will not send down my punishment or retribution upon a place that contains three people who fast the month of Ramaḍân. O Mûṣâ! If you are on a journey, hasten forward! And if you are ill, order them to carry you! And say to the women in their menses and the young children to come out with you wherever there are those who fast (the month of) Ramaḍân. And with the end of Ramaḍân, I grant permission to the earth and the sky to greet them, and to give them glad tidings of what I have informed them of. For I say, 'O My slaves who have fasted Ramaḍân, return to your saddlebags for I am pleased with you, and have made your reward for your fasting your freedom from the Fire, and that I will give you a gentle account. And I will ease your difficulties. And I will leave for you wealth. And I will not abandon you to be disgraced by anyone. By My Might! You will not ask anything after the fast of Ramaḍân and your station here, regarding your next life except that I will grant it. And you will not ask anything about the affairs of this temporal world of yours except that I will look to it.'"

Narration 157

It has been reported that Muḥammad bin Yazîd Khunays said: "The people dispersed on 'Eid Day, and I saw Wuhayb, meaning ibn al-Ward,[285] and they were passing him by in (their 'Eid) attire. He looked at them for a while and then said, "May Allah pardon us and you! If you woke this morning certain that Allah, the Mighty and Majestic, had accepted your month (of fasting) then it would be appropriate for you to busy yourselves (better than the way you) occupy yourselves today – by seeking gratitude! And if you did not

[285] His real name was Abdul Wahhâb ibn al-Ward. He was a well-known ascetic who lived in Makkah where he died in 153H/ 770CE. The few *ḥadîth* he related were mainly transmitted through Ibn al-Mubârak, and concerned focusing our actions on the Next World.

(wake in that state, but rather) you fear that He did not accept your month then you would be busy with all your heart with something more than what you are doing today".'

Narration 158

Sufyân told us that Wuhayb saw a group of people laughing on the Day of Fiṭr and he said: 'If there is among them someone whose fast was accepted, are these really the actions of the grateful? And if they are those whose fast was not accepted, is this really the action of those who fear (Him)?'

Narration 159

Salmân bin Sâlim al-Ḥalabî said Ghazwân al-Raqâshî[286] passed by some people on 'Eid day and saw that they were pushing one another and so he cried. He said, 'I have not seen anything more like the standing on the Day of Resurrection than this day'. He then returned home sick.

[286] Shaykh al-Ninowy said Ghazwân was a well-known storyteller accepted in the narration of the biography of the Prophet ﷺ.

Chapter Seventeen
The Blessing of Fasting During Shawwâl

Abdul Aziz Ahmed comments:

Shawwâl is the tenth month of the Islamic year and follows immediately after Ramaḍân. Its name is taken from the roots sh-w-l, meaning "to rise like the tail of a she camel." Shawwal is also the name of a scorpion, because it usually has its tail raised. However, this is not the reason Shawwâl has this name. It is believed to be based on the time the months were associated with the solar calendar, and the month of Shawwâl was when the pregnant camels were about to deliver, and they could be seen raising their tails. And Allah knows best. It was on the seventeenth of Shawwâl that the Battle of 'Uḥud took place.

Narration 160

'Amr bin Thâbit al-Ansâri said, "I heard Abû al-Ayyûb al-Ansâri[287] say, 'I heard the Messenger of Allah ﷺ say: "*Whoever fasts Ramaḍân and then follows it up with six days from Shawwâl, that will be like fasting the whole year.*"'"[288]

Narration 161

Yahyâ bin al-Ḥârith was told by Abû Asmâ al-Raḥabî on the authority of Thawbân,[289] the freed slave and client of the Messenger ﷺ that the Messenger of Allah ﷺ said: "*Fasting a month for (the reward of) ten months, and six days after it for (the reward of) two months, completes the year.*" And he meant by that Ramaḍân and the six days that follow it.[290]

---

[287] Abû Ayyûb al-Anṣârî was Khâlid bin Zayd from the tribe of Banû Najjâr who were maternal relatives of the Prophet ﷺ On his arrival in Madina, he chose to stay with Abû Ayyûb while his house and mosque were being built. He was a valiant fighter who fought at almost every battle from the time of the Prophet's arrival to the time of Mu'âwiya, including the conquest of Egypt, where he stayed for some time before rejoining the campaigns in Syria, and eventually the attack on Constantinople where he died in 49H (670CE).

[288] Related by Muslim (2/822), al-Tirmidhî (3/132), Abû Dawûd (2/813), Ibn Mâjah (1/547) and Aḥmad (5/418-419).

[289] Thawbân bin Bujdûd was a Yemeni slave bought by the Prophet ﷺ and then freed immediately. He stayed with him ﷺ and served him until his death, after which he moved to Syria where he died in 54H/633 CE.

[290] Related by Ibn Mâjah (1/547) and Aḥmad (5/280).

Narration 162

It has been reported on the authority of 'Ikrima from Ibn 'Abbas that the Messenger of Allah ﷺ said: *"The fasting person after Ramaḍan is like the one who returns (to battle) after fleeing ."* [291]

Narration 163

Muslim bin 'Ubaydullah al-Qurashî told Hârûn bin Salmân that his father informed him that the Prophet ﷺ was asked about fasting. (The questioner) said, "O Messenger of Allah? Should I fast perpetually?" And he was silent. And then he asked a second time and he was again silent. Then he asked a third time and said, "O Prophet of Allah, should I fast perpetually?" And to this, the Prophet ﷺ said, *"Who asked about fasting?"* And he said, "I did, O Prophet of Allah." And he said, *"Surely your family have a right over you! Fast the month of Ramaḍân and what follows it, and fast every Wednesday and every Thursday, and that is (the same as) the perpetual fast."* [292]

And he, may Allah be pleased with him, said, "This is how Muslim bin 'Ubaydullah said it on their authority, but it has also been said that it is on the authority of 'Ubaydullah bin Mûsâ, from Hârûn, from 'Ubaydullah bin Muslim al-Qurashî, from his father.

And the Shaykh, may Allah be pleased with him, said that Shawwâl contains other blessings, in that it is one of the months of the Ḥajj referred to in the verse, *"For Ḥajj are the months well known."* [293]

---

[291] Ibn Rajab said, "Such as someone who fleed from fighting in the path of Allah then returns to it. That is because many people celebrate the end of Ramadan due to the burden of fasting, and the weariness and length of it. Such people rarely rush back to fasting. Thus, for a person who does return to fasting after breaking it of Eid, his return to it shows his desire to fast, and that it hasn't become burdensome, and he hasn't grown weary of it and doesn't loathe it." See Lata'if al-Ma'arif, p 222. *(Editor)*

[292] Related by al-Tirmidhî (3/123 and, Abû Dawûd 3/812).

[293] Al-Baqara 2:197.

Narration 164

It has been reported on the authority of Nâfi' that Ibn'Umar[294] said of the verse *"For Ḥajj are the months well known,"* [295] that it refers to Shawwâl, Dhûl Qa'da, and ten days of Dhûl Ḥijja.

And he, may Allah be pleased with him said, "We have related on the authority of 'Umar ibn al-Khaṭṭâb, 'Abdullah bin Mas'ûd, 'Abdullah bin 'Abbâs, 'Abdullah bin al-Zubayr, and others like them that what he meant by the ten days of Dhûl Ḥijja is actually its nights, because when the dawn rises on the day of the tenth the period of the Ḥajj has ended."

Narration 165

It has been reported on the authority of Miqsam that Ibn 'Abbâs[296] said, "Do not wear the garb of pilgrimage for Ḥajj, except in the months of Ḥajj, for it is the Prophetic Way to only wear the garb of pilgrimage for Ḥajj in the actual months of the Ḥajj (and they are Shawwâl, Dhûl Qa'da, and the first nine days of Dhûl Ḥijja)."

---

[294] See note 81.
[295] Ibid.
[296] See note 17.

Narration 166

It has been reported on the authority of Ibn Jurayj that ‘Aṭâ said that whoever wears the garb of pilgrimage for Ḥajj outside of the months of the pilgrimage has done the Lesser Pilgrimage (al-‘Umra).

And the Shaykh, may Allah be pleased with him, said, “The months of Dhûl Qa’da and Dhûl Ḥijja have the additional blessing of being Sacred Months, and we mentioned the blessings of the Sacred Months when we discussed Rajab.

Chapter Eighteen

The Blessing of the Month of Dhûl Ḥijja

Abdul Aziz Ahmed comments:

Dhûl Ḥijja and the Days of the Ḥajj

The months for which one is permitted to wear the pilgrim garb for Ḥajj are Shawwâl, Dhûl Qa'da (which is the eleventh month of the Islamic year), and the first nine days of Dhûl Ḥijja.

The following chapters all talk about the special significance of the first twelve days of the month of Dhûl Ḥijja, which include the build up to the Ḥajj, the Ḥajj itself, and the days immediately following the main rites, which are considered to be part of the Ḥajj.

The main day of the Ḥajj is the Day of 'Arafat, which is the ninth of Dhûl Ḥijja. The Pilgrims are expected to stand on the Plain of 'Arafat near Makkah, spending the afternoon in worship and supplication. The evening is spent at Muzdalifa, again in prayer and supplication. In Arabic and Islamic understanding, the day begins at sunset, and so the night of Muzdalifa is the beginning of the tenth of Dhûl Ḥijja. As the daytime begins, the pilgrims leave for Mina where they throw stones at a pillar marking the place where the Prophet Ibrâhim, Abraham, was on his way to sacrifice his son, Ismâ'îl. The devil appeared before them and tried to tempt them away from this act of obedience. This pillar, which has now been expanded to resemble a huge wall, is called the *Jamara.*

On the tenth of Dhûl Ḥijja, the pilgrims only stone the *Jamara* at 'Aqaba but on the following two or three days they stone all three *Jamarât*, marking the three spots where the Devil tried to dissuade Ibrâhim from sacrificing his son.

The tenth of Dhûl Ḥijja is also called The Day of Slaughter or *Eid al-Adhâ*. Those who are performing the Pilgrimage do not actually celebrate the day as an 'Eid, as they are busy with the various rites of the day, which include the slaughter of a sacrificial animal. The rest of the Muslims around the world mark it as their 'Eid and they celebrate for as long as the pilgrims remain at Mina. This is either two or three days. These days are called the Days of *Tashrîq,* and the nights associated with them are to be spent in worship at Mina. These days are sometimes called *the Days of Eating and Drinking,* as they are opportunities for the pilgrims to relax after the strenuous rites, and to get to know pilgrims from different parts of the world. The following chapters deal with each section of the Ḥajj in the order mentioned above.

And we have mentioned that Dhûl Ḥijja is one of the Sacred Months, and we mentioned what has reached us regarding the blessings of the Sacred Months when we discussed Rajab.

Narration 167

It has been reported on the authority of 'Aṭâ ibn Yasâr that Abû Sa'îd al-Khudrî[297] said the Messenger of Allah ﷺ said: *"The master of all months is Ramaḍân, and the most sacred of them is Dhûl Ḥijja."* [298]

---

[297] See note 101.

[298] Al-Haythamî mentions it in *Majma' al-Zawâid* and says it was related by al-Bazzâr. It is also mentioned by al-Suyûṭî in *Durr al-Manthûr* (1/186).

Chapter Nineteen

The Special Status of the Ten Days of Dhûl Ḥijja for Striving to Do Good Actions and What There Contains Therein of Blessings

And Allah the Exalted has said:

(وَالْفَجْرِ)

(وَلَيَالٍ عَشْرٍ)

(وَالشَّفْعِ وَالْوَتْرِ)

By the break of day. By the ten nights. And by the even and odd (contrasted).

(Al-Fajr, 89: 1-2)

Narration 168

It has been reported on the authority of Abû Naṣr that Ibn 'Abbâs[299] said that *"By the break of day"* refers to the break of the day, and *"By the ten nights,"* refers to the ten days of Sacrifice (that is the first ten days of Dhûl Ḥijja), and the verse *"Is there (not) in these an adjuration (or evidence) for those who understand?"* refers to those who perform the pilgrimage.

Narration 169

Zurâra ibn Awfa said that Ibn 'Abbâs said *"the ten"* that Allah swears by are the (first) ten nights of Dhûl Ḥijja, and *"the even"*' is the Day of Sacrifice and *"the odd"* is the Day of 'Arafat.

Narration 170

And he, may Allah be pleased with him, said in the *ḥadîth* of Khayr bin Na'îm on the authority of Abû al-Zubayr, from Jâbir[300] who said the Messenger of Allah ﷺ said of the verse, *"By the break of day and by the ten nights"*: *"The ten days of the Slaughter (meaning the days of Dhûl Ḥijja), and* 'the odd' *is The Day of 'Arafat and* 'the even' *is the Day of Sacrifice."* [301]

And this is what I was told by Abû 'Abdullah al-Ḥâfiẓ with a licence[302] from Abû al-Ḥasan, 'Ali bin Muḥammad bin 'Ubaydullah al-Qurashi, who informed them that al-Ḥasan bin 'Ali bin 'Afân al-'Âmirî told us that Zayd bin al-Ḥabâb told us that 'Ayyâsh bin 'Uqba al-Ḥaḍramî told us that Khayr bin Naîm told us, and then he mentioned the above (*ḥadîth*).

---

[299] See note 17.

[300] See note 92.

[301] This *ḥadîth* is mentioned by Ibn Ḥajr in his *Fath al-Bârî* (8/704).

[302] An *ijâza* or licence in *ḥadîth* is expressed permission to transmit it.

Narration 171

Ibn 'Abbâs said that the Messenger of Allah ﷺ said: *"There are no days more beloved to Allah for worship than these ten."*
They said, "O Messenger of Allah! Not even fighting in the way of Allah?"
He said, *"Not even fighting in the way of Allah, except a man who goes out with his body and wealth, yet does not return with either of them."* [303]

Narration 172

Ibn 'Abbâs said that the Messenger of Allah ﷺ said, *"There are no days more preferred by Allah, and no actions more beloved to Him, the Mighty and Majestic, than those performed in them, than these ten days. So say abundantly during them,* 'la ilaha illAllah', there is no god but Allah *and* "Allâhu akbar", Allah is greatest, *for these are the days of pronouncing His unity and greatness, and remembering Him. And fasting for one day in them is like fasting for a year. And actions in them are rewarded by seven hundred fold."*

Narration 173

It is related on the authority of 'Abdullah ibn 'Umar[304], may Allah be pleased with him, that the Messenger of Allah ﷺ said: *"There are no days mightier with Allah or more beloved to Him. Anyone who (wishes to do) good action in these ten days should say* 'alhamdullilah', all praise is due to Allah, 'la ilaha illAllah', there is no god but Allah *and* 'Allâhu akbar', Allah is greatest." [305]

---

[303] Related by al-Bukhârî (2/7) al-Tirmidhî (3/130), Abû Dawûd (2/815), Ibn Mâjah (1/550) and Aḥmad (1/224).
[304] See note 81.
[305] Related by Aḥmad (2/85 and 131).

He, may Allah be pleased with him, said: 'Ali bin Âṣim related it on the authority of Yazîd, with the additional words "say *Subḥanallah, transcendent is Allah,*" and that he said it was on the authority of 'Ibn 'Abbâs, and not (from) Ibn 'Umar.

Narration 174

Abû Hurayra said the Messenger of Allah ﷺ said: *"There are no worldly days in which good actions are more beloved to Allah, the Exalted, than the worship in these ten days. A fast in them equals the fast of a year, and standing in prayer during them is like standing on the Night of Power."*

Narration 175

It has been related on the authority of Hunayda bin Khâlid on the authority of his wife, from some of the wives of Prophet ﷺ that the Messenger of Allah ﷺ used to fast the ninth of Dhûl Ḥijja, the tenth of Muḥarram, and three days from each month, the first Monday and the first two Thursdays.[306]

He, may Allah be pleased with him, said, "This *ḥadîth* takes priority over what we have already related on the authority of 'Aisha when she said, 'I did not see the Messenger of Allah ﷺ fasting during the ten days' because this *ḥadîth* establishes that he did whereas the other negates (seeing him to do it)."

[306] Related by Abû Dawûd (2/815), al-Nasâ'î (4/222) and Aḥmad (5/281).

Chapter Twenty
The Blessing of the Day of 'Arafat[307]

Allah the Exalted said by way of swearing an oath:

(وَشَاهِدٍ وَمَشْهُودٍ)

By one that witnesses, and the subject of the witness.

(al-Burûj, 85:3)

[307] The Day of 'Arafat is the main day of the Pilgrimage. It is the ninth of the month of Dhûl Ḥijja when the pilgrims gather on the plain of 'Arafat, which is twenty kilometres south east of Makkah.

Narration 176

It is related on the authority of Abû Hurayra[308] from the Prophet ﷺ about the verse, *"By one that witnesses, and the subject of the witness,"* that he said that the *"one that witnesses"* is Friday, and *"The subject of the witness"* is the Day of 'Arafat.

Narration 177

And the Shaykh, may Allah be pleased with him, said: 'And 'Ali bin Zayd related it on the authority of 'Ammâr, from Abû Hurayra, from the Prophet ﷺ.

Narration 178

It has also been related on the authority of 'Abdullah bin Râf'î from Abû Hurayra that the Prophet ﷺ said: *"The Promised Day is the Day of Ressurection, and* 'the one that witnesses' *is Friday, and* 'the subject of the witness' *is the Day of 'Arafat."*

And it has been related in various other forms going back to the Prophet ﷺ, but omitting the Companion.

[308] See note 83.

Narration 179

It is related on the authority of Ṭâriq bin Shihâb from 'Umar ibn al-Khaṭṭâb that a Jewish man came and said to 'Umar ibn al-Khaṭṭâb: "O Commander of the Faithful! There is a verse that you read from your Book that if it had descended to us Jews we would have taken that day as a day of celebration."
"Which verse is that?" He said.
"This day have I perfected your religion for you, completed My favour upon you, and have chosen for you Islam as your religion," [309] he said.
And so 'Umar said, "We know that day and the place on which it was revealed. It was sent down to the Messenger of Allah ﷺ at 'Arafât on a Friday."[310]
The Shaykh said, "we have related this on the authority of Ibn 'Abbâs that it was revealed on the Day of 'Arafat on a Friday."

Narration 180

Sa'îd ibn al-Musayyib told Yûnus (bin Yûsuf)[311] on the authority of 'Aisha, the wife of the Prophet ﷺ that the Messenger of Allah ﷺ said: *"There is no day on which Allah frees more of His slaves from the Fire than the Day of 'Arafat. Then He draws close*[312] *and boasts to the angels, and asks them, 'What do they want?'"*
And the Shaykh, may Allah be pleased with him, said, "'He draws close' means, *"with His Mercy"* which relates to the words of the Exalted *'And if My*

---

[309] Al-Mâida, 5:3.
[310] Related by al-Bukhârî (2/16), Muslim (4/2313), al-Tirmidhî (5/250), al-Nasâ'î (5/251), and Aḥmad (1/28-32).
[311] Al-Bayhaqî states that Mukhrama bin Bukayr said on the authority of his father who said he heard Yunus tell us that he heard... Al-Nasâ'î mentions that it is Yûnus bin Yûsuf who was indeed a student of Sa'îd bin al-Mussayyib. And Allah knows best.
[312] This is a metaphorical statement, as Allah has no physical body, and distance is not relevant when talking about Him.

slaves ask you about Me, surely I am near' [313] meaning near with My Mercy and quick in My response to My slaves."

Narration 181

Jâbir[314] said that the Messenger of Allah ﷺ said: *"On the Day of 'Arafat, Allah, the Exalted and High, boasts to the angels (about the pilgrims). He says, 'Look at My slaves, they come to Me dishevelled and dusty raising their voices as they come from every deep valley. I call you to witness that I have indeed forgiven them.' The angels will say, "Among them is so and so and such and such a young man."* Allah, the Exalted says, 'I have indeed forgiven them!'" The Messenger of Allah ﷺ said: *"There is no day on which there are more people freed from the Fire than the Day of Arafat."*

And the Shaykh, may Allah be pleased with him, said that it has been narrated in a different form on the authority of Abû al-Zubayr. and it includes additional wording which is, *"They ask for My Mercy and seek refuge from My punishment, and they have not seen Me."*

Narration 182

It has been reported on the authority of Ṭalḥa ibn 'Ubaydullah that the Messenger of Allah ﷺ said: *"The Devil has never been more insignificant, or more beaten back and wretched, or more frustrated than on the Day of 'Arafat. That is all because of what he sees of the descending of Mercy and Allah's pardoning of sins. The exception is (his state) on the Day of Badr."* [315]

---

[313] Al-Baqara, 2:186.

[314] See note 92.

[315] This is the day, when Allah sent angels to help the Muslims in battle, when they faced a large enemy force from Makkah. It occurred on the 17th Ramadan, in the second year after the Migration to Madina.

This is a good *mursal ḥadîth* (that is one that omits the name of the Companion. In this case it is related by Ṭalḥa ibn 'Ubaydullah bin Karîz, who was a Follower (and not Ṭalḥa ibn 'Ubaydullah the famed Companion) but it has been related in a weak form from Ṭalḥa on the authority of Abû al-Dardâ' from the Prophet ﷺ

Narration 183

Ibn 'Abbas said that al-Faḍl ibn 'Abbâs[316] was riding behind the Prophet ﷺ on the Day of 'Arafat. The young man[317] was looking at the women and staring at them. The Messenger of Allah ﷺ turned the face of the young man away using his hand, yet he began looking at the women again. So the Messenger of Allah ﷺ said: *"On this day, whoever controls his hearing, sight, and tongue will be forgiven."* [318]

---

[316] Al-Faḍl ibn 'Abbâs was the first cousin of the Prophet ﷺ and the older brother of 'Abdullah ibn 'Abbâs. He performed the farewell pilgrimage riding on the Prophet's camel, relating many *ḥadîth* about the pilgrimage. He died in Jerusalem in 18H (639CE).

[317] The scholars have understood that Al-Faḍl was the young man in question. See *Siyar A'lâm al-Nubulâ'* of Imam Al-Dhahabi (2/292). *(Editor)*

[318] Related by Aḥmad (1/356).

Chapter Twenty-One
The Blessing of Fasting the Day of 'Arafat

Narration 184

It has been reported on the authority of Abû Qatâda al-Ansâri[319] that the Messenger of Allah ﷺ was asked about the fast of the Day of 'Arafat and he said: *"It covers (the sins of) the previous year and the coming year."* [320]

Narration 185

It has been reported on the authority of Abû Isḥâq that Masrûq came to 'Aisha[321], may Allah be pleased with her, on the Day of 'Arafat and said, "Give me something to drink."
She said to a slave girl, "Give him a drink of honey."
"O Masrûq, are you not fasting?" She said.
"No, I feared that it might be the day of the Slaughter (*Eid al-Aḍḥâ*)," he said.
"It is not like that. The Day of 'Arafat is known by (the pronouncement of) the Imâm, and the Day of the Slaughter is the day on which the Imâm sacrifices his animal. Have you not heard, O Masrûq, that the Messenger ﷺ equated (fasting on the Day of 'Arafat) with fasting a thousand years?"

---

[319] He is al-Ḥarith ibn Rabî'a, better known by his *kunya* (honorific nick name) Abu al-Qatada. He died in Madina in 54H (673CE).
[320] Related by Muslim (2/819) and al-Tirmidhi (3/124).
[321] See note 23.

Narration 186

And Sulaymân bin Aḥmad al-Wâsiṭî also narrated it on the authority of al-Walîd bin Muslim and he said in the *ḥadîth,* "And the Messenger of Allah ﷺ used to say, *'Fasting the Day of 'Arafat is like fasting a thousand years.'*" [322]

Narration 187

And it has been related in a different form on the authority of Masrûq that 'Aisha said, "There is no day in the year that is more beloved to me for fasting than the Day of 'Arafat." Abû Ṭâhir al-Faqîh informed us that Abû Bakr al-Qaṭṭân informed us that 'Ibrâhîm bin al-Ḥârith told us that Yaḥyâ bin Abû Bakîr told us that Shu'ba told us on the authority of Abû al-Qays who said that he heard Huzayl say on the authority of Masrûq and then he mentioned the above.

Narration 188

Hârûn bin Mûsâ said that he heard al-Ḥasan speak on the authority of Anas ibn Mâlik[323] saying that it used to be said of each of the ten days that they were (worth) a thousand days, and that the Day of 'Arafat was (worth) ten thousand days. And he said, "Meaning in blessing."

And the Shaykh, may Allah be pleased with him, said that the difference is according to the differences (in the states of) those who are fasting in terms of sincerity and taking care (of the inner proprieties) during the fast. For the one who is more intense in his taking care (of the fast) and (his)

---

[322] This is mentioned by al-Suyûṭî in *Durr al-Manthûr* (1/231) and al-Mundhirî in *al-Targhîb* (2/112).

[323] See note 30.

certainty will have greater reward. And only by Allah is there enabling success.
And this is the case for the person who is not on the pilgrimage. For indeed al-Shâfi'î, may Allah show him mercy, said that the pilgrim not fasting on the Day of 'Arafat is more beloved to me than him or her fasting the Day of 'Arafat, because the Messenger of Allah ﷺ did not fast on the Day of 'Arafat and there is goodness in all that the Messenger of Allah ﷺ did. This is because the one who is not fasting is stronger (and more capable) of supplication than the one who is fasting. Supplication on the Day of 'Arafat is better than fasting.

Narration 189

'Abdullah bin Maslama al-Qa'nabî told us on the authority of Mâlik ibn Anas from what he had read to him on the authority of Abû Naḍr, the freed slave of 'Umar bin 'Abdul 'Azîz from 'Umayr, the freed slave of Ibn 'Abbâs from Umm al-Faḍl bint al-Ḥarith that people differed in her company about (what the) Messenger of Allah ﷺ (was doing) on the Day of 'Arafat. Some said he was fasting and others said he was not fasting, and so she sent him a large drinking bowl of milk. He had halted at 'Arafat on his camel and he drank from it.[324]

Narration 190

It has been reported on the authority of 'Ikrima that Abû Hurayra said, "The Messenger of Allah ﷺ forbade fasting on the Day of 'Arafat for those who are on 'Arafat."

---

[324] Related by al-Bukhârî (2/184), Muslim (2/781), Abû Dawûd (2/817) and Aḥmad (6/339-340).

Chapter Twenty-Two

The Blessing of Supplication on the Day of 'Arafat

Narration 191

It has been reported on the authority of Ziyâd ibn Abû Ziyâd, the freed slave of Ibn 'Abbas from Ṭalḥa bin 'Ubaydullah bin Karîz that the Messenger of Allah ﷺ said: *"The best supplication for the Day of 'Arafat is the best thing I, and the prophets before me, have ever said and that is:* 'lâ ilâha illAllâh waḥdahu lâ sharîka lahu' there is no god but Allah, alone without partner."

And he, may Allah be pleased with him, said this is a good *mursal ḥadîth* (that is, one that omits the name of the Companion. In this case, Ṭalḥa bin 'Ubaydullah bin Karîz related it directly from the Prophet ﷺ, whom he did not actually meet). And it has been related in the *ḥadîth* of Mâlik which has a chain all the way to the Prophet ﷺ, but is weak. And it has been related in other ways including:

Narration 192

It has been reported that 'Amr ibn Shu'ayb told us on the authority of his father that his grandfather said: 'The supplication that the Messenger of Allah ﷺ did most abduntantly on the Day of 'Arafat was '*lâ ilâha ilAllâh waḥdahu lâ sharîka lahu, lahu_mulk wa lahu_lḥamd bi yedihi_khayr wa huwa 'alâ kulli shayin qadîr.' There is no god but Allah, alone without partner. The Dominion belongs to Him. And all praise is due to Allah. In His Hands is goodness and He has power over all things'*[325]

[325] Related by al-Tirmidhî (5/572).

And the Shaykh, may Allah be pleased with him, said: 'This is (technically) praise, but it is called supplication since it is a prelude to supplication, and it is therefore described as such."

Narration 193

It has been reported that al-Ḥusayn bin al-Ḥasan al-Murwazî, who stayed in Makkah and died there said, "I asked Sufyân ibn 'Uyayna about the exegisis of the words of the Messenger of Allah ﷺ, 'The best supplication for the Day of 'Arafat is the best thing I and the prophets before me have ever said and that is *"lâ ilâha illAllâh waḥdahu lâ sharîka lahu' there is no god but Allah, alone without partner,"* for it appears to be only rememberance and there is no supplication in it. And Sufyân asked if I had heard the *ḥadîth* of Manṣûr bin Mâlik bin al-Ḥârith in which Allah the Exalted says, *'Whoever busies himself with My rememberance over asking me, I will give him more than I give those who ask.'"* [326]

"Yes", I said.

And he said, "That is the exegisis of it." And then he said, "Do you know what Umayya said when he came to Ibn Jad'ân requesting a favour?"

"No," I said.

He said, "When he came, he said:

'Shall I mention my need or does it indeed suffice -
Your modesty is an innate characteristic
If a person were to praise you one day
There would be no need for him to present to you more praise'

[326] This part of the *ḥadîth* is related by al-Bukhârî in his *Tarîkh al-Kabîr* and mentioned by Ibn Hajr in his commentary *Fatḥ al-Bârî* (11/147).

And other than him have said, “Whoever presents him with praise.”” And Sufyân said, “This is the case with created beings, that when one wants generosity (to be shown) it is said, ‘It suffices us to present praise to you so that you will give us what we need’ so how is it with the Creator?”
And the Shaykh, may Allah be pleased with him, said, “It is with this meaning that Sâlim bin ‘Abdullah replied in the following:”

Narration 194

It has been reported on the authority of Bukayr bin ‘Atîq who said: “I performed Ḥajj, and I was carefully watching a man who I was following (in the rites). His beard was dusty. It was Sâlim bin ‘Abdullah.[327] He was in the place of standing (at ‘Arafat) saying *‘lâ ilâha illAllâh waḥdahu lâ sharîka lahu, lahu_mulk wa lahu_lḥamd bi yadihi_lkhayr wa huwa ‘alâ kulli shay’in qadîr. Lâ ilâha illAllâh ilâhan wâḥidan wa naḥnu lahu muslimûn lâ ilâha illAllâh wa law kariha_lmushrikûn. Lâ ilâha illAllâh Rabbuna wa Rabbu Âbâ’inâ al-awwalîn.’*
There is no god but Allah, alone without partner. The Dominion belongs to Him. And all praise is due to Him. In His Hands is goodness, and He has power over all things. There is no god but Allah, One God, to Him we submit. There is no god but Allah, even if the polythesists dislike it. There is no god but Allah, our Lord and the Lord of our fathers of old.
He continued saying that until the sun set, and then he looked at me and said, “I noticed you staring at me today.” And then he said, “My father told me on the authority of his father ‘Umar bin al-Khaṭṭâb that the Prophet ﷺ said that Allah, the Exalted, says: *‘Whoever busies himself with My rememberance over asking me, I will give him more than I give those who ask.’”’*
And the Shaykh al-Imâm Aḥmad al-Bayhaqî, may Allah be pleased with him, said it has been related in other *ḥadîth* which are not particularly strong:

[327] See note 177.

Narration 195

'Ali ibn Abû Ṭâlib[328] said that the Messenger of Allah ﷺ said: "The supplication I did most, and the supplication that the Prophets before me did, on the Day of 'Arafat is, *'lâ ilâha illAllâh waḥdahu lâ sharîka lahu, lahu_lmulk wa lahu_lḥamd wa huwa 'alâ kulli shay'in qadîr. Allâhumma_jal fî qalbi nuran wa fî sam'î nuran. Allâhumma_shraḥ lî ṣadrî wa yassir lî amrî wa a'ûdhu bika min waswâsi_ṣudûr wa shatâti_l'umûr wa fitnati_lqubûr. Allâhumma inni a'ûdhu bika min sharri mâ yaliju fi_llayl wa sharri mâ yaliju fi_nahâr wa sharri mâ tahubba bihi_riyâḥ wa min sharri bawâ'iq al-Dahr.'*

There is no god but Allah, alone without partner. The Dominion belongs to Him, and all praise is due to Him. And He has power over all things. O Allah! Place in my heart a light, and in my hearing a light. O Allah! Open up my chest, and ease my affair. And I seek refuge in You from the whisperings of the chest, and varying situations, and the tribulation of the grave. O Allah! I seek refuge in You from the evil that comes by night, and from the evil that comes by day, and the evil that is bestowed by the wind, and the evil of the calamaties of time."

And he, may Allah be pleased with him, said that it was also related by Khalîfa bin Ḥuṣayn from the Prophet ﷺ.

Narration 196

It has been reported that Jâbir bin 'Abdullah[329] said that the Messenger of Allah ﷺ said: "No Muslim stands on the evening of 'Arafat, in the place of standing turning his face in the direction of prayer, and then says *'lâ ilâha illAllâh waḥdahu lâ sharîka lahu, lahu_mulk wa lahu_lḥamd wa huwa 'alâ kulli shayin qadîr.' There is no god but Allah, alone without partner. The Dominion belongs to Him. And all praise is due to Him. And He has power over all things.'* a

[328] See note 65.
[329] See note 92.

hundred times and then says, "*Qul huwa_llahu aḥad,*" '*Say: Allah is One*'[330] a hundred times, and then he says, "*Allâhumma ṣalli 'alâ Muḥammadin wa 'alâ âli Muḥammadin kamâ ṣallayta 'alâ 'Ibrâhîm wa 'alâ âli 'Ibrâhîm innaka ḥamîdun majîd,*" '*O Allah send prayers upon Muhammad and his family, as you sent prayers upon 'Ibrâhîm (Abraham) and the family of 'Ibrâhîm, for surely You are praised and majestic*' except that Allah, the Blessed and Exalted, says, "*O My angels, what is the reward of this slave of mine? He celebrates My oneness, he glorifies Me, exalts Me, acknowledges Me, praises me and prays for My Prophet? Bear witness that I have forgiven him and I have interceded on his behalf with Myself and if this slave of mine asks me anything I will intercede for him and (in doing so I will) encompass all the people of the place of standing.*""

---

[330] This is the 113th Chapter of the Quran, and what is meant is reciting the whole chapter, which is three lines, and not just the first line mentioned here. And Allah knows best.

Chapter Twenty-Three
The Prophet's Petition ﷺ for His Nation on the Eve of 'Arafât

Narration 197

It has been reported on the authority of 'Ikrima that Ibn 'Abbas[331] said: "I saw the Messenger of Allah ﷺ supplicating at 'Arafat, and his arms were stretched like a poor person begging for food."

Narration 198

It has been reported on the authority of Ibn Kinâna bin Mirdâs al-Sulamî from his father from his grandfather, Abbâs ibn Mirdâs, that the Messenger of Allah ﷺ supplicated on the evening of the Day of 'Arafat for the forgiveness of his nation and for mercy for them, and he was abundant in his prayers, so Allah revealed to him: *"Indeed I have done it (that is, I have forgiven them), except the case of which some of them wronged others. As for the sins between them and Me, I have forgiven them."* So he ﷺ said, *"O my Lord! You are able to reward the one who has been wronged with greater than the wrong (he has endured), and to forgive the wrongdoer."* And Allah did not answer his prayer on that night. So when he went to Muzdalifa the next night he repeated his prayer and Allah, the Exalted, answered, *"I have indeed forgiven them."* And the Messenger of Allah ﷺ smiled at a time one would not expect him to smile. He said, *"I smiled at the enemy of Allah, Iblîs (the Devil). When he came to know that Allah, the Exalted, had answered my prayer for my nation, he fell (to the ground) cursing and wailing, and he scattered dust over his head."* [332]

---

[331] See note 17.
[332] Related by Ibn Mâjah (2/1002) and Aḥmad (4/14).

And the Shaykh, may Allah be pleased with him, said, "It is probable that this answering of the prayer in the case of wronging (other people) is with regard to the next life, in that that person will not be in the Fire forever for his wronging of others, which is the case for attributing partners to Allah. But it is also probable that this is in the beginning, before he is punished for any of his own sins. Thus, our way is to avoid wronging others as much as we can. And by Allah is enabling success.

And the Shaykh, may Allah be pleased with him, said, "(There is) in the Book of Allah and the Way of the Messenger of Allah ﷺ evidence that sins which are less than (the ultimate sin of) associating partners with Allah are left to (be dealt with according to) the Will of Allah. Allah, the Exalted, has said, *'Allah forgives not that partners should be set up with Him; but He forgives anything else, to whom He pleases.'"* [333]

Narration 199

It has been reported on the authority of Abû al-Ash'ath al-Ṣan'ânî that 'Ubâda ibn al-Ṣâmit[334] said, "The Messenger of Allah ﷺ used to take (the oath of allegiance) from us, as he took it from the women, that we would not associate partners with Allah in any way, that we would not steal, nor commit adultery, nor kill our children, and that we would not undercut each other (in trade). (He would say that) whoever among you fulfils this (contract) will have his reward with Allah, and that whoever has the *hadd*[335]

---

[333] Al-Nisâ 4:48.

[334] 'Ubâda ibn al-Ṣâmit was one of the leaders of the Anṣâr at the Oath of Allegiance at 'Aqaba. He participated in all battles during the Prophet's lifetime and went on to participate in the Conquest of Egypt. He was a prolific narrator of *ḥadîth* and many Companions also related from him. He was one of those who collected the verses of Quran during the time of the Prophet ﷺ, and was sent to Syria during the time of 'Umar to teach them the Quran. He was known to be tall, strong, and handsome.

[335] *Ḥadd* literally means 'limit'. Its plural is *ḥudûd.* It is a fixed punishment set in the Quran and *ḥadîth* for transgressions against God and society. The six crimes that lead to these set punishments include theft, illicit sexual relationships, making unproven accusations of illicit

punishment inflicted upon him will have it count as recompense, and of whomsoever Allah hides his mistake, his affair will be with Allah, if He wishes He will punish him and if He wishes, He will forgive him."[336]

He, may Allah be pleased with him, said, "Whatever is done apart from associating partners with Allah is within the discretion of Allah, the Exalted. And if, through His discretion, some are punished this will not be forever, and that person will eventually be taken from the Fire and returned to the Garden as a result of his faith. Allah, the Mighty and Majestic, said: *'Allah is never unjust in the least degree.'*[337] And He said: *'Verily We shall not suffer to perish the reward of any who do a (single) righteous deed.'* [338] Keeping the believer in the Fire with the disbelievers would be *'perishing the reward'* of *'the righteous deed'* of faith in Allah, His Books, and His Messengers; and Allah, the Mighty and Majestic, has said He will not do that."

Narration 200

It has been reported by Sufyân ibn 'Uyayna who said that 'Amr bin Dînâr heard Jâbir ibn 'Abdullah[339] say, "I heard the Messenger of Allah ﷺ with these two ears say, *'Indeed Allah will take some people out of the Fire and enter them into the Garden.'*" [340]

---

sex, drinking intoxicants, apostasy, and highway robbery. These all require strict requirements of evidence, and can only be implemented by the state based on a legitimate ruling by a judge.

[336] Related by Muslim (3/1333), Ibn Mâjah (2/868) and Aḥmad (5/313).

[337] Al-Nisâ, 4:40.

[338] Al-Kahf, 18:30.

[339] See note 92.

[340] Related by Muslim (1/187).

Narration 201

Abû Hurayra[341] said that the Messenger of Allah ﷺ said: *"Every Prophet has a (special) supplication that is answered. Indeed, I have reserved mine for intercession for my nation on the Day of Ressurection. And it will be success for you - if Allah, the Exalted, wills. Whoever dies without associating partners with Allah (will enter the Garden)."* [342]

Narration 202

Abû Hurayra told Ka'b al-Aḥbâr[343] that the Prophet of Allah ﷺ said: *"Indeed, every Prophet has a (special) supplication that is answered. All Prophets hastened to make theirs but I reserved mine for intercession for my nation on the Day of Resurrection. And it will be a victory - if Allah, the Exalted, wills for whoever dies without associating partners with Allah."* And Ka'b said to Abû Hurayra, "Did you hear this from the Messenger of Allah ﷺ ?" And Abû Hurayra said, "Yes."[344]

Narration 203

It has been reported that Ka'b al-Aḥbâr said to Abû Hurayra, "Shall I not tell you what Isḥâq (Isaac), the son of Ibrâhîm (Abraham) said?"
"Indeed," said Abû Hurayra.
Ka'b said, "When Ibrâhîm saw himself sacrificing his son, Isḥâq,[345] the Devil said, 'By Allah! I will test one of them!' And so the Devil appeared in the

[341] See note 83.
[342] Related by al-Tirmidhî (5/580), Ibn Mâjah (2/144) and Aḥmad (2/426).
[343] See note 282.
[344] Related by Muslim (1/189).
[345] This story is normally associated with his son Ismâîl (Ishmael).

form of a man they knew. He approached them as Ibrâhîm was leaving with Isḥâq to sacrifice him. He came to Sarah, the wife of Ibrâhîm and said to her, "Where did Ibrâhîm go with Isḥâq this morning?"

'He went out for one of his errands,' she said.

"No, by Allah! He has not gone out for that reason!" The Devil said to her.

'So why did he go out?' Sarah said.

"He went out to sacrifice him," he said.

'That is not at all why he went out. It was not to sacrifice him,' Sarah said.

"Indeed it was! By Allah!" The Devil said.

'Why would he sacrifice him?' Sarah said.

"He thinks that his Lord ordered him to do so," the Devil said.

'Then indeed it would be best if he obeyed his Lord if he ordered him to do so,' said Sarah.

The Devil left Sarah. Soon he came to Isḥâq while he was walking behind his father. "Where is your father heading this morning?" He asked.

'He has gone out with me for one of his errands,' he said.

"No! By Allah! He has gone out with you to sacrifice you," the Devil said.

'It can't be that my father would sacrifice me,' Isḥâq said.

"Indeed, it is so!" He said.

'Why?' He said.

"He thinks his Lord ordered him to do that," he said.

'And by Allah! If he has been ordered to do that, he should definitely obey Him,' said Isḥâq. So the Devil left him and rushed to Ibrâhîm and said to him, "Where are you heading with your son this morning?"

'I have gone out for an errand of mine,' he said.

"No! By Allah! You went out for no reason other than to sacrifice your son!" He said. "You think that Allah has ordered you to do it," he said.

'And by Allah! If he ordered me to do it, I would most definitely do it,' he said.

And he said that when Ibrâhîm took Isḥâq to sacrifice him, Allah saved Isḥâq and kept him safe, and instead *"ransomed with a great slaughter."* [346] And Ibrâhîm said to Isḥâq, 'Stand up O my son! Allah has saved you.' And Allah revealed to Isḥâq, *"I have granted you a supplication that I will answer."*
Isḥâq said, 'O Allah! I ask you to answer me! Whichever slave meets you from the first and last ones that does not associate partners with you (I ask You) to enter them into the Garden.'"

Narration 204

It has been reported on the authority of 'Aṭâ ibn Yasâr that the Prophet Ibrâhîm went out with his son Ismâ'îl, yet some people say it was Isḥâq, and they relate the meaning of (what has been related above) on the authority of Ka'b and then Ibrâhîm said, *"O my son! I see in a vision that I offer you in sacrifice. Now see what is your view!" (The son) said, "O my father! Do as you are commanded. You will find me, if Allah so wills, one practising Patience and Constancy!"* [347]
"O my dear father, tie me well so my blood does not spill upon you," (said Ismâ'îl). And Ibrâhîm stood with the sharp knife, and he leaned over him and placed it ominously between his chest and his throat. The knife made no impression on him. Then Ibrâhîm turned around and behind him was a ram. And then Ibrâhîm said, "O my son stand up! For Allah, the Mighty and Majestic, has ransomed you." He sacrificed the ram and left his son. And then Ibrâhîm said, "Surely Allah has given you inner sight today, and so ask today whatever you wish and He will give it to you."

---

[346] Allah replaced Isḥâq with a ram as Ibrâhîm was about to sacrifice his son, and Allah refers to this as *"ransoming with a great slaughter."*
[347] Ṣâffât 37:102.

"Indeed I ask that no slave of His meets Him believing in Him, bearing witness that there is no god but Allah, alone without partner, except that He forgives him and He enters him into the Garden."

Narration 205

It has been related on the authority of Ibn Sâliḥ that Ibn 'Abbâs[348] said that *Tarwiyya*[349] and 'Arafat are called by those names because revelation came to Ibrâhîm ﷺ that he should sacrifice his son, and so he said to himself, "Is this from Allah or from the Devil?" He fasted that morning and that evening, which was the eve of 'Arafat, further revelation came to him, and so he knew it was the truth from His Lord, and therefore it was known as 'Arafat (that is, *the place where he knew*). This is what has been said in this narration.

Narration 206

Abû Tufayl relates on the authority of Ibn 'Abbâs that when Ibrâhîm ﷺ was tested, meaning with the sacrifice of his son, Jibrîl (Gabriel) came to him and showed him the rites of the pilgrimage. Then he went with him to 'Arafat. Ibn 'Abbâs said, "Do you know why 'Arafat is called 'Arafat?"
"No," I said.
And Ibn 'Abbâs said, "Jibrîl (Gabriel) said to Ibrâhîm, 'Are you now aware?'
"Yes," he said." And Ibn 'Abbâs said, "And from then on it was called 'Arafat (place of awareness)."

---

[348] See note 17.

[349] The day preceding the Ḥajj where the Pilgrims travel to Mina in preparation for the Day of ''Arafat that is the 8th of Dhûl Ḥijja.

Narration 207

Umm al-Fayḍ, the freed slave of 'Abdul Malik bin Marwân said: "I heard Abdullah bin Mas'ûd[350] say, 'no slave, male or female, supplicated on the eve of 'Arafat with these ten words a thousand times, except that Allah gave him what he asks for, apart from the one who cuts family ties and the wrongdoer. (The ten words are) *Subhânallahil_ladhi fi_samâ 'arshahu. Subhânallahil_ladhi fi_larḍ mawṭiuhu. Subhânallahi_ladhi fi_lbaḥr sabîluhu. Subhânallahi_ladhi fi_nâr sulṭânuhu. Subhânallah_ladhi fi_ljannati raḥmatuhu. Subhânallahi_ladhi fi_lqubûr qaḍâuhu. Subhânallahi_ladhi fi_hawâ rûḥuhu. Subhânallahi_ladhi rafa'a_samâ. Subhânallahi_ladhi waḍa'a_lardîn. Subhânallahi_ladhi lâ malja' wa lâ manja illa ilayhi.'"*

Transcendent is He who is in the Heaven and Earth. Transcendent is He whose Throne is in the sky. Transcendent is the One whose Predestination has effects on the Earth. Transcendent is He whose path is through the sea. Transcendent is He who over the Fire has complete rule. Transcendent is He whose Mercy is in the Garden. Transcendent is He whose decree is in the graves. Transcendent is He whose Spirit is in the air. Transcendent is He who raised the skies. Transcendent is He who laid down the earths. Transcendent is He from whom there is no escape nor refuge except to Him.

And Umm al-Fayḍ said, "I said to 'Abdullah bin Mas'ûd, 'did you hear this from the Messenger of Allah?' And he said, "yes.""

And the Shaykh, may Allah be pleased with him, said that 'Âṣim bin 'Ali related it on the authority of 'Azra bin Qays with his chain of transmission and added, "You should be in a state of ritual ablution, and once you have finished you should send prayers upon the Prophet ﷺ, and then specify your need."

[350] See note 117.

Chapter Twenty-Four
The Blessing of the Day of Sacrifice

Allah the Exalted has said:

(فَصَلِّ لِرَبِّكَ وَانْحَرْ)

Therefore, to thy Lord turn in Prayer and Sacrifice.
(al-Kauthar, 108:2)

Qatâda said the *"Prayer"* referred to here is the "Prayer of the Sacrifice" (that is the 'Eid Prayer) and the *"sacrifice"* is the slaughter of the sacrificial animal on that day. And this is the narration of al-Kalbî on the authority of Abû Ṣâliḥ from Ibn 'Abbâs. He said, "Pray to your Lord before you sacrifice and then slaughter your sacrificial animal, that is, turn to the direction of prayer and slaughter and say, *'Allâhu Akbar' 'Allah is Greatest.'*"

It is related on the authority of 'Ali, Ibn 'Abbâs, and Anas ibn Mâlik, may Allah be pleased with them all[351], that they said it means that one places one's right hand upon one's left in prayer when sacrificing.

Narration 208

And it has been related in a different form on the authority of 'Ali but not going all the way back to the Messenger of Allah ﷺ that Jibrîl (Gabriel) said: "It is not (referring to) the sacrifice, but it is a command to raise your hands

[351] See notes 65, 17 and 30.

when you say, *'Allâhu Akbar' 'Allah is Greatest,'* and when you bow, and when you raise your head from the bowing.

And we have related it on the authority of Sa'îd bin Jubayr, Mujâhid, and 'Ikrima that they said about this verse, "Pray the Prayer and slaughter the sacrificial animal."

Narration 209

It has been reported that Zubayd al-Ayâmî told us that he heard al-Sha'abî say, on the authority of al-Barâ bin Âzib,[352] who said that the Messenger of Allah ﷺ said: *"Indeed, the first thing that we do on this day of ours is to perform the Prayer. Then we return and slaughter the sacrificial animal. Whoever does that has followed the Prophetic Way, and whoever slaughters before the Prayer, it is no more than meat presented to his family. It is not part of the rites."* And a man from the Ansâr said, and it is said it was Burda bin Niyâr, *"O Messenger of Allah, I have already sacrificed my animal, but I have a ewe which is better than the old animal."* And he said, *"Offer that in its place, but that will not avail or suffice anyone after you."* [353]

And Muṭarraf related it on the authority of al-Sha'abi, and he said in the *ḥadîth*, "a baby goat."

---

[352] Al-Barâ' ibn 'Âzib embraced Islam when he was very young, and along with 'Abdullah ibn 'Umar wanted to attend the Battle of Badr but was sent back for being too young. He fought at all the battles from Khandaq onwards. He said that he travelled eighteen times with the Prophet ﷺ. He related *ḥadîth* directly from the Messenger ﷺ, and some of the major Companions including Abû Bakr and 'Umar.

[353] Related by al-Bukhârî (2/3), Muslim (3/1553), al-Tirmidhî (4/93), Abû Dawûd (3/333), al-Nasâ'î (7/223) and Aḥmad (4/281-283 and 303).

Narration 210

It has been reported on the authority of Isḥâq bin Buzurj that al-Ḥasan bin 'Ali[354], may Allah be pleased with him, said: "The Messenger of Allah ﷺ ordered us to wear the best clothes we can find, to use the best perfume, and to slaughter the fattest animal we can find. A cow counts as seven animals and a camel counts as seven. And that you should call *'Allâhu Akbar' 'Allah is Greatest,'* and to show tranquillity and dignity."

Narration 211

It has been related on the authority of 'Abdul Raḥmân bin 'Jâbir bin 'Abdullah from his father that the Prophet ﷺ had two huge beautiful plump tender rams, and he turned one of them on its side and said, *"bismillâhi wallâhu akbar, Allahumma hadhi 'an Muḥammad, In the name of Allah, O Allah this is from Muḥammad."* And then he turned the other on its side and said, *"bismillâhi wallâhu akbar, Allahumma hadhi 'an Muḥammad wa ummatihi fa man shahida laka bi_tawḥîd wa shahida lî bi_lbalagh. In the name of Allah, O Allah this is from Muḥammad and his nation. For whoever bears witness to Your Oneness and bears witness to my deliverance of the Message."*

And it has been related in a different form, and in that *ḥadîth* it says of the first ram, " *'An Muḥammad wa âli Muḥammad' 'from Muhammad and the family of Muhammad.'"*

[354] See note 164.

Narration 212

It has been related on the authority of Abu 'Ayyâsh that 'Jâbir said that the Messenger of Allah ﷺ slaughtered two rams on 'Eid day. When he turned them (to face the direction of prayer) he said: *"Inni wajjahtu wajhiya lilladhi faṭara_samawâti wa_lard ḥanifan musliman wa mâ ana min al-mushrikîn inna_ṣalâtî wa nusukî wa maḥyâya wa mamâtî lillahi rabb_il 'âlamîn lâ sharîka lahu wa bidhâlika 'umirtu wa anâ min al-Muslimîn.'*
"Surely I turn my face to the One who created the Heavens and the Earth, following the religion of submission, and I am not of those who associate partners. All my prayers, my sacrifice, my life, my death are for the Lord of the Worlds. He has no partner. This is what I have been ordered to do and I am one of those who submits."
And he said, *"Allâhumma minka wa laka 'an Muḥammadin wa ummati," "O Allah, this is from you, and to you from Muḥammad and his nation."* And then he mentioned the name of Allah over it and slaughtered it.
And Ibrâhîm bin Ṭahmân related it on the authority of Muḥammad bin Isḥâq, and in the *ḥadîth* "he turned the two animals to the direction of the prayer and then he slaughtered them."
And it has been said it was on authority of Muḥammad bin Isḥâq from Yazîd bin Khâlid bin 'Imrân from 'Ayyash from Jâbir, may Allah be pleased with them.

Narration 213

Imrân bin Ḥuṣayn said the Messenger of Allah ﷺ said: "O Fâtima![355] Rise and witness your sacrifice, for surely all your sins will be a forgiveness from the

[355] Fâṭima was the fifth child of the Prophet ﷺ. As she was only three years old when her father received revelation. She grew up during the period of persecution, and was sixteen years old when she migrated to Madina. When her mother, Khadija bint al-Khuwaylid, died, she took great care of her father, despite her young age. As a result, she was given the nickname *"Umm Abîha"* "the Mother of her Father." She married the Prophet's cousin, 'Ali

first drop of blood, and say, *'Truly, my prayer, my service of sacrifice, my life, and my death are (all) for Allah, the Cherisher of the Worlds. No partner has He. This am I commanded, and I am the first of those who bow to His will.'"* [356]

I said, "O Messenger of Allah, is this specifically for your household only, or is it for all the Muslims generally?"

He said, *"It is for all Muslims generally."*

And the Shaykh, may Allah be pleased with him, said it is from the Prophetic Way for the one who wants to make a sacrificial slaughter to remove nothing of his hair or nails from the time of the new moon of Dhûl Ḥijja until he has made the sacrifice.

Narration 214

It has been reported on the authority of Sa'îd ibn al-Musayyib from Umm Salama that the Messenger of Allah ﷺ said: *"When the ten (days of Dhûl Ḥijja) arrive, and one of you wishes to make sacrifice an animal, one should hold back (from cutting) one's hair and nails."* [357]

And al-Shâfi'î, may Allah be pleased with him, said that in this *ḥadîth* is an evidence that the sacrificial slaughter is not compulsory. As the Messenger of Allah ﷺ said, "If one of you wishes to sacrifice, then he should hold back from cutting his hair and nails." If it had been compulsory, he would have said, "and so do not touch your hair until you have made the sacrifice." and he would not have connected it to wishing (to do or not to do).

And the Shaykh, may Allah be pleased with him, said that the Prophetic Way with the sacrificial slaughter is not to eat anything until you have

---

ibn Abû Ṭâlib (see note 65), and all his surviving lineage are from this union. At the battle of 'Uḥud, she tended to the wounds of her father and husband. She died, as prophesied by the Messenger ﷺ, six months after her father.

[356] Al-An'âm, 6:162-163.

[357] Related by Muslim (3/1565), al-Tirmidhî (3/102), Ibn Mâjah (2/1052), Abû Dawûd (3/333), al-Nasâ'î (7/211) and Aḥmad (6/289).

slaughtered your animal after the Prayer, and to eat from the sacrificial animal.

Narration 215

It has been reported on the authority of 'Abdullah bin Burayda[358] from his father[359] that the Messenger of Allah ﷺ would not leave on the Day of Fiṭr until he had eaten, and he would not eat on the Day of Sacrifice until he returned, and that he would eat of the sacrificial animal.[360]

And 'Uqba bin al-Aṣamm related it on the authority of Ibn Burayda from his father, and in the *ḥadîth* (are the words), "Until he returned and when he returned, he would eat from the liver of the sacrificial animal."

It is not permitted to fast on this day, just as it is not permitted to fast on the Day of Fiṭr.

[358] 'Abdullah bin Burayda was a Tâbi'î who related related ḥadîth his father Burayda bin Khaṣîb, as well as from other Companions including Ibn 'Abbâs, Ibn Mas'ûd and Abû Hurayra. He died in Merv in 105H 723 CE).

[359] Burayda bin Khaṣîb was a companion who embraced Islam when the Prophet ﷺ met him while he was making migration to Madina. He came to al-Madina some years later to join the Muslim community, after which he moved to Basra where his son 'Abdullah was born, and where he eventually died in 63H (682 CE).

[360] Related by al-Tirmidhî (2/462) and Aḥmad (5/352).

Narration 216

Mûsâ bin 'Ulayyi bin Rabâh told us that he heard his father tell him on the authority of 'Uqba ibn 'Âmir,[361] that the Messenger of Allah ﷺ said: '*The Day of 'Arafat, the Day of Sacrifice, and the days of* Tashriq *are the days of celebration for the people of Islam. They are the days of eating and drinking.*" [362]

And the Shaykh, may Allah be pleased with him, said that what he intended (in the statement about) not fasting on the Day of 'Arafat is in respect of the pilgrim, and this is the meaning of not fasting on these specific days.

Narration 217

It has been reported that Aḥmad bin Abû al-Ḥawârî said, "I heard Abû Sulaymân al-Dârânî 'Abdul Raḥmân bin 'Aṭiyya say that 'Ali ibn Abû Ṭâlib[363], may Allah be pleased with him, was asked why the place of standing in the Ḥajj was at the mount (of 'Arafat), and not in the Holy City.

He said, 'The Ka'ba is the House of Allah. The Sacred City is the Door of Allah. And when they approach Him in delegations they stand at His door, humbling themselves in supplication.'

It was said, "O Commander of the Faithful! And so why is there (another act of) standing at al-Mash'ar al-Ḥarâm?"

He said, 'When He gives permission to enter, He makes them stop at a second veil, and that is Muzdalifa. Once they have extended their humble

---

[361] 'Uqba ibn 'Âmir al-Juhaynî was a well-known Companion who related *ḥadîth* directly from the Prophet ﷺ and from whom many other Companions related *ḥadîth,* including Ibn 'Abbâs (see note 17) and Abû Umâma al-Bahilî (see note 20) and many Followers in Syria and Egypt. He was known for his beautiful recitation of Quran, his vast knowledge and expertise in the law of inheritance. He was one of the commanders of the forces that conquered Egypt and went on to lead a naval expedition to the island of Rhodes in the Mediterranean Sea. He died in Egypt in 58H (677 CE).

[362] Related by al-Tirmidhî (3/142), Abû Dawûd (2/804) and al-Nasâ'î (5/252).

[363] See note 65.

supplication, He grants permission for them to draw close through sacrificial slaughter (called *Qurbân* which means an "act of drawing close"), and this is at Minâ. By this they seek to cleanse themselves from the sins that they have brought with them. Then He grants permission for them to make the visit in a state of purity.'

And it was said to him, "O Commander of the Faithful! And so why is it forbidden to fast during the Days of *Tashrîq*?"

He said, 'Because they are a folk who are visiting Allah, and are enjoying His hospitality. It is not permitted for the guest to fast without permission of the one who is hosting them.'

And it was said to him, "O Commander of the Faithful! A man clings to the cover of the Ka'ba, why is that?"

He said, 'It is similar to a man whose companion has agreed on the wages of his work with him, and (after he has finished his work) he hangs on to his clothing and begs him until he gives him wages.'"

And the Shaykh, may Allah be pleased with him, said, "the Day of Sacrifice has other blessings, and among them is that Allah calls it the Day of The Greatest Ḥajj."

Narration 218

It has been reported on the authority of Nâfʾî that Ibn Umar[364] said: "The Messenger of Allah ﷺ halted on the Day of Sacrifice at the *Jamarât*[365] during his farewell pilgrimage. And he said, *'What day is this?'*

"The Day of Sacrifice," they said.

'In which city is this? He said.

"The Sacred City," they said.

'In which month is this?' He said.

"The Sacred Month," they said.

He said, *'This is the Greatest Day of the Pilgrimage and so your blood, your possessions and your honour are sacred between you just as sacred as this city on this day.'* Then he said, *'Have I informed you?'*

"Yes," they said.

And he immediately said, *'O Allah! Bear witness!'* And then he said farewell to the people. And the people said that this was the farewell pilgrimage."

And the Shaykh, may Allah be pleased with him, said, "It has been called the Greatest Day of the Pilgrimage because it contains many of the actions of the pilgrimage in it. They include the stoning of the *Jamara*[366] at 'Aqaba, during the mid-morning of the Day of Sacrifice, the sacrificial slaughter, shaving of the head, the circumambulation during the visit to Makkah, although it is permitted to delay it, it remains the Prophetic Way to do it on that day. And it is one of the ten days that Allah the Exalted has named, 'the Known Days' *'al-Ayyâm al-Ma'lûmât'.*[367] And it has been singled out as one that He provided you with *'beast of cattle.'*"

---

[364] See note 81.

[365] These are stone pillars marking the place where the Devil unsuccessfully tried to convince Ibrâhîm (Abraham) not to sacrifice his son.

[366] See note 365.

[367] *Ma'lûmât* literally means, *"known."* The Months of the Ḥajj are referred to in Surah al-Baqara as *al-Ashur al-Ma'lûmât, "the known months"* and in Surah al-Ḥajj, the Days of Ḥajj are referred to as *Ayyâm Ma'lumât, 'well known days'* and as the remainder of the *ḥadîth*

Chapter Twenty-Five
The Days of *Tashrîq*

Allah the Exalted said:

(وَاذْكُرُواْ اللّهَ فِي أَيَّامٍ مَّعْدُودَاتٍ)

Celebrate the praises of Allah during the Appointed Days.
(Al-Baqara, 2:203)

Narration 219

It has been reported on the authority of Sa'îd bin Jubayr that Ibn 'Abbâs[368] said that the *al-Ayyâm al-Ma'lûmât, the Known Days* are the ten days of Dhûl Ḥijja and the *"Appointed Days"* (referred to in the verse above) are the Days of *Tashrîq.*

Narration 220

'Amr ibn Dînâr said, "I saw Ibn 'Abbâs glorifying Allah (saying *'Allâhu Akbar'*) on the Day of Sacrifice in Makkah, and he recited the verse *"Celebrate the praises of Allah during the Appointed Days."*

---

mentions they are associated with *"the beast of cattle"* (see Surah Ḥajj 22:28). This is expanded upon in the next chapter. And Allah knows best.

[368] See note 17.

Narration 221

It has been reported on the authority of Yaḥyâ bin Sa'îd that he heard Yûsuf bin Mas'ûd bin Ḥakam al-Anṣârî say that his grandmother said that she saw a rider riding during the time of the Prophet ﷺ and they were at Minâ. He was calling out, "O people! These are the days of eating and drinking and women and family and the remembrance of Allah." She said, "I said, 'Who is that?' And they said that it was 'Ali ibn Abû Ṭâlib."

And the Shaykh, may Allah be pleased with him, said, "He only called out like that on the order of the Messenger of Allah ﷺ. What is meant by the phrase *'and women and family'* is clarification that intimacy (with one's wife) is permitted for the pilgrim once he has left the state of *iḥrâm,*[369] which is after the stoning of the *jamarah* at 'Aqaba, shaving one's head, and the circumambulation of the visit to Makkah. This is as in the words of Allah, the Mighty and Majestic, *"But when you are clear of the sacred precincts and of garb of pilgrimage, you may hunt,"* meaning it is permitted after it was forbidden while in the state of *iḥrâm.*[370]

And as for the phrase, 'and the remembrance of Allah', we have also related this in the *ḥadîth* of Nubaysha that the Messenger of Allah ﷺ said, *'The Days of Tashrîq are the days of eating drinking, family, and remembrance of Allah."*[371]

And what is intended by 'remembrance of Allah' is saying *"Allâhu Akbar" "Allah is Greatest."* And Allah knows best. One starts this on the Day of Sacrifice after the Midday Prayer and continues until the Morning Prayer on the last of the Days of *Tashrîq.* This is the opinion that has been related from Ibn 'Umar and Ibn 'Abbâs. And it has also been related from 'Uthmân, Zayd ibn Thâbit and Abû Sa'îd al-Khudrî.

---

[369] This is the sanctified state that one enters by making intention for the Pilgrimage, which is the first integral of the Hajj. Once the intention has been made and one enters this state, certain things become forbidden including perfume, sexual relations, cutting the hair and, for men, wearing sewn clothes, which is why the state of *Iḥrâm* is associated with the pilgrims' garb consisting of two white cloths.

[370] Al-Mâida, 5:2.

[371] Related by Muslim (2/800) and Aḥmad (5/85-86).

And al-Shâfi'î, may Allah shower him with mercy, based on what has been said by the righteous predecessors, considered it preferable to start after the Morning Prayer on the Day of 'Arafat. The origin of this is the following:"

Narration 222

It has been reported on the authority of Bishr bin 'Umar and Abû Naîm that Muḥammad bin Abû Bakr al-Thaqafî said to Anas ibn Mâlik[372] as they were setting off from Minâ to 'Arafat, "What did you used to do on this day with the Messenger of Allah ﷺ?"
"The one who said, *'labayk Allahumma labayk' 'I am at Your Service O Allah! I am at Your Service!'* used to say it, and he did not dislike it, and the one who said, *"Allâhu Akbar" "Allah is Greatest"* used to say it, and he did not dislike that either." [373]

Narration 223

It has been reported on the authority of 'Âṣim that Shaqîq said that 'Ali used to say *"Allâhu Akbar" "Allah is Greatest"* from after the Morning Prayer going to 'Arafat and continue until the Imâm had finished his prayer on the last day of *Tashrîq*. And then he would say it again after the afternoon prayer.

---

[372] See note 30.
[373] Related by al-Bukhârî (2/7), Muslim (2/932) Ibn Mâjah (2/1000) and al-Nasâ'î (5/251).

Narration 224

It has been reported on the authority of 'Ikrima that Ibn 'Abbas used to say "*Allâhu Akbar*" from the time he set off for 'Arafat until the last day of *Tashrîq*.

Narration 225

It has been reported on the authority of Jâbir ibn 'Abdullah that the Messenger of Allah ﷺ prayed on the morning of 'Arafat, and then said to his Companions: "In your places!" And then he said, "*Allâhu Akbar, Allâhu Akbar, Allâhu Akbar, lâ ilâha illAllah, Allâhu Akbar, Allâhu Akbar wa lillâhil_ḥamd.*" And he would continue glorifying Allah (in that way) until the afternoon prayer on the Days of *Tashrîq*.
And it has been related in another form:

Narration 226

It has been reported on the authority of Abû Tufayl, from 'Ali and 'Ammâr, may Allah be pleased with them both,[374] that the Prophet ﷺ used to say "*bismillâhi_raḥmân_irraḥîm, In the name of Allah, Most Gracious, Most Merciful*" aloud in the prescribed prayers, and used to supplicate with the prayer known as the *qunût* in the Morning Prayer. And he used to say "*Allâhu*

[374] For the biography of 'Ali ibn Abû Ṭâlib see note 65. Âmmar and his parents, Sumayyah bint Khayyât and Yâsir bin 'Âmir, were among the earliest converts to Islam, and as poor members of the Makkan society with no clan protection were often targets of the cruel persecution of the people of Quraysh. The Prophet ﷺ encouraged them to be patient saying, *"Be steadfast O family of Yâsir, for you are promised the Garden."* His parents were the first martyrs of Islam. Âmmar went on to migrate to Madina, and then to Kûfa from where he left for the Battle of Siffîn where he was martyred in 37H (657CE).

Akbar" from the Morning Prayer on the Day of 'Arafat, and would not stop until the Afternoon Prayer on the last day of *Tashrîq*.

Narration 227

It has been reported on the authority of 'Âsim bin Sulaymân that 'Uthmân al-Nahdî said that Salmân[375] used to teach us how to glorify Allah. He would say, "*Allâhu Akbar, Allâhu Akbar, Allâhu Akbar kabîran*" -or he said *takbîran* - "*Allâhumma anta 'Alâ wa ajall min an takûna laka waladun aw takûna laka sharîkun fil mulk aw yakûna laka waliyun min al-dhulli wa kabbirhu takbîran Allâhumm_ighfir lanâ war_ḥamnâ.*" "*Allah is Greatest! Allah is Greatest! Allah is Greatest and glorified! O Allah You are the Most High and Most Majestic, beyond taking a child or partner from this dominion or that there could be one who protects you from humiliation - Glorify and Magnify Him! O Allah, forgive us and show us mercy!*" And then he said that this will indeed be written, and so do not neglect these two, and they will intercede for you.

And the Shaykh, may Allah be pleased with him, said that these days have other blessings in that they are the days of stoning the three *jamarât* after midday, and these are the days of sacrifice for all those who did not manage to slaughter a sacrificial animal on the Day of Sacrifice; for slaughtering on these days is permitted as the Messenger of Allah ﷺ said: "*All the Days of* Tashrîq *are the days of sacrifice.*"

[375] See note 36.

Chapter Twenty-Six

The Blessing of the Month of Muḥarram

Abdul Aziz Ahmed comments:

Muḥarram

Muḥarram is the first month of the Islamic calendar. It is one of the Sacred Months referred to in the Quranm, and discussed in the chapter on Rajab.

The meaning of Muḥarram is *"sanctified"* or *"inviolable"* or *"forbidden."* It is taken from the intensive form of the verb *ḥ-r-m* from where the words *ḥarâm* and *iḥrâm* are also derived.

It is the month of fasting and repentance. It contains one of the holiest days of the year. The tenth of Muḥarram, known as 'Âshûrâ, has significance to all Muslims. It is believed that Moses was saved from the Pharaoh on this date, and it was on this date that Ibrahîm, Abraham, was saved from the fire of Namrûd, Nimrod. The Prophet ﷺ correctly predicted that his grandson, al-Ḥusayn would be martyred on this date, and after that it took on a special significance for those who revered the family of the Prophet ﷺ.

Allah, the Mighty and Majestic, swore an oath saying:

(وَالْفَجْرِ)

(وَلَيَالٍ عَشْرٍ)

By the break of day. By the ten nights.

(Al-Fajr, 89: 1-2)

Narration 228

'Uthmân bin Muḥṣin related that Ibn Abbâs[376] said about the verses: "*By the break of day. By the ten nights*" that the "*break of day*" refers to Muḥarram, which is the "dawn" of the New Year.

The Shaykh, may Allah be pleased with him, said, 'The month of Muḥarram is one of the sacred months mentioned specifically by Allah in His Book. The People of *Jâhillîya*[377] used to glorify it. However, some of the Arabs used to sanctify it one year and not the next, sanctifying Ṣafar in its place. Allah, the Exalted, negated their fanciful notion with His Words, may He be Exalted, '*The number of months in the sight of Allah is twelve (in a year) - so ordained by Him the day He created the heavens and the earth; of them, four are sacred: that is the straight usage. So wrong not yourselves therein.*'" *(al-Tauba 9:36)*

[376] See note 17.

[377] The Arabs before the advent of Islam

Narration 229

It has been related on the authority of Muḥammad, from Ibn Abû Bakra,[378] from his father that the Prophet ﷺ said: *"Indeed time rotates in its current form as it has done since the day Allah created the heavens and the earth. The year has twelve months. Four are sacred. Three of them are consecutive: Dhûl Qa'da, Dhûl Ḥijja, Muḥarram; and Rajab, which is the month of Muḍr,[379] between Jumâdi and Sha'bân."*

And then he said, *"Which month is this?"*

We said, "Allah and His Messenger know best."

He (Abû Bakra) said, "We were silent for a while until we thought he would name it with other than the name it was (usually) called."

"Is it not Dhûl Ḥijja?" He said.

And we said, "Indeed it is, O Messenger of Allah."

He said, *"And which city is this?"*

We said, "Allah and His Messenger know best." He (Abû Bakra) said, "We were silent for a while until we thought he would name it with other than the name it was (usually) called."

"Is it not the Holy City?" He said.

And we said, "Indeed it is, O Messenger of Allah."

"And what day is this?" He said.

We said, "Allah and His Messenger know best."

He (Abû Bakra) said, "We were silent for a while until we thought he would name it with other than the name it was (usually) called."

"Is it not the Day of Sacrifice?" He said.

We said, "Indeed it is, O Messenger of Allah."

---

[378] See note 13.

[379] Muḍar is the clan of the Prophet Muhammad ﷺ They considered the month of Rajab to be sacred, whereas some other Arab clans mentioned different months in addition to the three months agreed upon, which are the three months of Ḥajj also mentioned in this *ḥadîth*.

Then he said, *"Surely your blood and your wealth are sacrosanct."* And Muḥammad bin Abû Bakra said, *"I think he also said, 'and your honour.'"* *"They are as sacred as this day of yours, in this city of yours, in this month of yours. You will meet your Lord and He will ask you about your actions. So do not return to error after me when some of you will strike the necks of others amongst you. Indeed, let the one who is present inform the one who is absent; and so might it be that some of those who hear might be more heedful than those who pass on (this message)."* Muḥammad bin Sirîn[380] would say when he heard this, "Indeed it was as the Messenger of Allah ﷺ said." Then he would say, *"have I not passed on (the message)?"*

The Shaykh said, "The fighting and killing of Muslims and taking their possessions without a legitimate right has been forbidden throughout the year, according to this *ḥadîth* and others, and the sanctity of these sacred months means there is an additional penalty for accidental killing during them. Blame is greater for wrongdoing in them, and reward is increased for obedience in them. And by Allah is enabling success."

Narration 230

It has been related on the authority of Abû Hurayra,[381] who said, "I heard the Messenger of Allah ﷺ say: *'The best fast after the month of Ramaḍân is the Month of Allah, Muḥarram, and the best prayer after the compulsory prayer is the night prayer.'"* [382]

---

[380] Ibn Sirîn was either a freed slave or the son of a freed slave, according to different sources, and a client of the Companion Anas ibn Mâlik (see note 24). According to Ibn Ḥibbân, his father was freed by Anas, and the son remained with the Companion from the time of his birth in 28H (648 CE) until Anas' death. He related *ḥadîth* from many of the great Companions, and was known as a mystic, a scholar, and an interpreter of dreams. He died in Basra in 110H (729 CE).

[381] See note 83.

[382] Related by Muslim (2/821), al-Tirmidhî (2/301), Abû Dawûd (2/811), Nasâ'î (3/206) and Aḥmad (2/342 - 344).

Narration 231

It has been related on the authority of Abû Hurayra, who said, "I heard the Messenger of Allah ﷺ say: *'The best prayer after the compulsory ones is the night prayer, and the best fast after the month of Ramaḍân is the month of Allah that you call Muḥarram.'"* [383]

Narration 232

It has been related on the authority of Ibn Sa'd, who said that a man came to 'Alî[384] and said to him: "O Commander of the Faithful, tell me which month I should fast in addition to Ramaḍân." He said, "Indeed you have asked something that I have not heard anyone ask since someone asked the Messenger of Allah ﷺ about it." And he said, "If you are to fast any month in addition to the month of Ramaḍân, fast the month of Muḥarram, for surely it is the month of Allah. In it is a day on which some people turn (to Him) and some people are turned to others." [385]

---

[383] Related by Muslim (2/821) and Aḥmad (2/229-303).
[384] See note 65.
[385] Related by Al-Tirmidhî (3/117).

Chapter Twenty-Seven

The Day of 'Âshûrâ'

Abdul Aziz Ahmed comments:
The Day of 'Âshûrâ' is the tenth of Muḥarram. It is one of the most Sacred Days of the year. Abdul Ḥamîd Qudus says in *Kanz al-Najâḥ wa al-Surûr* (p. 21):

> *"Know that what is required on the Day of 'Âshûrâ' is to bring to life the night preceding it, as this is one of the greatest things that the Islamic Way recommends because of the spiritual blessings it contains and the outpouring of goodness. (One should worship Allah), especially through recitation of the Noble Quran and listening to it, and to do the things which have been related of supplications and litanies of remembrance."*

Narration 233

It is reported on the authority of Sâîd ibn Jubayr that Ibn Abbâs[386] said, "When the Prophet ﷺ came to Madina and he found that the Jews used to fast on the Day of 'Âshûrâ', he said: *'What is this day that you fast?'*
They said, "This is a mighty day. Allah saved Moses on it and He drowned Pharaoh on it, and so Moses fasted this day in gratitude."
And so the Messenger of Allah ﷺ said, *'We have a greater right to Moses than you.'* And so the Messenger of Allah ﷺ fasted and ordered others to fast." [387]

Narration 234

Al-Rubayyi' the daughter of Mu'awwidh bin 'Afrâ'[388] said that on the morning of the Day of 'Âshûrâ', the Messenger of Allah ﷺ sent to the villages of the Helpers[389] who lived around Madina (the following message): *"Whoever started the fast this morning should complete his fast and whoever did not start the fast should complete the remainder of the day."* She said, "After that we fasted. Our young children fasted, and we made toys out of palm branches for them, and we took them to the mosque. If any of them cried for food, we would give it to them so that they could break their fast with it." [390]

---

[386] See notes 14 and 23.
[387] Related by al-Bukhârî (2/251), Muslim (2/796) Abû Dawūd (2/818), Ibn Mâjah (1/552) and Aḥmad (1/291-336).
[388] Mu'awwidh bin 'Afrâ' was a Companion from the Anṣâr tribe of Khazraj, who was one of the two brothers credited with the killing of Abû Jahl at the Battle of Badr. After killing Abû Jahl, Mu'awwidh was martyred in the same battle along with his brother 'Auf. He was actually Mu'awwidh bin al-Ḥârith, but was attributed to his mother, who was fortunate enough to have six children fight at the Battle of Badr. She was one of the first women to embrace Islam among the people of Madina.
[389] The Muslims of Madina were of two groups, those who migrated from Makkah, and the people of Madina who welcomed them and supported them. The first are referred to as *Muhâjirûn*, Migrants, and the second as *Anṣâr*, Helpers.
[390] Related by al-Bukhârî (2/242), Muslim (2/242) and Aḥmad (6/359).

Narration 235

'Ubaidallah ibn Abû Yazîd heard Ibn 'Abbâs[391] say that the Messenger of Allah ﷺ did not strive to attain the benefit of any day's fast like this day, the Day of 'Âshûrâ', and the month of Ramaḍan.[392]

Narration 236

On the authority of Abû Qatâda who said the Messenger of Allah ﷺ said: *"Fasting the Day of 'Âshûrâ' wipes out (the sins) of the previous year, and fasting the Day of 'Arafat wipes out two years: the year before it and the year after it."* [393]

The Shaykh, the Imâm, may Allah be pleased with him, said, "This applies to one who fasts and has made transgressions which require atonement. For if he fasts and his transgressions have already been atoned for, then it is turned into an increase in his spiritual rank. And by Allah is enabling success."

The Shaykh, may Allah be pleased with him, said, "Traditions have been narrated about the blessings of fasting the Day of 'Âshûrâ', in some of the chains there are people who are unknown."

Narration 237

It was been reported that Ibn 'Abbâs said that the Messenger of Allah ﷺ said: *"Whoever fasts the Day of 'Âshûrâ' will be given the reward of sixty years of worship by its fasting and standing (during its night). Whoever fasts the Day of*

---

[391] See note 17.

[392] Related by al-Bukhârî (Book of Fasting *ḥadîth* number 224),Muslim (2/797) and al-Nasâ'î (4/204).

[393] Related by Muslim (2/818) and al-Tirmidhî (3/142).

'Âshûrâ' will be given the reward of ten thousand angels. Whoever fasts the Day of 'Âshûrâ' will be given the reward of a thousand major pilgrimages (Ḥajj) and a thousand minor pilgrimages ('Umra). Whoever fasts the Day of 'Âshûrâ' will be given the reward of ten thousand martyrs. Whoever fasts the Day of 'Âshûrâ' will be given the reward of the seven heavens. Whoever provides food for a believer to break his fast with him on the Day of 'Âshûrâ', it will be as if he provided iftâr (the meal to break the fast) for all the poor of the nation of Muḥammad ﷺ Whoever satisfies a hungry person on the Day of 'Âshûrâ', it is as if he fed all the poor of the nation of Muḥammad ﷺ and filled their stomachs. And whoever wipes his hand over the head of an orphan on the Day of 'Âshûrâ' will be raised a rank in the Garden for every hair of his head."

'Umar, may Allah be pleased with him, said, "O Messenger of Allah, indeed Allah, the Majestic and Mighty, has blessed us on the Day of 'Âshûrâ'!"

He said, *"Yes, Allah created the heavens on the Day of 'Âshûrâ', and likewise the earths. He created the Throne ('Arsh) on the Day of 'Âshûrâ', and likewise the Footstool (Kursî). He created the mountains on the Day of 'Âshûrâ', and likewise the stars. He created the Pen on the Day of 'Âshûrâ', and likewise the Tablet. He created the Archangel Jibrîl, and his angels on the Day of 'Âshûrâ'. He created Adam, upon him be peace, on the Day of 'Âshûrâ', and likewise Ḥawâ' (Eve). He created the Heaven on the Day of 'Âshûrâ' and Adam took residence in it on the Day of 'Âshûrâ'. Ibrâhîm (Abraham) was born on the Day of 'Âshûrâ', and He saved him from the fire on the Day of 'Âshûrâ'. He provided him safety on the Day of 'Âshûrâ'. He drowned the Pharaoh on the Day of 'Âshûrâ'. He raised 'Idrîs (Enoch) ﷺ on the Day of 'Âshûrâ'. He lifted the tribulation of 'Ayyûb (Job) on the Day of 'Âshûrâ'. 'Isa ibn Maryam (Jesus) was raised on the Day of 'Âshûrâ', and he was born on the Day of 'Âshûrâ'. Allah turned to Adam on the Day of 'Âshûrâ'. The mistake of Dawûd (David) was forgiven on the Day of 'Âshûrâ'. The Prophet ﷺ was born on the Day of 'Âshûrâ'. The Lord, Mighty and Majestic is He, reclined on the Throne on the Day of 'Âshûrâ'. And the Day of Resurrection will be on the Day of 'Âshûrâ'."*

Qaḍi Abû Bakr[394] said, "The Reclining is without physical touching or movement in a manner that is appropriate to His Esteemed Essence."
The Shaykh, may Allah be pleased with him, said, "This *ḥadîth* is denounced (*munkar*) and its chain is extremely weak, and I absolve myself before Allah of what it contains; for in its text is that which is not correct, including what it relates regarding the creation of all the heavens and the earths and mountains on the Day of 'Âshûrâ'. Allah the Exalted has said, '*Your Guardian-Lord is Allah, Who created the heavens and the earth in six days, and is firmly established on the throne (of authority)*' (al-'Araf 7:54). It is inconceivable that the whole year occurred on the Day of 'Âshûrâ' which itself indicates the weakness of this transmission.' And Allah knows best.
And there is some difference of opinion about fasting the Day of 'Âshûrâ', was it compulsory in the beginning and then abrogated, or was it never compulsory? Those who think that it was compulsory and then abrogated use the following as their evidence:"

Narration 238

'Aisha[395], may Allah be pleased with her, said that the Messenger of Allah ﷺ ordered us to fast the Day of Âshûrâ' before the fast of Ramaḍân was made compulsory. And so after the fast of Ramaḍân was made compulsory, whoever wished to fast, did so, and whoever wished not to, did not fast.[396]

---

[394] Muḥammad bin Abu Bakr b. al-'Arabi was an Andalusian jurist and scholar specialising in the Mâlikî school of law and was a famed commentator on Quran and *ḥadîth.* He wrote a commentary on the collection of al-Tirmidhî. He was born in Seville in 468H (1076 CE) and died in Fez in 543H (1148 CE).

[395] See note 23.
[396] Related by Muslim (2/250), al-Tirmidhî (3/127), Abû Dawûd (2/817) and Aḥmad (6/248).

And the Shaykh, may Allah be pleased with him, said, “And those who assert that it was never compulsory – and that is the correct opinion – use the following:”

Narration 239

Ḥumayd, the son of ‘Abdul Raḥmân ibn ‘Awf said he heard Mu’âwiyya ibn Abû Sufyân on the Day of ‘Âshûrâ’ in the year that he performed Ḥajj say from the pulpit: “O People of Madina! Where are your scholars? I heard the Messenger of Allah ﷺ say, *‘Surely this day is the Day of ‘Âshûrâ’. Allah has not made fasting it compulsory for you. So whoever wishes to fast, should do so, and whoever wishes not to fast, should not do so.’*” [397]

The Shaykh said about his words, “Allah has not made fasting it compulsory” indicates that it was never made obligatory, as the use of the word *‘lam’* negates the past tense. In this is an indication that the command to fast was meant as a recommendation (and not a compulsion).”

And the Shaykh said, “‘Abdullah ibn ‘Umar and ‘Aisha, may Allah be pleased with them both,[398] said that the Prophet ﷺ said that the Day of ‘Âshûrâ’ is a day on which the People of *Jâhilliya* used to fast, and so whoever wishes to fast it, should do so, and whoever wants to leave it, should do so.[399]

---

[397] Related by al-Bukhârî (2/250), Muslim (2/795) and al-Nasâ’î (2/793).

[398] See notes 81 and 23.

[399] Related by Muslim (2/794).

Chapter Twenty-Eight
The Preference of Fasting the Ninth of Muḥarram Along With the Tenth

Narration 240

Abû Ghaṭafân bin Ṭarîf said, "I heard 'Abdullah ibn 'Abbâs[400] say, 'When the Messenger of Allah ﷺ fasted the Day of 'Âshûrâ' and he ordered others to fast it, they said, "O Messenger of Allah! Indeed it is a day that the Jews and the Christians glorify." And the Messenger of Allah ﷺ said, *'Next year we will fast the ninth if Allah, the Exalted, so wills.'*"[401]

Narration 241

It has been reported on the authority of Ibn 'Abbâs who said the Messenger of Allah ﷺ said: *"If I live, God-Willing, to next year, I will fast the ninth."* He said it was out of fear that he might miss the Day of 'Âshûrâ.'[402]

And the Shaykh, may Allah be pleased with him, said that al-Shâfi'î said something similar regarding fasting on the ninth.

---

[400] See note 17.
[401] Related by Muslim (2/797 -798) and Abû Dawûd (2/818).
[402] Related by Muslim (2/896-7), Ibn Mâjah (1/552) and Aḥmad (1/224 - 236).

Narration 242

On the authority of Ibn Jurayj who said, "Ibn 'Aṭâ' informed me that he heard Ibn 'Abbâs say, 'Fast the ninth and tenth to distinguish yourself from the Jews.'"

The Shaykh, may Allah be pleased with him, said, "This (narration is) attributed to Ibn 'Abbâs. It is consistent with the narration of Abû Ghaṭafân from Ibn 'Abbâs that the Prophet ﷺ was determined to fast the ninth to differentiate (the Muslims) from the Jews. It is one of the two reasons for fasting the ninth with the tenth. There are other narrations that are attributed to the Messenger ﷺ."[403]

Narration 243

On the authority of Dawûd ibn 'Ali from his father from his grandfather, Ibn 'Abbâs, who said, *"The Messenger of Allah ﷺ said, 'Fast the Day of 'Âshûrâ', and distinguish (yourselves) from the Jews by fasting the day before it or the day after it.'"* [404]

---

[403] A *marfû' ḥadîth* is one where the chain of narrators goes all the way back to the Prophet ﷺ as the following one does. Whereas a *mawqûf* one ends with the Companion as the previous one did. Here he points out that although the one related above is *mawqûf,* there are others that are not.

[404] Related by Aḥmad (1/241).

Chapter Twenty-Nine

On What Has Been Related About Spending Generously on One's Family on the Day of 'Âshûrâ'

Narration 244

On the authority of 'Alqama from 'Abdullah[405] who said the Messenger of Allah ﷺ said: "*Whoever spends generously on his dependents on the Day of 'Âshûrâ', Allah will spend generously on him for the rest of the year.*"

Narration 245

Abû Sâîd al-Khudrî[406] said that the Messenger of Allah ﷺ said: "*Whoever spends generously on his family on the Day of 'Âshûrâ', Allah will spend generously on him for the rest of the year.*"

The Shaykh, may Allah be pleased with him, said that this has been related in two different ways from Jâbir and Abû Hurayra,[407] both attributed to the Prophet ﷺ.[408]

---

[405] Meaning 'Abdullah ibn Mas'ûd (see note 116). Al-'Alqama here is Ibn Qays, The Tâbi'î, al-Nakha'î, the faqîh, reciter, and scholar of al-Kûfa. It is said that he was the maternal uncle of Ibrâhîm al-Nakha'î. He was born during the life of the Prophet ﷺ, later moving to Madina to seek knowledge, accompanying Ibn Mas'ûd, where he developed and grew in knowledge. Ibn al-Madînî said he was one of the four most knowledge of the knowledge of Ibn Mas'ûd. He relates hadith from many of the great companions, including 'Umar, 'Uthman, 'Alî ibn Abu Ṭalib, 'Aisha, Abu Dardâ, and others. He died in al-Kûfa around the year 60AH. See *Siyar* of Imam Al-Dhahabî (4/53). *(Editor)*

[406] See note 101.

[407] See notes 92 and 83.

[408] According to al-Suyûṭî, the *ḥadîth* is related by al-Ṭabrânî and Ibn Ḥibbân, and is *ṣaḥîh*, authenticated. Al-Munâwî explains that this *ḥadîth* relates to the fact that Allah destroyed

Chapter Thirty

On Using Koḥl on the Day of 'Âshûrâ'

Narration 246

It has been related on the authority of Juwaybir from al-Ḍaḥḥâk (who said that) Ibn 'Abbâs said that the Messenger of Allah ﷺ said: "Whoever wears *koḥl* [409] on his eyes on the Day of 'Âshûrâ' will never suffer from sore eyes."

And the Shaykh ﷺ said this is how it has been related from Bishr bin Ḥamdân bin Bishr ibn al-Qâsim al-Naysaburî from his uncle al-Ḥusayn bin Bishr and I have not seen it in any other narration beside this and Juwaybir is considered to be a weak narrator and al-Ḍaḥḥâk did not meet Ibn 'Abbas. And Allah knows best.

---

everything on the earth by the flood, except the Ark, and then provided for everyone and everything once again. Therefore, whenever we spend on our family, we should remember this event and the fact that He can provide after everything has gone. And Allah knows best.

[409] *Koḥl* is an traditional cosmetic used to color under or around the eyes. It can be made from different materials, such as Antimony, which comes from stibnite (a source of Antimony). In a sound ḥadith, the Prophet ﷺ said that, *"The best of your kohl is Antimony; for it improves the eyesight and makes the hair (eyelashes) grow."* Al-Nasâ'î (8/149), Ibn Mâjah (3/536), and Abû Dawûd (4/536). *(Editor)*

[The Shaykh does not mention anything about the months of Safar or Rabî' al-Awwal]

Abdul Aziz Ahmed comments: Safar and Rabî' al-Awwal

Ṣafar

There were many superstitions that the pre-Islamic Arabs associated with the month of Ṣafar. The Prophet ﷺ clarified these, and set some important principles about the blessings of specific times, and the drawing of bad omens from times and events.

Ṣafar was considered by some to be a sacred month, with some Arabs recognising its sanctity one year and then Muḥarram the next. Some used to "save up" the bad actions they had intended during the three sacred months. As soon as Ṣafar entered, they immediately plunged into the acts forbidden in the Sacred Months. Others felt that all the good that was accumulated during the three Sacred Months that preceded Ṣafar was counteracted by "evil" associated with Ṣafar. They would avoid travel, marriage, or anything of importance.

The fact that it was not a sacred month was clarified in the verses and *ḥadith* mentioned in the Chapter on Rajab and the Chapter on Muḥarram. The four sacred months have always been sacred and will always be sacred according to the words of the Messenger ﷺ. This was the first misunderstanding that he rectified.

He warned us not to draw bad omens from events such as illness, birds flying in a particular direction, or at a particular time. Islam prohibited these superstitions. Imam Aḥmad and Imam Muslim relate on the authority of Jâbir that the Messenger of Allah ﷺ said: *"There is no bad omen in contagious disease, nor in birds, nor in carrion bugs, nor in Ṣafar, and there are no desert demons."* He taught us that contagious diseases are exactly that – diseases spread from one person to another or from one animal to another. He advised us that we should avoid mixing with others if we have a contagious disease, and we should avoid mixing with carriers of the disease if we are healthy. These are the practical implications of the *ḥadîth.*

Ṣafar was not the only month considered unlucky. The month of Shawwâl was considered a month that you should not marry in because it brings bad luck and disease. This was because some Bedouin Arabs drew a bad omen from the fact that, on one occasion, plague spread among them in the month of Shawwâl. The Prophet ﷺ ended this superstition in a practical way by marrying his beloved 'Aisha, and also Umm Salama, in the month of Shawwâl.

One of the reasons it was important to make sure the Arabs and the later generations understood that time is something created by Allah and that He placed greater value in some times more than others, was to guide us to be "in tune" with His patterns and rhythms, and not to those of soothsayers and stargazers. In a more modern context, we should not allow the media and social pressures to dictate our time management. We should seek the blessings of time as set out by the Prophet ﷺ, and live in tune with the natural patterns of the Sun and the Moon which run according to His will.

The Arabs would not travel in the days before the new moon nor on the last Wednesday of the lunar month. They would refer to them as *al-Muḥâq* days, and many Bedouins would seek permission from the stargazers to check if it was safe to travel. The various *ḥadîth* mentioning Ṣafar, including the one quoted above, highlight this point. As for the Wednesdays, Abdul Ḥamîd Qudus mentions that al-Bayhaqî in his *Branches of Faith* relates that, *"supplication made on Wednesdays will not be rejected."* It is well known that the Prophet's ﷺ supplication at the Battle of the Trench was accepted on Wednesday between midday and mid-afternoon. This was after he made the same supplication on the Monday and Tuesday. And Allah knows best.

The Prophet ﷺ did not forbid the drawing of good omens from things. This is because he had an optimistic outlook. For example, seeing rain as a sign of Allah's mercy descending was natural for those who could see signs in Allah's creation.

As for those who continue to see signs in time, some have established that the last Wednesday of Ṣafar is not a time of bad omens, but is actually the time on which Allah causes the tribulations of the year to descend, similar to the way in which He causes the blessings on the Night of Power to descend in Ramaḍân. Abdul Ḥamîd Qudus says in *Kanz al-Najâḥ wa Surûr* (p25):

> *Some of the Gnostics from the People of Unveiling and Certainty mention that six hundred major tribulations and twenty thousand minor tribulations are sent down each year. All of them on the last Wednesday of Ṣafar. Therefore that day is the most difficult of all days.*

He then goes on to recommend that we pray for protection on the first night of Safar, throughout the month, and in particular on the last Wednesday. There are many verses of protection in the Quran, and supplications in the *ḥadîth* literature that are recommended to protect us from evil. Some of these are included in the appendices.

Rabî' al-Awwal

Rabî' al-Awwal literally means the "first spring." It is derived from the root letters r-b-'a. The origin of the verb is to take a fourth part of the spoils of war, and by extension for a camel to drink on the fourth day after not having water for three days. This last image is what makes the meaning of "spring" so significant. For this reason, one would use the verb saying *"raba'a al-matr al-'ard" (the rain brought life to ground),* and when using the passive voice *rubi'at al-'ibl* (the camels were rained upon), as opposed to them drinking after three days with no water. Spring is the time of rejuvenation, and rain in the desert context is about life and the pouring down of blessing. Another extension of the original meaning is to make a group complete by becoming the fourth or fortieth person in that group. Therefore, the month of Rabî' al-Awwal is seen as the month of completion and perfection, and the month of rejuvenation, the pouring down of blessing, and of life itself. Allah planned that this was to be the month of the birth of the Prophet ﷺ, the month of his migration to Madina, and the month of his departure from this world to the next.

The month of Rabî' al-Awwal is traditionally one for reconnecting with the Prophet ﷺ through praying upon him, reading his biography, and trying to emulate his behaviour, inwardly and outwardly.

Abdul Ḥamîd Qudus says in *Kanz al-Najâḥ wa al-Surûr* (p43)

> *Know that it is required in this month to be abundant in prayers and salutations upon our Prophet the master of all people ﷺ, and to increase our reverence and honour towards him, for this is a mighty month. Indeed, in it a general goodness became manifest, and in it rose the felicity of the felicitous ones through, the rising of our Prophet ﷺ, shining upon all present.*

Chapter Thirty-One
The Blessing of Friday

Allah the Exalted said:

(وَشَاهِدٍ وَمَشْهُودٍ)

By one that witnesses, and the subject of the witness.

(al-Burûj, 85:3)

Narration 247

Abû Hurayra said that the Messenger of Allah ﷺ said: *"The Promised Day"* is the Day of Resurrection and *"one that witnesses"* (as in the above verse) is Friday, and *"the subject of that witness"* (as in the above verse) is the Day of 'Arafat.

The Shaykh, may Allah be pleased with him, said, "From what Allah, the Exalted, has blessed this day with is that it contains the time in which Allah has made compulsory the Jumu'a Prayer, and specified it for the nation of Muḥammad ﷺ, as He said:

(يَا أَيُّهَا الَّذِينَ آمَنُوا إِذَا نُودِي لِلصَّلَاةِ مِن يَوْمِ الْجُمُعَةِ فَاسْعَوْا إِلَى ذِكْرِ اللَّهِ وَذَرُوا الْبَيْعَ ذَلِكُمْ خَيْرٌ لَّكُمْ إِن كُنتُمْ تَعْلَمُونَ)

O you who believe! When the call is proclaimed to prayer on Friday (the Day of Assembly), hasten earnestly to the Remembrance of Allah, and leave off business. That is best for you if you but knew!

(al-Jumu'a, 62:9)

Qatâda said that *"Hasten earnestly"* means "Hasten O son of Adam with your heart and action," which means going to it (that is, the Friday Prayer).

Narration 248

It is reported that Hudhayfa al-Yamâni[410] said the Messenger of Allah ﷺ said: *"Allah allowed those before you to err with regard to the day of congregation. The Jews had Saturday and the Christians had Sunday. So Allah brought us forth, and guided us to Friday, and so we have Friday followed by Saturday and Sunday, and likewise they will follow us on the Day of Resurrection. We are the late comers as people of this world, but the forerunners on the Day of Resurrection, judged before other people"* [411] And the Shaykh, may Allah be pleased with him, said:

Narration 249

"We have related in the *ḥadîth* of 'Aisha,[412] may Allah be pleased with her, that the Messenger of Allah ﷺ said, '*Do you know over what it is that the Jews are jealous towards us?'*

"Allah and his Messenger know best," she replied.

'Surely their jealousy towards us is over the Qibla *that we have been guided towards and they erred from; over the Friday towards which we have been guided and they erred from, and our saying* 'Amin' *behind the Imâm.'"*

---

[410] Hudhayfa bin Yaman was one of the early Companions, and had a special place with the Prophet ﷺ. His father was very old and was told not to attend the Battle of Badr, but he wanted to attain martyrdom, and so after the army had left, he and another aged Companion went to the battlefield but he was mistakenly killed by a Muslim. Hudhayfa was offered blood money, which he refused; saying his father attained what he wished for. Hudhayfa was known for his intelligence, control under pressure, and ability to keep a secret. The Messenger ﷺ used these skills in battle, and in informing him of the names of all the hypocrites. He was not allowed to divulge them and did not break the trust he was given. He died in Kufa 37 AH (658 CE).

[411] Related by Muslim (2/586), al-Nasâ'î (3/86) and Ibn Mâjah (1/344).

[412] See note 23.

Narration 250

Abû Lubâba ibn 'Abdul Mundhir[413] said the Messenger of Allah ﷺ said: *"Surely Friday is the lord of all days, and more mighty with Allah than the 'Eid of Breaking the Fast and the 'Eid of Sacrifice. Five things emanated on it - Allah the Exalted created Adam on it, it contains an hour during which a slave does not ask Allah anything, except that He grants it to him, as long as he does not ask for what is forbidden, and there is no close angel nor heaven nor earth nor mountain nor sea, except that it fears that that particular Friday will bring about the Final Hour."* [414]

Narration 251

It is reported on the authority of Abû Hurayra[415] who said, "I went out to the Mount and met Ka'b al-Aḥbâr[416] and sat with him. He told me things from the Torah, and I told him things that the Messenger of Allah ﷺ had told me. Among the things I told him was that the Messenger of Allah ﷺ said, 'The best day upon which the sun rises is Friday. On it, Adam was created. On it, he was sent out (of the Garden) and on it, he was turned towards (in acceptance by Allah). On it, he died. On it, every beast listens in reverence[417] from the moment it wakes until the sun rises with its evening glow except

---

[413] Abû Lubâba ibn 'Abdul Mundhir's name was Bashîr, although there is some difference of opinion about this. He was one of the Anṣâr from the tribe of Aws. At the battle of Badr, he had prepared himself for war, but the Prophet ﷺ instructed him to stay behind as caretaker of the city. He related *ḥadith* directly from the Messenger ﷺ and through 'Umar ibn al-Khattab (see note 41). He died in Madina sometime between 36 and 40H. And Allah knows best.

[414] Related by Ibn Mâjah (1/344) and Aḥmad (3/430).

[415] See note 83.

[416] See note 282.

[417] There is a misprint in the Ibn Ḥazm edition. If we take the Dar al-Kutub edition to be correct, the word used is *muṣaykh* from *ṣ-y-kh* which implies, according to Lane's Lexicon, 'to listen in silence' or 'to be silent like the frequent chider of camels' or 'to be silent out of respect to the rights of another'. And Allah knows best.

for the *Jinn* and the humankind. During it is an hour that no Muslim slave will be praying, petitioning Allah, except that He will grant him it.'

"A day in every year?" asked Ka'b.

'No, it is every Friday,' I said.

And Ka'b al-Aḥbâr read from the Torah and then he said, "The Messenger ﷺ spoke the truth.""

And Abû Hurayra said, "I met Basra bin Abû Basra al-Ghifârî[418] and he said, 'Where did you meet?'

"At the Mount," I said.

'If I had come across you before you had left you would not have gone out, for I heard the Messenger of Allah ﷺ say, "Do not make a journey (to visit historic sites as an act of worship) except three mosques; and they are the Sacred Mosque (of Makkah), this mosque of mine, and the Mosque of Ilya (Jerusalem) or the Holy House."' And he was unsure which of the two he said (although they both refer to the same mosque.)

And then Abû Hurayra said, "I met 'Abdullah ibn Salâm[419] and I spoke to him about my meeting with Ka'b al-Aḥbâr, and I told him about what Ka'b had said, that it was once in a year. And 'Abdullah ibn Salâm said, 'Ka'b has not spoken the truth.' And I said, "Yes, after that Ka'b read from the Torah and he said, 'Indeed, it is every Friday.'"

---

[418] Here there are several misprints in the Dar al-Kutub edition, including the name of the Companion.

[419] 'Abdullah bin Salâm was a Rabbi and descendent of the Prophet Yûsuf (Joseph), from the Jewish tribe of Banû Qaynuqâ' who were allies of the tribe of Khazraj before they embraced Islam and welcomed the Prophet ﷺ to Madina. His original name was Ḥaṣîn before he became Muslim, and the Prophet ﷺ renamed him 'Abdullah. He became Muslim shortly after the arrival of the Messenger, although it has been said it was in the 8th year. The Prophet ﷺ described him as one of the People of the Garden walking on the earth. Mu'adh ibn Jabal on his death bed advised those around him to hold fast to the knowledge of certain individual Companions, and among them was 'Abdullah ibn Salâm whom he said he heard the Prophet ﷺ say, *"He used to be a Jew, and he is one of the ten promised the Garden."* He related directly from the Messenger ﷺ and many Companions, including Abû Hurayra. His son Yûsuf related from him. He died in Madina in 43H (663 CE).

‘Ka’b spoke the truth,’ said ‘Abdullah ibn Salâm. And ‘Abdullah ibn Salâm said, “Indeed I know what hour it is.”
‘And so tell me about it and do not hold your silence,’ I said.
“It is the last hour of Friday (that is the hour before sunset),” said ‘Abdullah ibn Salâm.
‘How can it be the last hour of Friday when the Messenger ﷺ said, *“It is an hour that no Muslim slave will be praying,”* and during that hour there is no prayer?’ Abû Hurayra said.
And so ‘Abdullah ibn Salâm said, “Did the Messenger of Allah ﷺ not say *‘Whoever sits waiting for the prayer is in a state of prayer until he actually prays?’”*
Abu Huraira said, “I said, ‘Indeed he did.’” He said, “And that is it.”
And the Shaykh, may Allah be pleased with him, said the word *musîkha* means *muṣyikha* (the word used above meaning *“listened to in reverence.”*) Abû Sulaymân says the meaning is *muṣîgha*, to listen, as *aṣâkha* and *istâkha* have the (same) meaning, which is to listen attentively in silence.
And the Shaykh, may Allah be pleased with him, said, “What has been related from the Prophet ﷺ is what is consistent with the words of ‘Abdullah ibn Salâm in his clarification of the special hour on Fridays.”

Narration 252

It has been related on the authority of Jâbir ibn ‘Abdullah[420] that the Messenger of Allah ﷺ said: *“On Fridays, a Muslim slave will not be found asking Allah, except that he will be granted what he asks, and so seek it during the last hour after ‘Asr (the mid afternoon prayer).”*

[420] See note 92.

And the Shaykh, may Allah be pleased with him, said, it has been related on the authority of Fâṭima,[421] the daughter of the Prophet ﷺ that "It is when the sun appears close due to its setting."
And it has been related in other forms:

Narration 253

Abû Barda, the son of Abû Mûsâ al-Ash'arî said that 'Abdullah ibn 'Umar[422] said to me, "Have you heard your father mention what the Messenger of Allah ﷺ said about the special hour on Friday?"
"Yes," I said. "I heard the Messenger of Allah ﷺ say, *'It is between the time that the Imâm sits and the end of the Prayer.'*" [423]
The Shaykh, may Allah be pleased with him, said the Prophet ﷺ used to know exactly when the time was, but he was made to forget it just as he was made to forget the Night of Power so that the servant would spend all his day in remembrance and supplication.

Narration 254

On the authority of Abû Mûsâ al-Asharî,[424] it has been reported that the Messenger of Allah ﷺ said: *"Indeed Allah, the Exalted, will resurrect the days on the Day of Resurrection in their current form, and Friday will be resurrected as a shining light. Its people will surround it like the bride gifted to her husband. It will glow for them flowing through their varying colours like white ice. Their scent will radiate like musk absorbed into a mountain of camphor. People will look at them*

[421] See note 355.
[422] See note 81.
[423] Related by Muslim (2/584) and Abû Dawûd (1/636).
[424] See note 76.

unable to turn away their gazes out of amazement until they enter the Garden, and no one will accompany them other than the Callers to Prayer who kept account (of the prayer times)."

Narration 255

On the authority of Abû Hurayra,[425] it has been reported that the Prophet ﷺ said: "*The five daily prayers and Jumu'a to Jumu'a wipe out what is between them.*" And Ibn Hishâm and others add, "*as long as they avoid the major sins.*" [426]

Narration 256

Anas[427] said that the Messenger of Allah ﷺ said: "*Surely Allah, the Mighty and Majestic, frees six hundred thousand people from the Fire every Friday, all of whom had earned their places there.*"

---

[425] See note 83.
[426] Related by Muslim (1/209), al-Tirmidhî (1/417) and Aḥmad (2/359 and 414).
[427] See note 30.

Section on the Compulsion to Pray the Jumu'a Prayer

Allah the Exalted has said:

(يَا أَيُّهَا الَّذِينَ آمَنُوا إِذَا نُودِيَ لِلصَّلَاةِ مِن يَوْمِ الْجُمُعَةِ فَاسْعَوْا إِلَىٰ ذِكْرِ اللَّهِ)

O you who believe! When the call is proclaimed to prayer on Friday (the Day of Assembly), hasten earnestly to the Remembrance of Allah.

(al-Jumu'a 62:9)

Narration 257

Al-Ḥakam bin Mînâ' said he was told by both 'Abdullah ibn 'Umar and Abû Hurayra, may Allah be pleased with them all,[428] that they heard the Messenger of Allah ﷺ say while he was on the steps of his pulpit: "*Most certainly people will cease their neglect of Friday Prayers or Allah will definitely seal their hearts.*" [429]

Narration 258

On the authority of Abû al-Aḥwaṣ, it has been reported that 'Abdullah, and he is Ibn Mas'ûd[430], that the Prophet ﷺ said about the people who stayed back from the Friday Prayer: "*I wished I was able to appoint a man to lead the*

[428] See note 81 and 83.
[429] Related by Muslim (in the Book of Friday Prayers, *ḥadîth* number 40), Ibn Mâjah (1/591) and Aḥmad (1/239, 1/354 and 2/84).
[430] See note 117.

people in prayer and then to burn the houses of the men who stayed back from praying the Jumu'a." [431]

Narration 259

Abû al-Ja'd al-Ḍamrî said that the Messenger of Allah ﷺ said: "*Whoever neglects the Jumu'a out of lack of concern for it three times, Allah will seal his heart."* [432]

Narration 260

Abû Ṭâhir al-Faqîh informed us of a similar chain on the authority of Muḥammad ibn 'Amr ibn 'Alqama.

Narration 261

Jâbir ibn 'Abdullah[433] said: "I heard the Messenger of Allah ﷺ saying while on the pulpit, '*O People! Turn to Allah, the Majestic and Mighty, before you die. Hasten to good actions. Fix that which is between you and your Lord by abundant remembrance of Him and by abundant charity, given privately and openly, and you will be rewarded, praised, and provided for. Know that Allah, the Mighty and Majestic, has made the Jumu'a prayer compulsory upon you. It is a compulsion ordained here where I stand, in this month of mine, in this year of mine, and will be binding until the Day of Resurrection for the one who has the means. Whoever neglects it during my life, or after it, denying it or out of making light of it while*

[431] Related by Muslim (1/452) and Aḥmad (1/402,422,448 and 461).
[432] Related by al-Tirmidhi (3/373), Abû Dawûd (1/638), al-Nasâ'î (3/88) and Aḥmad (3/424).
[433] See note 92.

there is an Imâm, whether just or corrupt, Allah will not gather their disunited state of affairs. Indeed, He will not place blessing in any of their affairs. He will have no ritual prayer, no ablution, and indeed no charity, nor pilgrimage or act of goodness until he repents. If he turns back to Allah, Allah will turn to him. A woman will not give protection to a man, a desert Arab will not give protection to a migrant, a wrong doer will not give protection to a believer, except where the ruler oppresses him and he fears his sword and whip.'" [434]

And the Shaykh, may Allah show him mercy, said:

Narration 262

'Ubaid bin Ya'îsh also related on the authority of al-Walîd ibn Bakîr with a different chain to the one above that he said: "The Messenger of Allah ﷺ addressed us on Friday, and he said, *'O you people! Turn to your Lord before you die and hasten to righteous, pure actions before you become occupied.'"* Then the *ḥadîth* continues with the same meaning. This *ḥadîth* has this unique chain. And Allah knows best.

Narration 263

It has been reported on the authority of Abû Mûsâ al-Ash'arî [435]that the Prophet ﷺ said: *"The Jumu'a is an incumbent duty upon every Muslim apart from the following four: a slave, a woman, a child, and a sick person."* [436]

The Shaykh, may Allah be pleased with him, said that the only way that this chain could be connected directly to the Prophet ﷺ was through 'Ubaid al-

---

[434] Related by Ibn Mâjah (1/343).

[435] See note 76.

[436] Related by Abû Dawûd (1/644).

‘Ajal. It was related by Abû Dawûd al-Sajastâni on the authority of ‘Abbas without mentioning Abû Mûsa.

Narration 264

Muḥammad ibn Kathîr said: “I heard al-Awzâ’î say, ‘There was among us a man who went out hunting, travelling on Fridays to hunt, and he would not wait for the Jumu’a prayer. One day, he went out, and he and his mule disappeared with no trace other than its ear.’”

And the Shaykh, may Allah be pleased with him, said, “And we have narrated the following:”

Narration 265

It has been reported on the authority of Mujâhid that a group of people travelled on Friday before the sun had reached its zenith. Their hideout burnt down, but no fire was seen.

And the Shaykh, may Allah be pleased with him, said that this is because attending the Jumu’a becomes a compulsion after the Sun’s passing the zenith, and if they neglected it without any legitimate reason they were deserving of punishment unless Allah pardoned them. However, if they were travellers then there is no problem with them not attending the Jumu’a.

Narration 266

It has been reported on the authority of Tamîm al-Dâri[437] that the Prophet ﷺ said: *"The Jumu'a is a compulsion (on all male Muslims) except on the child, the slave, and the traveller."*

Narration 267

And the Shaykh, may Allah be pleased with him, said: "And Ismâ'îl bin Abân related it on the authority of Muḥammad bin Ṭalḥa, and he added, *'and the woman and the sick person.'*"

[437] See note 233.

Section on the Form of the Ṣalatul Jumu'a (Friday Congregational Prayer) and the Importance of Hastening to It

Narration 268

It has been reported on the authority of Salmân al-Khayr[438] that the Messenger of Allah ﷺ said: *"A man does not take a bath on Friday and then wipe himself with his oil or the perfume of his family and then comes to the Mosque and avoids going in between two people and is silent while the Imâm speaks, except that he is forgiven that which was between this Friday and the previous one."* [439]

And others have narrated it on the authority of Abû Dhi'b and additionally state, *"and purify (themselves) as best they can."* [440]

Narration 269

Abû 'Umâma bin Sahl reports that Abû Hurayra and Abû Sa'îd[441] both said that they heard the Messenger of Allah ﷺ say: *"Whoever takes a bath on Friday, brushes his teeth and wipes on perfume if he has some, and wears his best clothes, and then comes to the mosque and does not strain the necks of people (by pushing in between them in the rows). and prays whatever prayer cycles Allah wills, and then is silent once the Imâm comes and until he prays, it will be atonement for whatever happened between this Friday and the one before it."*

And Abû Hurayra would say, "And three days more, surely Allah the Exalted has magnified reward by ten times." [442]

---

[438] See note 36.
[439] Related by al-Bukhârî (1/213) and al-Nasâ'î (3/104).
[440] Related by al-Bukhârî (1/213).
[441] See notes 83 and 101.
[442] Related by Abû Dawûd (244-245) and Aḥmad (3/81).

Narration 270

Aws ibn Aws said that the Messenger of Allah ﷺ said regarding Friday: *"Whoever washes and cleans himself, and sets off early in the afternoon and (thereby is able to sit) close (to the Imâm), and is silent and listens, will be forgiven that which occurred between the last Friday and this one and in addition three more days. Whoever wipes a stone has been frivolous."* [443]

Hassân ibn 'Aṭiyya relates it on the authority of Abû al-Ash'ath except that he said, *"Then went early and promptly, and walked and did not ride, and (sat) close to the Imâm and listened and did not speak (or act) frivolously, he will have with every footstep, the reward of a year's fasting and praying at night."* [444]

Narration 271

Aws ibn Aws al-Thaqafî[445] said: "I heard the Messenger of Allah ﷺ say, *'Whoever takes a bath on Friday and washes, then goes promptly and early ....'*" and then he mentions the above.

And the Shaykh, may Allah be pleased with him, said regarding his words, *"takes a bath"* means washes his head including the foremost part (that is the nose and mouth) and then washes himself. And this is the opinion of Makḥûl and Sa'îd bin 'Abdul 'Azîz.

---

[443] Related by al-Tirmidhî (2/367-368) and al-Nasâ'î (2/95). The *ḥadîth* cites touching a stone as an act of frivolity to show the importance of focusing one's full attention on the Imâm. And Allah knows best.

[444] Related by Abû Dawûd (1/246), al-Nasâ'î (3/95), Ibn Mâjah (1/246) and Aḥmad (4/9-10).

[445] Aws bin Aws was born in Tâif, to the South of Makkah, into the tribe of Banû Thaqîf. They were allies of the Quraysh and strongly opposed the Prophet ﷺ in the early years of his mission. After the Battle of Tabûk, they sent a small delegation to Madina, and among them was Aws bin Aws, who embraced Islam. He joined the Muslims in Madina before moving to Damascus where he died in 59H or 63H (679CE or 682CE).

Narration 272

And in the *ḥadîth* of Ibn 'Abbâs (it is related) that the Messenger ﷺ said: "*Take a bath on Friday and wash your heads.*"

Narration 273

And in the *ḥadîth* of Abû Hurayra (it is related) that the Messenger ﷺ said: "*When it is Friday, a man should take a bath and wash his head.*" And this indicates the correctness of this interpretation.

And there are some who narrate the *ḥadîth* using the intense form "*ghassala*" with a doubling of the 's', and what is intended by that is that he necessitates a bath upon his wife by his intimacy with her, so that he does not look at that which is forbidden.[446] The first interpretation is correct.

Narration 274

It reached Sa'îd ibn Musayyib from Abû Hurayra[447] that the Prophet ﷺ said: "*When Friday comes, there will be angels on every door of the mosque writing the names of those who enter, one at a time (in order as they enter). Whoever hastens to the prayer (at the time of the call) is as one who has ritually sacrificed a she-camel, and the one who comes after is as the one who has sacrificed a cow, and the one who comes after is as one who has sacrificed a sheep...*", until he mentioned a chicken

[446] What is implied in this statement is that the narration of the *ḥadîth* in the form mentioned suggests that the husband should approach his wife and fulfil his sexual needs, so that when he goes to the mosque, he feels satisfied and will not feel the need to look at that which is forbidden including the opposite sex. And Allah knows best.

[447] See note 83.

and an egg. *"And when the Imâm sits, the pages (of the scribing angels) are closed and they gather to listen to the sermon."* [448]

Narration 275

It has been reported on the authority of Abû Bakr al-Ṣiddîq,[449] may Allah be pleased with him, that a desert Arab came to the Prophet ﷺ and said: "O Messenger of Allah, it has reached me that you say, 'From Jumu'a to Jumu'a, and the five daily prayers wipe out (the sins) of what is between them, as long as the major sins are avoided." And he said, *"Yes."* And then the Messenger of Allah ﷺ added: *"The ritual bath on Friday is an atonement, and every step the walker takes is like twenty years of good action, and once he leaves the Jumu'a Prayer he is rewarded with the reward of two hundred years of good action."*

---

[448] Related by Muslim (Book of Friday Prayer, *ḥadîth* 24) al-Nasâ'î (2/98), Ibn Mâjah (1/347) and Aḥmad (2/239).

[449] Abû Bakr was called *al-Ṣiddîq, the faithful one*, because of his unflinching belief in the Messenger ﷺ. He was a close friend of the Messenger ﷺ before he received Prophethood, and was the first adult male to believe in him and to support him. He facilitated the conversion of many of the early Muslims through his outstanding character and standing in the community. He was the closest and most beloved Companion, sharing the journey of migration to Madina, and succeeding the Prophet as the leader of the Muslim community.

Section on Prayer upon the Prophet ﷺ

He said (as the full title of the section)...*On the eve of Friday and the day of Friday and on the blessing of reading the Chapter of Qurân known as Surah al-Kahf.*

Narration 276

Aws ibn Aws[450] said that the Messenger of Allah ﷺ said: *"Surely among your most bountiful days is Friday, the day on which Adam was created. On it he died. On it will be the blowing of the trumpet and the Resurrection, and so pray upon me, for surely your prayers will be shown to me."* And they said to him, "O Messenger of Allah, how can our prayers be shown to you when you have turned to dust?" They said, "When you have decomposed?" He said, *"Surely Allah, Mighty and Majestic, forbade the earth to consume the bodies of the prophets."*

Narration 277

Anas ibn Mâlik[451], the servant of the Prophet ﷺ said that the Prophet ﷺ said: *"The closest to me on the Day of Resurrection in every place will be the one of you who did the most prayer upon me in the temporal world. Whoever prays upon me on Friday, or the eve of Friday, Allah will fulfil a hundred of his needs; seventy otherworldly and thirty from the temporal world. And then Allah will appoint an angel to take responsibility for (that prayer) and present it to me in my grave as presents are presented, informing me who it was that prayed upon me, mentioning his name, his lineage and his origin, and after that it is established with me on a piece of white paper."*

---

[450] See note 445.
[451] See note 30.

Narration 278

Anas said that the Messenger of Allah ﷺ said: *"Pray abundantly upon me on Fridays and during the night preceding Friday, for whoever prays upon me one prayer, Allah will pray upon him ten times."*

Narration 279

It has been reported on the authority of Razîn al-Khulqâni that Ja'far ibn Muḥammad,[452] may Allah be pleased with him, said: "(Every) Thursday afternoon, Allah sends down angels from the sky to the earth, with them are parchments from freshly cut trees, and in their hands are pens of gold. They record the prayers upon Muḥammad ﷺ made during that day, that night, and until the setting of the sun (on Friday)."

Narration 280

Abû Sa'îd al-Khudrî said that the Messenger of Allah ﷺ said: *"Whoever reads the Chapter of the Cave*[453] *on Fridays will have a light shining from him to the Ancient House."* [454]

And the Shaykh, may Allah be pleased with him, said: "And Sa'îd bin Manṣûr related it from Hishâm with a chain which stops short at Abû Sa'îd al-Khudrî." [455]

---

[452] Ja'far bin Muḥammad bin 'Ali bin al-Ḥusayn bin 'Ali bin Abu Talib, Al- Ṣâdiq. A fiqh and imam, from the noble family of the Prophet ﷺ. He was of the highest caliber narrators of the ḥadîth of the Prophet ﷺ, and multitudes took from him include the Imams of Ahl al-Sunna such as Mâlik, Abu Ḥanifa, Suyfan al-Thawri and ibn 'Uyayna. He died in 148AH in Madina, May Allah be pleased with him. *(Editor)*

[453] *Surah al-Kahf*, the twentieth chapter of Quran.

[454] That is, the Holy House of Makkah known as the Ka'ba.

[455] Al-Suyûṭî says it was related by Ibn Ḥibbân and is classified as a good (*ḥasan*) *ḥadîth*.

Narration 281

On the authority of 'Awn ibn 'Abdullah, it has been reported that 'Asmâ the daughter of Abû Bakr[456] said that whoever reads the Opening Chapter of the Quran, and the last three chapters seven times, will be protected from that time until the next Friday.

And the Shaykh, may Allah be pleased with him, said: "Ḥumayd bin Zanjawayhi related it on the authority of Ja'far bin 'Awn with his chain, yet it ends short of the Messenger of Allah ﷺ." [457]

[456] Asmâ was the older sister of 'Aisha bint Abû Bakr (see notes 19 and 433). Her parents were divorced before the Prophecy of Muḥammad ﷺ. She lived with her father, and was therefore one of the first to embrace Islam. At the time of the Migration to Madina, she used to carry food to the Prophet ﷺ and her father, who were hiding in the Cave of Thawr. She used to carry the food tied around her waist using two bands, and was affectionately given the title *Dhat al-Naṭâqayn, Possessor of the two belts.* She had recently married the Prophet's cousin Zubayr ibn Awwâm, and was pregnant with his son 'Abdullah bin Zubayr who was the first baby born in the new Muslim community in Madina. She is famed for her fierce fighting in the Battle of Yarmuk. She died shortly after the murder of her son in 73H (692CE) aged 100 years.

[457] This is described as '*mawqûf*' meaning that it is a chain going as far as the Companion of the Prophet ﷺ but not actually saying he or she heard it from the Messenger ﷺ himself. And Allah knows best.

Section on the Blessings of Fasting on Fridays

Narration 282

'Abdullah ibn Ma'sûd said: "The Messenger of Allah ﷺ used to fast the first three days of every month, and would rarely miss fasting on Fridays." [458]

Narration 283

It is related on the authority of a man from Banî Jusham that Abû Hurayra said that the Messenger of Allah ﷺ said: "*Whoever fasts on Friday will have the reward of ten days of the next world recorded, and these are not like the days of this temporal world.*"

And the Shaykh, may Allah be pleased with him, said that the Follower (that is, the unnamed man in the *ḥadîth* above) was Sa'îd bin 'Abdul Azîz al-Darâwardî.

Narration 284

Walîd ibn Qays was informed by Abû Sa'îd al-Khudrî that the Messenger of Allah ﷺ said: "*Whoever fasts on Friday and visits a sick person, attends a funeral, gives charity, and frees a slave on that day will enter the Garden, if Allah the Exalted wills.*"

---

[458] Related by al-Tirmidhî (3/118), Abû Dawûd (2/822) al-Nasâ'î (4/204) and Aḥmad (1/406).

Narration 285

It has been reported on the authority of Abû Hurayra that the Prophet ﷺ said: *"Whoever fasts on Friday, visits a sick person, attends a funeral, and gives charity has indeed made it incumbent (that is, the Garden)."*

And the Shaykh, may Allah be pleased with him said: Al-Khalîl bin Murrah related it with a chain on the authority of Jâbir connecting it to the Prophet ﷺ with the same meaning, except that he reported that he said: *"And he will not stick to sin for the (next) forty years."*

Narration 286

Abû Hurayra said that the Messenger of Allah ﷺ said: *"One should not fast on a Friday, except if he fasts the day before it or the day after it."* [459]

Narration 287

'Âmir bin Ladîn al-Ash'arî asked Abû Hurayra about fasting on Fridays. He said: "I heard the Messenger of Allah ﷺ say, *'Indeed Friday is a day of celebration and remembrance, so don't make your day of celebration a day of fasting but rather make it a day of remembrance, unless you combine it with other days.'"*

[459] Related by al-Bukhârî (2/248), Muslim (2/801) al-Tirmidhî (3/119), Abû Dawûd (2/805) and Ibn Mâjah (1/459).

Narration 288

Al-Walîd ibn 'Abdul Raḥmân mentioned that Ibn 'Umar[460] said to al-Ḥumrân: "Has it not reached you that the Messenger of Allah ﷺ said, *'Surely the most preferred prayers with Allah are the Morning Prayer and the Jumu'a prayer in congregation.'*"

Narration 289

It has been reported on the authority of Sahl ibn Sa'd al-Sâ'idî[461] that the Messenger of Allah ﷺ said: *"Surely you have in every Friday a lesser and major pilgrimage (*Ḥajj *and* 'Umra*). The major pilgrimage is in hastening to the Jumu'a, and the lesser pilgrimage is in waiting for the afternoon ('Asr) prayer after the Jumu'a."*

The Shaykh, may Allah be pleased with him, said, "These two are *gharîb ḥadîth*[462] about praying the Morning prayer and the Jumu'a prayer in congregation, and waiting for the afternoon prayer after Jumu'a.

And we ask Allah, the Exalted, that we apply them, and by Allah is enabling success.

---

[460] See note 81.

[461] See note 255.

[462] A ḥadîth that has many individuals transmitting the ḥadîth at each stage, to the extent that it would be impossible for them to have colluded together to lie about it, or to have accidentally made the same error, is called *Mutawâtir*. A ḥadîth that is not transmitted as such is called *Âḥâd*. One type of *Âḥâd* ḥadîth is called *Gharîb*, meaning it has only one person in its chain of transmission in one or more places. The term *gharîb* (strange/unique) may also refer to a ḥadîth that has an addition to either the chain or wording of the ḥadîth, which is only related by one person, thus making it "unique," which is the case with these two particular ḥadîth. And Allah knows best.

Chapter Thirty-Two

The Blessings of Mondays and Thursdays

Narration 290

It has been reported on the authority of Abû Qatâda al-Ansâri[463] that a man said to the Prophet ﷺ, "O Messenger of Allah! (What is the significance of) fasting on Mondays?" He said, *"I was born on it and the Quran was sent down to me on it."* [464]

Narration 291

It was reported on the authority of the freed slave of Qudâma bin Maẓ'ûn that the freed slave of Usâma bin Zayd used to ride out to some of his camels[465] which were in a valley outside the town and that he would fast on Mondays and Thursdays. He said, "I said to him, 'You fast yet you are old and thin?'"

---

[463] Abû Qatâda al-Anṣârî is al-Ḥârith ibn Rib'î although some say his name was 'Umar or Nu'mân ibn Rib'î. He was best known by the name Abû Qatâda. He was called "the rider of the Messenger of Allah ﷺ," and the Prophet ﷺ described him as "the best rider amongst us." He is said to have been the guard for the Prophet ﷺ on the night before the Battle of Badr, and the Prophet supplicated, *"O Allah, protect Abû Qatâda as he protected me this night."* It is also said that this prayer, was made on another occasion. Ibn Hajar said that Abû Qatâda fought in all the battles after 'Uḥud, and the reports of his participation in Badr are not correct (See *Taqrîb al-Tahdhîb*, 8311.) And Allah knows best. He was appointed governor of Makkah and died in Madina in 54H (674CE).

[464] Related by Muslim (2/820) and Aḥmad (5/299).

[465] Literally *"Mâl"*, which refers to possessions of value, such as wealth, money, livestock and property. The Arabs used it most frequently to refer to camels, and that meaning fits in the context of the ḥadîth. *(Editor)*

He said, "Indeed I have seen the Messenger of Allah ﷺ fast on Mondays and Thursdays, and I said, 'O Messenger of Allah do you fast on Mondays and Thursdays?'"
He ﷺ said, *"Surely actions are presented on Mondays and Thursdays."* [466]

Narration 292

It has been reported on the authority of Abû Hurayra[467] that the Prophet ﷺ said, *"The doors of the sky are opened every Monday and Thursday, and forgiven are the sins of every slave who does not associate partners with Allah in any way, except for the person who between him and his brother is enmity."* He said that it is said of them, *"Wait for those two until they resolve (their differences)."* [468]
The Shaykh, the Imâm Aḥmad, may Allah be pleased with him, said, "It has reached me from al-Ḥâkim Abû 'Abdullah on the authority of al-Ḥalîmî, may Allah show him mercy, who said that it is conceivable that the angels responsible for (recording the actions of) the children of Adam alternate. One group are with them from Monday to Thursday, and a group from Thursday to Monday, and after (they have completed their duty) they ascend. Each time a group ascends they read what has been written in their (own special) station in the sky. And in this way, it is literally 'a presentation'. Allah, the Exalted, counts this as the worship of the angels. As for Himself who is Mighty and Majestic, He is in no need of the presentation of what they have recorded for He knows what His slaves have done."
He said, "This is similar to the angels responsible for (recording) the actions of the children of Adam performed during the night and the angels

---

[466] Related by Aḥmad (5/204 and 205).
[467] See note 83.
[468] Related by Muslim (4/1986) al-Tirmdhî (4/383), Abû Dawûd (5/216) and Aḥmad (2/268, 329, 400-465).

responsible for the actions of the day. The meaning of 'presenting' is their leaving of their convenant of worship (that is the role of recording) and Allah, the Exalted, manifests what He wishes to them of His actions, and so in reality it is His presentation of His forgiveness and His manifesting it to His angels. And Allah knows best."

Chapter Thirty-Three

The Blessing of Fasting Three Days of Every Month and Mention of the Days Which the Messenger of Allah ﷺ Fasted and Which Three Days He Ordered Others to Fast

Narration 293

Abû Hurayra said: "My beloved ﷺ advised me of three things. (He recommended) the *witr*[469] prayer before sleep, fasting three days each month, and the *Ḍuḥâ*[470] prayer." [471]

Narration 294

It has been reported on the authority of Abû 'Uthmân al-Nahdî that Abû Hurayra was on one of his journeys and on his return, while he was in prayer, a messenger was sent to him to give him food. He said to the messenger, "I am fasting." He said that when the food was brought and they were almost finished, he came and began eating. The people stared at their messenger and he said to them, "What are you staring at? He had informed me that he was fasting."

Abû Hurayra said, "He speaks the truth. Surely I heard the Messenger of Allah ﷺ say, *'Fasting the Month of Steadfastness and fasting three days of every month is the perpetual fast.'* And I have fasted the three days of this month. I

---

[469] The *witr* are the prayers performed after the final compulsory prayer of the day (the *'Isha* prayer) but before the dawn. It finishes with an odd number of prayer cycles.

[470] The *Ḍuḥâ* prayer is prayed during the mid-morning and consists of between two and eight prayer cycles.

[471] Related by al-Bukhârî (2/54), Muslim (1/499) al-Tirmdhî (3/134), Abû Dawûd (2/138) and Aḥmad (2/258, 265 and 288).

break my fast as Allah has made things easy, and I fast as Allah provides increase (in reward so that three days is equivalent to a perpetual fast)." [472]

Narration 295

It has been reported on the authority of al-Azraq ibn Qays that a man from Banî Tamîm said: "We were at the door of Mu'âwiya and with us was Abû Dharr,[473] and he mentioned that he was fasting. When we entered, the table was spread and Abû Dharr began to eat." He said, "I looked at him and he said, 'O Aḥmar![474] Do you want to busy me away from my food?'"

He said, "Did you not tell me" or "I thought you were fasting?"

He said, "Indeed, but have you not read the Quran?"

"Yes," I said.

"Perhaps you only read a word (or two) from it, and you did not read the many where He says, *'He that does good shall have ten times as much to his credit.'"* [475] And then he said, "I heard the Messenger of Allah ﷺ say: *'Fasting the month of steadfastness (that is, Ramaḍân) and three days of each month, I count this as the perpetual fast - and this is what there is no doubt about - 'and it removes the malevolence of the chest.'*

"What is the malevolence of the chest?" I said.

'The filth of the Devil,' he said."[476]

---

[472] Related by Aḥmad (2/263, 384 and 513).

[473] See note 140.

[474] Literally, *"O Red One!"* Yet the Arabs used *Aḥmar* to refer to a white skin complexion. See Lane's Lexicon, entry *"ḥ-m-r". (Editor)*

[475] *Al-An'âm (6:160)*

[476] *Related by Aḥmad (5/154).*

Narration 296

It has been reported on the authority of 'Abdullah ibn Mas'ûd[477] that the Messenger of Allah ﷺ used to fast the *shining days* [478] of the month.[479]

Narration 297

It has been reported on the authority of 'Abdul-Malik bin Qadâda bin Milḥân al-Qaysî from his father[480] that the Messenger of Allah ﷺ ordered us to fast the white (days), and they are the thirteenth, fourteenth and fifteenth (days of the lunar month); and they are like (fasting) perpetually.

Narration 298

It has been reported on the authority of Ḥafṣa,[481] the wife of the Messenger of Allah ﷺ that he used to fast three days every month. He would fast the Monday and Thursday (of one week), and then the Monday of the following week.[482]

---

477 *See note 117.*

478 The days when the moon is at its fullest, i.e. the 13th, 14th and 15th of the lunar month.

479 Related by al-Tirmidhî (3/118), Abû Dawûd (2/822) and al-Nasâ'î (4/204).

480 Qatâda bin Milḥân al-Qaysî was one of the Companions from Basra. He was also known as Qatâda ibn al-Sudûsî. He came to the Prophet ﷺ as a child and the Prophet ﷺ wiped his face. Although very young at the time, he is still considered a Companion as he was old enough to relate directly from the Messenger ﷺ.

481 See note 245.

482 Related by al-Nasâ'î (4/203), Abû Dawûd (2/822) and Aḥmad (6/287).

Narration 299

Umm Salama[483] said: "The Messenger of Allah ﷺ ordered me to fast three days of (every) month, Monday, Thursday, and then Thursday." [484]

Narration 300

Mu'âdha al-'Adawiyya asked 'Aisha: "Did the Messenger of Allah ﷺ fast three days every month?"
"Yes," she said.
"Which days of the month did he fast?" I asked her.
"He wasn't overly concerned about which days of the month he fasted," she said.[485]
The Shaykh, may Allah be pleased with him, said, "In this is an indication that he ﷺ used to rotate around all the different (days) that we have mentioned. Thus, everone who saw him doing one of these types (of fasts), or commanding (others) to it, narrated it accordingly. 'Aisha, may Allah be pleased with her, had memorised all these different (patterns) and therefore she said, 'He wasn't overly concerned about which days of the month he fasted.'"

---

[483] Umm Salama was Hind bint Abû Ummaya from the powerful tribe of Banu Makhzûm who were generally opposed to the Messenger ﷺ. As one of the early adherents to Islam, she had to give up the privileges of her clan, eventually being forced to migrate twice to Ethiopia with her husband Abû Salama. Her husband died of wounds received during the Battle of 'Uḥud. He had prayed that after he died she would be married to someone even better. His prayer was answered, in that the Prophet ﷺ proposed to her, and they were married in 4H. She died in 62H (680CE).

[484] Related by al-Nasâ'î (4/221), Abû Dawûd (2/822) and Aḥmad (6/289).

[485] Related by Muslim (2/818), al-Tirmidhi (3/135) Abû Dawûd (2/823), and Ibn Mâjah (1/545).

Narration 301

It has been reported on the authority of Ibn 'Umar that the Messenger of Allah ﷺ said: *"Whoever fasts Wednesday, Thursday and Friday, and gives charity on them, whether a little or a lot, Allah will forgive his sins and he will leave from his state of sin as (pure) as the day his mother gave birth to him."*

Narration 302

It has been reported on the authority of 'Abdullah ibn 'Abbas from his father that he used to prefer fasting Wednesday, Thursday, and Friday, and he was informed that the Messenger of Allah ﷺ used to order them to fast and give charity, whether a little or a lot, for surely in that is great blessing.

Narration 303

Anas ibn Mâlik[486] said that the Messenger of Allah ﷺ said: *"Whoever fasts Wednesday, Thursday, and Friday, Allah will build for him a palace of pearls, precious stones, and emeralds in the Garden; and Allah will grant him freedom from the Fire."*

And the Shaykh, may Allah be pleased with him said:

---

[486] See note 30.

Narration 304

"We have related on the authority of Jâbir ibn 'Abdullah[487] that he said the Prophet ﷺ supplicated on Monday, Tuesday, and Wednesday, and (his prayer) was answered on Wednesday between the Midday (*Ẓuhr*) and Mid-afternoon (*'Asr*) prayers. We could see the joy in his face. Jâbir said that no important matter came to me, except that I turned to Allah in prayer at that time and I found an answer." [488]

Narration 305

It has been reported on the authority of 'Ali ibn 'Abdullah ibn 'Abbas that Kurayb, the freed slave of 'Abdullah ibn Abbas was sent by Ibn 'Abbas and other Companions to Umm Salama[489] to ask her which days the Messenger of Allah used to fast most often.

"Saturday and Sunday," she said.

I returned to them and informed them but it was as if they disputed the answer. They got up and went to her, and said that we sent so and so to ask about such and such and he reported that you said such and such.

"He spoke the truth. Indeed the days that the Messenger of Allah ﷺ used to fast most often were Saturday and Sunday and he used to say, *'These are the 'Eid days of the polytheists and I want to differ from them.'*"

And as for the *ḥadîth* that are related:

---

[487] See note 92.
[488] Related by Aḥmad (3/332).
[489] See note 483.

Narration 306

Al-Ṣammâ'a[490] said that the Messenger of Allah ﷺ said: *"One of you should not fast on Saturday except when Allah has made it compulsory upon you. If you find nothing to eat but the bark of a tree, you should chew that."* [491]

And 'Ali bin Aḥmad bin 'Ubayd informed us that al-Bâghandî informed us that Abû 'Âṣim informed us on the authority of Thowr on the authority of Khâlid bin Ma'dân on the authority of Abdullah bin Busr (the brother of al-Ṣammâ'a), and he mentioned the same.

And the Shaykh, the Imâm, may Allah be pleased with him, said, "If this narration is correct, fasting on Saturday alone out of glorification for that day would be prohibited, as that would be imitation of the Jews, thus disliked for that reason. And Allah knows best."

---

[490] She is known as al-Ṣammâ'a bint Busr al-Mâzinî but her given name was Bâhiyya. Her father was a close Companion of the Prophet ﷺ, and as a child she was blessed to share the Prophet's ﷺ company and heard directly from him, as well as her father, her brothers, and 'Aisha, the wife of the Prophet ﷺ. She is buried in Homs in Syria.

[491] Related by al-Tirmidhî (3/120), Abû Dawûd (2/805) and Ibn Mâjah (1/551.

Narration 307

It is related on the authority of Ya'qûb on the authority of Râshid on the authority of Anas who said that the Messenger of Allah ﷺ said: "*Whoever fasts three days from the Sacred Months, Thursday, Friday, and Saturday will have written for him the (reward of) seven hundred years of worship.*" Yaqûb said, "May my ears fall deaf if I did not hear this from Râshid," and Râshid said, "May my ears fall deaf if I did not hear this from Anas," and Anas had said, "May my ears fall deaf if I did not hear this from the Messenger of Allah ﷺ."

The Blessings of Specific Times has (now) been completed, with all praise to Allah and by the excellence of His enabling success. Allah sends prayers upon Muḥammad, the best of His creation and upon his family and his companions and sends salutations. And that was at midday on Thursday, the fourteenth of Dhûl Ḥijja 809H (22nd May 1407).[492]

[492] These words are from the scribe, meaning his work copying the book was completed on that date. Imam Al-Bayhaqî, May Allah be pleased with him, passed on to the mercy of his Lord on the 10th of Jumâdi al-Awwal, 458 H, roughly April 9th, 1066 CE. *(Editor)*

References and Bibliography

Al-Asqalâni, Ibn Hajr, *Al-Isâba fi Tamyîz al-Saḥâba,* Cairo: Dâr El-Fikr, 2008

Al-Bayhaqî, Imâm Abu Bakr, *Kitâb al-'Arba'ûn al-Sughrâ,* Beirut: Dâr al-Kutub al-'Arabî, 1988

Al-Bayhaqî, Imâm Abu Bakr, *Kitâb Faḍâ'il al-Awqât,* Beirut: Dâr Ibn Ḥazm 2003

Al-Bayhaqî, Imâm Abu Bakr, *Kitâb Faḍâ'il al-Awqât,* Cairo: Dâr al-Kutub al-'Ilmiyya, 1997

Al-Bayhaqî, Imâm Abu Bakr, *Kitâb Faḍâ'il al-Awqât,* Mecca: Maktaba al-Manâra, 1990

Al-Nawawî, Imâm Muhyidîn, *al-Adhkâr,* Jeddah: Dâr al-Minhâj, 2005

Ibn Ḥibbân al-Bustî, Muḥammad bin Aḥmad, *Kitâb al-Thiqât,* Dâr al-Kutub al-'Ilmiyya, 1998

Lane, Edward William, *Arabic-English Lexicon,* London: Williams & Norgate, 1863, accessed online at www.ejtaal.com

Qudus, Abdul Ḥamîd, *Kanz al-Najâḥ wa al-Surûr,* Mombasa: Private Publication, 1969

Glossary of Arabic terms used in the text

al-Aḍḥâ	The *"sacrifice."* This refers to the sacrifice associated with the Pilgrimage, *Ḥajj.* The word is often used with the word *'Eid,* celebration, meaning the Celebration of the Day of Sacrifice, when the Pilgrims sacrifice their animals during the *Ḥajj.*
'Asr	The afternoon prayer.
'Eid	*Celebration.* There are two main days of celebration in the Islamic Calendar, they are 'Eid al-Fitr, which begins on the first of Shawwâl, and 'Eid al-Adhâ which follows the Ḥajj, Pilgrimage, and begins on 10 Dhûl Ḥijja.
al-Fiṭr	Literally means *"breaking"* and here refers to the breaking of the fast, either at the end of the day of fasting or at the end of the month of fasting, that is, Ramaḍân. Therefore, it is often connected to the word *Eid,* celebration, meaning the Celebration of the End of the Fast (of Ramaḍân).
Ḥadîth	The words, actions, description of, or report of silent approval of the Prophet Muḥammad ﷺ reported by one of his companions.
Ḥajj	Pilgrimage to Makkah.
Hijra	The Migration of the Prophet ﷺ from Makka to Madina. It is from this year that the Islamic calendar begins.
Ḥouris/ *Ḥur al-'Ayn*	These are *beings* that reside in the Garden and provide pleasure to their spouses. They are described as being "wide eyed," which implies great beauty.
Iḥrâm	This is the sanctified state that one enters by making intention for the Pilgrimage, which is the first integral of the *Ḥajj.* Once the intention has been made and one enters this state, certain things become forbidden, including perfume, sexual relations, cutting the hair, and, for men, wearing sewn clothes, which is why the state of *Iḥrâm* is

	associated with the pilgrim garb consisting of two lengths of white cloth.
Imâm	Literally *"leader,"* usually denoting the person leading the congregational prayer or leader of the community.
'Ishâ'	*The night prayer*. The last of the compulsory five daily prayers.
Jâhiliyya	Literally *"ignorance"*. It refers to the time before the Prophecy of Muḥammad ﷺ.
Jumu'a	Literally*"gathering."* It is reported that Friday (literally *the day of gathering*) was named such even before the advent of Islam. It also refers to the Jumu'a prayer, which is performed in congregation, and replaces the Dhuhr prayer on Friday for those who have prayed it.
Khalîfa	*"Representative"* of the Prophet ﷺ, that is, the ruler who leads the Muslim community after him, starting with Abû Bakr, his closest Companion.
Maghrib	The sunset or the Dusk Prayer that falls shortly after the sun has set. This is the fourth of the five daily compulsory prayers.
Qibla	The direction of the ritual prayer, that is, towards Makkah
Rak'a	A *rak'a* is a complete prayer cycle. Each of the five daily prayers has a set number of prayer cycles. The plural is *raka'ât.*
Ṣâ'a	An Islamic measure of volume equal to four *Mudd*, which is what an average size man will scoop up with his two hands. In metric weight a *Ṣâ'a* is equal to 3150gms of grain. (See note 252)
Sunnah	*"The path"* or *"the way,"* referring to the way of the Prophet ﷺ. This is understood to complement and explain the Quran in a practical way providing the Messenger ﷺ as a physical example of its teachings.
Tâbi'î (plural-	*"Follower"* or one of second generation of Muslims, that is someone who met a Companion of the Prophet ﷺ, but did

Tâbi'în)	not actually meet the Prophet ﷺ himself.
Tarâwîḥ	The supererogatory night prayer, which takes place in the month of Ramaḍân.
Tashrîq	The days of the Pilgrimage which follow the Day of Sacrifice.
Witr	Literally, *witr* means an odd number. It refers to the last prayer of the night that ends with an odd number of prayer cycles usually 3 or 2 followed by 1.
Zakât	Literally, *Zakât* means *"purification"* and *"growth."* It is the money that one gives to designated groups, including the poor, once one has more than a set amount of money for a full lunar year.

Appendices

The text of *Faḍâ'il al-Awqât* mentions the supplications that the Prophet ﷺ made when breaking his fast, on the Days of Ḥajj, and the night which falls midway through Sha'bân. The best source for further supplications recommended at different times is the collection of *ḥadîth* compiled by the *ḥadîth* Master, Imâm al-Nawawî, called *al-Adhkâr.*

The footnotes made reference to *Kanz al-Najâḥ wa al-Surûr* by Abdul Hamîd Qudus, which also has many beneficial supplications. However, most are not directly from the Prophet ﷺ and the benefits are authenticated by experience rather than by the rigours of research into chains of transmission. In the appendices that follow, we have included a selection of supplications from these two sources. We hope they might benefit readers and give them a sense of these two useful sources.

The footnotes made cross references to the famous six collections of *ḥadîth,* as well as other sources. As these works may not be known to all readers, we have included as a final appendix, a brief introduction to each of the scholars who compiled the texts, and a little about each text. We pray that Allah benefits us by them and their work, and rewards them for their service to His Religion.

Appendix One: Supplication for the beginning of the year

Abdul Ḥamid Qudus mentions in his *Kanz al-Najâḥ wa al-Surûr* that one should read the following supplication on the first day of the Islamic year:

اللَّهُمَّ يَا مُحَوِّلَ الأَحْوَالِ حَوِّلْ حَالِي إِلىٰ أَحْسَنِ الأَحْوَالِ ، بِحَوْلِكَ وَ قُوَّتِكَ يَا عَزِيزُ يَا مُتَعَال ، وَ صَلَّى اللهُ تَعَالىٰ عَلىٰ سَيِّدِنَا مُحَمَّدٍ وَعَلىٰ آلِهِ وَصَحْبِهِ وَسَلَّمَ.

Allahumma yâ muḥawwil al-ahwâl, ḥawwil ḥâlî ilâ aḥsanil-aḥwâl biḥawlika wa quwwatika yâ 'azîzu yâ muta'âl wa ṣalla_Allâhu ta'âla 'alâ sayyidinâ Muḥammadin wa 'alâ âlihî wa ṣaḥbihî wa sallam

O Allah! O Changer of States, change my state into the best of states by Your power and ability! O Mighty One! O Exalted One! And May Allah, the Exalted, send prayers and salutations upon Muḥammad and upon his family and Companions.

Appendix Two: Supplication for protection

When discussing the month of Ṣafar, the footnotes, drawing on the writings of Ibn Rajab and ‘Abdul Ḥamid Qudus, examined the various beliefs about seeking protection from evil. It concluded that the best way to seek protection from evil is to do so on a regular basis with the words given to us by the Messenger ﷺ.

The Prophet ﷺ recommended for us to recite the following two supplications three times each, both in the morning and the evening. Whoever does so, will not be harmed during that day.

أَعُوذُ بِكَلِمَاتِ اللهِ التَّامَّاتِ مِنْ شَرِ مَا خَلَقَ

A'ûdhu bi kalimâtillah_ittâmmâti min sharri mâ khalaq

I seek refuge in the Perfect words of Allah from the evil that He created.

بِسْمِ اللهِ الَّذِي لَا يَضُرُّ مَعَ اسْمِهِ شَيءٌ فِي الْأَرْضِ وَلَا فِي السَّمَاءِ وَهُوَ السَّمِيعُ العَلِيْمُ.

Bismillahil_ladhi lâ yaḍurru ma' a_smihi shay'un fil_arḍi wa lâ fis_samâ'i wa huwas_samî'ul_'alîm.

In the name of Allah, the name with which no harm in the earth or skies can come to (the one who is under its protection). And He is the all-Hearing and all-Knowing.

Appendix Three: Selection of Prayers upon the Prophet ﷺ

The text tells us of the importance of sending prayers and salutations upon the Prophet ﷺ. The footnotes, drawing on 'Abdul Ḥamid Qudus' *Kanz al-Najâḥ wa al-Surûr* and other texts, and the practice of the Scholars recommends reconnecting with the Prophet ﷺ through increasing our sending of prayers upon him ﷺ . One of the best sources for transmitted prayers upon the Messenger ﷺ is Yusuf al-Nabahâni's *Afḍal Salawât 'ala Sayyid al-Sâdât.* Among the prayers included in his book are the following well-known prayers. These two prayers are read all around the world but with very slight variations. The ones quoted below are taken from a book of prayers published in Singapore by the Ba Alawi Mosque.

اَللّٰهُمَّ صَلِّ صَلَاةً كَامِلَةً وَسَلِّمْ سَلَامًا تَامًّا عَلٰى سَيِّدِنَا وَمَوْلَانَا مُحَمَّدٍ وَعَلٰى آلِ سَيِّدِنَا مُحَمَّدٍ الَّذِيْ تَنْحَلُّ بِهِ الْعُقَدُ وَ تَنْفَرِجُ بِهِ الْكُرَبُ وَ تُقْضٰى بِهِ الْحَوَائِجُ وَ تُنَالُ بِهِ الرَّغَائِبُ وَ حُسْنُ الْخَوَاتِمِ وَ يُسْتَسْقَى الْغَمَامُ بِوَجْهِهِ الْكَرِيْمِ وَ عَلٰى آلِهِ وَصَحْبِهِ فِيْ كُلِّ لَمْحَةٍ وَنَفَسٍ عَدَدَ مَا وَسِعَهُ عِلْمُكَ

Allahumma ṣalli ṣalâtan kâmilatan wa sallim salâman tâmman 'alâ sayyidinâ wa maulânâ Muḥammadin wa 'alâ âli sayyidinâ Muḥammadin_ladhi tanḥallu bihi_l'uqadu wa tanfariju bihi_kurab wa tuqḍâ bihi_lḥawâ'ij wa tunâlu bihir_raghâ'ib wa ḥusnu_lkhawâtimi wa yustasqâ_ghamâmu bi wajhihi_lkarîm wa 'ala âlihi wa ṣaḥbihi fî kulli lamḥatin wa nafasin 'adada mâ wasi'ahu 'ilmuka

O Allah, send a perfect prayer and complete salutation upon our liege lord and master Muḥammad, and upon the family of our liege lord Muḥammad, one that unties knots and releases from difficulties, and by which our needs (are met) and hopes (are fulfilled), and (by which we are granted) good endings and the clouds pour by his noble face, and likewise upon his family,

Companions in every moment and breath with the number that encompasses Your knowledge.

اللَّهُمَّ صَلِّ وَسَلِّمْ عَلىٰ سَيِّدِنَا مُحَمَّدٍ طِبِّ ٱلْقُلُوْبِ وَ دَوائِها. وَعَافِيَةِ ٱلأَبْدَانِ
وَ شِفَائِهَا. وَ نُوْرِ الْأَبْصَارِ وَضِيَائِهَا. وَعَلىٰ آلِهِ وَصَحْبِهِ وَسَلِّمْ.

Allahumma ṣalli wa sallim ʻalâ sayyidinâ Muḥammadin ṭibb al-qulûbi wa dawâ'ihâ wa ʻâfiyatil abdân wa shifâ'ihâ wa nur al-abṣâr wa ḍiyâ'ihâ wa ʻalâ âlihi wa ṣaḥbihi wa sallim.

O Allah, send prayers and salutations upon Muḥammad, the medicine of the hearts and their remedy, wellbeing of bodies and their cure, and the light of sight and its glow, and likewise upon his family and Companions.

Appendix Four: Dua of Rajab of Abdul Qadir al-Jaylani

إِلٰهي تَعَرَّضَ لَكَ فِي هٰذِهِ اللَّيلَةِ الْمُتَعَرِّضُونَ، وَقَصَدَكَ القَاصِدُونَ وَأَمَّلَ فَضْلَكَ وَمَعْرُوفَكَ الطَّالِبُونَ، وَلَكَ فِي هٰذِهِ اللَّيْلَةِ نَفَحَاتٌ وَجَوائِزٌ، وَعَطَايَا وَمَواهِبٌ، تَمنُّ بِهَا عَلٰى مَنْ تَشَاءُ مِنْ عِبَادِكَ، وَتَمْنَعُهَا مِمَّنْ لَمْ تَسْبِقْ لَهُ الْعِنَايَةَ مِنْكَ، وَهَأَنَذا عَبْدُكَ الْفَقِيرُ إِلَيْكَ ، المُؤَمِّلُ فَضْلَكَ وَمَعْروفَكَ، فَإِنْ كُنْتَ يَا مَوْلَايَ تَفَضَّلْتَ فِي هٰذِهِ اللَّيلَةِ علىٰ أَحَدٍ مِنْ خَلْقِكَ ، وَجُدْتَ عَلَيهِ بِعَائِدَةٍ مِنْ عَطْفِكَ، فَصَلِّ عَلٰى سَيِّدِنَا مُحَمَّدٍ وَآلِهِ وَصَحْبِهِ، وَجُدْ عَلَيَّ بِطَوْلِكَ وَمَعْروفِكَ، يَا رَبَّ الْعَالَمِينَ

Ilâhi ta'arraḍa laka fî hadhihi_laylati_l muta'arriḍûn wa qaṣadaka al-qâṣidûn wa ammala faḍlaka wa ma'rûfaka al_ṭâlibûn wa laka fî hadhihi_laylati nafaḥât wa jawâ'iz wa 'aṭâyâ wa mawâhib tamunnu bihâ 'alâ man tashâ'u min 'ibâdika wa tamna'uhâ mimman lam tasbiq lahu_'inâyatan minka wa hâ anâ dha 'abduka al-faqîr ilayka al-mu'ammilu faḍlaka wa ma'rûfaka wa in kunta yâ mawlâyâ tafaḍḍalta fî hadhihi_laylati 'alâ aḥadin min khalqika wa judta 'alayhi bi 'â'idatin min 'aṭfika fa ṣalli 'alâ sayyidina Muḥammadin wa 'alihi wa ṣahbihi wa jud 'alayya biṭawlika wa ma'rûfika ya rabbal_'âlamîn.

O God, on this night those who present to you, present. And those who direct to you, direct themselves to you, and those who ask hope for Your blessings and generosity. And during this night You have special breezes, prizes, gifts, and favours that you bestow upon whom You wish from among Your slaves, and You hold back from those who have not been destined with special attention from You. And here I am,

Your slave in total dependence on You, one who hopes for Your blessing and kindness. And so if You – O my Master – bless anyone from among Your creation and You show kindness to anyone by showing Your compassion to him, send salutations upon our liege lord Muḥammad and upon his family and Companions. And show kindness to me by Your benevolence and generosity, O Lord of the Worlds.

Appendix Five: Brief Biographies of those who related ḥadîth mentioned in the text

Imâm Aḥmad and his Musnad

Aḥmad bin Muḥammad bin Ḥanbal was a jurist and scholar of *ḥadîth* to whom one of the four major schools of jurisprudence is attributed. He was born in Baghdad in 164H (781 CE) and died there in 241H (855 CE), spending some of his youth travelling through Syria and Arabia collecting *ḥadîth* and studying jurisprudence. He was a staunch opponent of wrongdoing, and was a soldier for a short while; and famously stood up against the ruler Ma'mun for his erroneous beliefs. As a result, he was harshly punished. He was much loved by the masses, and his funeral was attended by over 880,000 people, including 20,000 Christians and Jews, some of whom embraced Islam on that day. His *Musnad* contains approximately 30,000 *ḥadîth* that he heard from 285 different teachers. It also contains sayings of the Companions and early scholars, and for this reason is a massive work. Whenever Aḥmad is mentioned in the footnotes, it is to this book that they refer.

Al-Bukhârî and his Jâmi' al-Ṣaḥîḥ

Muḥammad bin Ismâ'îl al-Bukhârî was born in Bukhâra, which is in modern day Uzbekistan, in 194H (810 CE). He related ḥadîth from many prominent scholars of his time including the students of Imâm Mâlik and of 'Abdullah ibn al-Mubârak, and studied *ḥadîth* under Aḥmad ibn al-Ḥanbal. He was very rigorous and methodical in his critical appraisal of *ḥadîth* and as a result, his collection *al-Jâmi' al-Ṣaḥîḥ* is considered by most scholars to be the most authentic collection of *ḥadîth.* It contains over 7500 *ḥadîth.* He restricted it to that number for brevity, but acknowledged that there were many more authentic *ḥadîth* than those in his collection. Although he has several collections of *ḥadîth,* this is by far the most important and well known. Whenever, reference is made to al-Bukhari in the footnotes, it refers to his *Jâmi',* unless otherwise stated. He died in 256H (870 CE).

Abû Dawûd and his Sunan

Abû Dawûd is Sulaymân ibn al-Ash'ath, He was born in Sijistân, which lies in modern day Eastern Iran, in 202H (819 CE). While studying and teaching, he emphasised those *ḥadîth* that were supported by the practice of the Prophet's ﷺ Companions. This was the focus of his collections rather than the chain of transmission. For this reason, it contains *ḥadîth* which do not meet the criteria of al-Bukhârî and Muslim, but which provide a good description of the Prophetic practice as shown through the human legacy that he left behind. It took Abû Dawûd twenty years to collect the *ḥadîth* contained in his *Sunan,* which is one of twenty-one books of *ḥadîth* attributed to him. During this period, he collected over

500,000 *ḥadîth* of which 5274 are included in his *Sunan*. Apart from being a scholar of *ḥadîth,* he was a jurist who studied both jurisprudence and *ḥadîth* under Aḥmad ibn Ḥanbal in Baghdad. He died in Basra in 275H (889 CE).

Imâm Muslim and his Jâmi' al-Ṣaḥîḥ

Muslim ibn Ḥajjâj bin Muslim al-Naysabûrî was born in 206H (821CE). He travelled widely around the Muslim world, visiting Arabia, Egypt, and Syria collecting *ḥadîth.* After his travels, he settled back in his native Nishapur where he attached himself to Imam al-Bukhârî. This provided an opportunity to further develop the science of *ḥadîth* studies and to compile his own collection. He systemised the study of the narrators, and advanced the science of what is now known as *'Ilm al-Rijâl*, the science of narrators. He had memorised over 300 000 *ḥadîth* of which about 7500 are included in his collection, also known as *al-Jâmi' al-Ṣaḥîḥ.* He died in 261 (875 CE) and was buried in the suburbs of Nishapur.

Al-Tirmidhî and his Jâmi'

Abû 'Isa Muḥammad ibn 'Isa al-Ḍaḥḥâk al-Sulamî al-Tirmidhî was born in the town of Tirmidh, which is in modern day Uzbekistan, in 209H (824 CE). He started his study of *ḥadîth* at the relatively late age of 20, focusing before that on grammar and other disciplines. From 235H onwards, he travelled widely in Iraq, Khorasân and Arabia collecting *ḥadîth*. He studied under al-Bukhârî and adopted his methodology but also incorporated the approaches of Muslim and Abû Dawûd. All the references in the footnotes are to his *Jâmi*, which is his most famous book, containing just under 4000 *ḥadîth.* Towards the end of his life, he went blind, and died in a town to the north of his native Tirmidh in 279H (892 CE).

Ibn Mâjah and his Sunan

Muḥammad bin Yazîd bin Mâjah al-Qazwînî, better known as Ibn Mâjah. He was born in Qazwîn in modern day Iran in 209H (824CE). As a young man, he excelled in the study of Quran and *ḥadîth* and after travelling around the Muslim world, collecting *ḥadîth* and studying. He became well known both for his Quranic exegesis and for the transmission of *ḥadîth.* His latter years were spent writing and teaching and he left behind three important texts, a commentary on Quran, a history, and his collection of *ḥadîth* known as *al-Sunan.* It contains approximately 4300 *ḥadîth* and is organised according to the books of jurisprudence. He died in 273H (887 CE) in his native Qazwîn.

Al-Nasâ'î and his Sunan

Aḥmad bin Shu'ayb bin 'Alî al-Nasâ'î was born in Nasâ', which is in modern day Turkmenistan, in 215H (829 CE). He travelled widely, spending most of his later years in Egypt and Syria, where he became involved in political controversy and was tortured, and from where he was eventually expelled. He decided to go to Makkah but either died on the way or soon after arrival. He was buried there in 303H (915 CE). The references in the footnotes are to his abridged collection of *ḥadîth* known as *al-Sunan al-Sughrâ* (the small Sunan) or *al-Mujtaba* (the Selection) or simply as the *Sunan* of al-Nasâ'î. This text, which contains about 5700 *ḥadîth,* was abridged from his first *Sunan* called *al-Sunan al-Kubrâ,* and omitted those which he did not consider met the criteria of *ṣaḥîḥ*, authenticated. The few *ḥadîth* that do not meet those criteria are identified by the compiler.

Other references mentioned in the footnotes

Other books of *ḥadîth* are mentioned in the footnotes. These include *al-Ṣaḥîḥ* of Ibn Ḥibbân, which is a collection of *ṣaḥîḥ*, authenticated, *ḥadîth* by the great jurist and scholar Abû Ḥâtim Muḥammad ibn Ḥibbân. He was from Khorasân and lived between 275H (888 CE) and 354H (965CE).

Among the most important references used in the translation of this text is the work of Ibn Ḥajr. He is Aḥmad bin 'Ali, Abû Faḍl, but he is best known as Ibn Ḥajr al-'Asqalâni. His biographies of the Companions, *al-Isâba* has been heavily relied upon in the footnotes. Reference is also made to his commentary on the *Jami'* of Imâm al-Bukhârî known as *Fatḥ al-Bâri.* He was born in Cairo in 852H (1372 CE) to a famous family of scholars. He excelled as a young student, memorising the whole Quran by the age of nine years old, and was considered competent enough to lead the prayers when he travelled to Makkah, aged 12. He went on to become a great commentator on *ḥadîth* and a jurist in the Shâfi'î School. His wife, Uns Khâtûn was also a famous *ḥadîth* scholar whose classes attracted large crowds and produced a number of notable scholars. He died after leading the 'Isha prayers on 2nd February 1449, 852 A.H. His funeral was attended by over 50,000 people, including the Sultan.

Reference is also made to al-Suyûṭî's *Durr al-Manthûr,* which is an exegesis of Quran based on *ḥadîth* and traditions. Al-Suyûṭî was born in Egypt in 849H (145CE) and died there in 911H (1445 CE). He has several collections of *ḥadîth,* but these are mainly aggregations of earlier works. *Durr al-Manthûr* contains all he could find about each verse of the Qur'an that could be attributed back to the Messenger of Allah ﷺ, and in this sense is very different from other collections.

Reference is made to a book entitled *'al-Du'afa al-Kabîr* which was compiled by Abu Ja'far, Muhammad bin 'Amr bin Mûsa Al-'Uqaylî. He died in Makkah in 322H (934CE). This text identifies weak chains of transmission, and lists *ḥadîth* which are related using those chains.

Some of the *ḥadîth* are found in a book entitled *al-Targhîb wa al-Tarhîb* by al-Imâm 'Abdul 'Azîm al-Mundhirî who was a *ḥadîth* scholar born in Egypt in 581H (1185CE).

The book contains *ḥadîth* that specifically encourage acts of worship and discourage acts of disobedience. Al-Mundhirî was famous for his collections of *ḥadîth* as well as his abridgement of *Ṣaḥîḥ Muslim* and *Ṣaḥîḥ al-Bukhârî*. He died in Egypt in 656H (1258CE).

May Allah reward them for their service to His Religion, and benefit us by their work. Amin.